Artificial Intelligence

Artificial Intelligence

Kaleb Stirling

CLANRYE
INTERNATIONAL
www.clanryeinternational.com

Clanrye International,
750 Third Avenue, 9th Floor,
New York, NY 10017, USA

ISBN: 978-1-63240-902-7

Cataloging-in-Publication Data

Artificial intelligence / Kaleb Stirling.
   p. cm.
Includes bibliographical references and index.
ISBN 978-1-63240-902-7
1. Artificial intelligence. 2. Neural computers. I. Stirling, Kaleb.
Q335 .A78 2019
006.3--dc23

For information on all Clanrye International publications
visit our website at www.clanryeinternational.com

Contents

Preface

Artificial intelligence (AI) refers to the intelligence that is demonstrated by machines. Devices that perceive the environment and act in a way that aids in the deliverance of its objectives and tasks, are called intelligent agents. Such agents execute tasks by mimicking the cognitive functions of the human brain such as learning and problem solving. Understanding human speech, intelligent routing in content delivery network, competing in strategic game systems such as chess and Go, etc. are all capabilities of artificial intelligence. The ultimate objective of AI is to achieve general intelligence. Artificial intelligence uses varied tools such as search algorithms, mathematical optimization, logic programming, Bayesian networks, etc. in order to solve the most complex problems related to computer science. This book presents the complex subject of artificial intelligence in the most comprehensible and easy to understand language. Most of the topics introduced in this book cover new techniques and the applications of AI. It is a complete source of knowledge on the present status of this important field.

A short introduction to every chapter is written below to provide an overview of the content of the book:

Chapter 1- The demonstration of intelligence by machines is termed as artificial intelligence. A machine displays human-like cognitive mental processes such as problem solving and learning. This is an introductory chapter, which will introduce briefly all the significant aspects of artificial intelligence, such as diagnosis, argumentation framework, AI- complete and synthetic intelligence; **Chapter 2-** In artificial intelligence, an automated system that mimics the decision-making capacity of a human expert is called an expert system. Using reasoning, expert systems can solve complex problems. This chapter has been carefully written to provide an easy understanding of the varied aspects of expert systems, such as model-based reasoning, legal expert system, SHINE expert system, split up, etc.; **Chapter 3-** In AI systems, algorithms that imitate the intellectual processes in humans were developed for simulating problem solving and logical deduction making. An important field of artificial intelligence is knowledge representation and reasoning, which has been covered in extensive detail in this chapter. The diverse aspects of strategic artificial intelligence processes, such as automated planning and scheduling, computational humor, artificial intelligence systems integration, commonsense reasoning and computer- assisted proof, etc. have also been thoroughly discussed in this chapter; **Chapter 4-** A subset of artificial intelligence is machine learning. It is concerned with the use of statistical techniques for simulating the ability to learn in computers. The topics elaborated in this chapter will help in gaining a better perspective about the key elements of machine learning, such as hyperparameter, ensemble averaging, supervised learning and reinforcement learning; **Chapter 5-** Artificial intelligence has diverse applications in the modern world, for instance in the fields of electronic trading, robot control, medical diagnosis and remote sensing. The significant applications of AI systems such as software agent, virtual assistant, video game bot, autonomous robot and domestic robot have been thoroughly discussed in this chapter.

I extend my sincere thanks to the publisher for considering me worthy of this task. Finally, I thank my family for being a source of support and help.

Kaleb Stirling

An Introduction to Artificial Intelligence

The demonstration of intelligence by machines is termed as artificial intelligence. A machine displays human-like cognitive mental processes such as problem solving and learning. This is an introductory chapter, which will introduce briefly all the significant aspects of artificial intelligence, such as diagnosis, argumentation framework, AI- complete and synthetic intelligence.

AI (artificial intelligence) is the simulation of human intelligence processes by machines, especially computer systems. These processes include learning (the acquisition of information and rules for using the information), reasoning (using the rules to reach approximate or definite conclusions) and self-correction. Particular applications of AI include expert systems, speech recognition and machine vision.

AI was coined by John McCarthy, an American computer scientist, in 1956 at The Dartmouth Conference where the discipline was born. Today, it is an umbrella term that encompasses everything from robotic process automation to actual robotics. It has gained prominence recently due, in part, to big data, or the increase in speed, size and variety of data businesses are now collecting. AI can perform tasks such as identifying patterns in the data more efficiently than humans, enabling businesses to gain more insight out of their data.

Types of Artificial Intelligence

AI can be categorized in any number of ways, but here are two examples.

The first classifies AI systems as either weak AI or strong AI. Weak AI, also known as narrow AI, is an AI system that is designed and trained for a particular task. Virtual personal assistants, such as Apple's Siri, are a form of weak AI.

Strong AI, also known as artificial general intelligence, is an AI system with generalized human cognitive abilities so that when presented with an unfamiliar task, it has enough intelligence to find a solution. The Turing Test, developed by mathematician Alan Turing in 1950, is a method used to determine if a computer can actually think like a human, although the method is controversial.

The second example is from Arend Hintze, an assistant professor of integrative biology and computer science and engineering at Michigan State University. He categorizes AI into four types, from the kind of AI systems that exist today to sentient systems, which do not yet exist. His categories are as follows:

- Type 1: Reactive machines. An example is Deep Blue, the IBM chess program that beat Garry Kasparov in the 1990s. Deep Blue can identify pieces on the chess board and make predictions, but it has no memory and cannot use past experiences to inform future ones. It analyzes possible moves -- its own and its opponent -- and chooses the most strategic move. Deep Blue and Google's AlphaGO were designed for narrow purposes and cannot easily be applied to another situation.

- Type 2: Limited memory. These AI systems can use past experiences to inform future decisions. Some of the decision-making functions in autonomous vehicles have been designed this way. Observations used to inform actions happening in the not-so-distant future, such as a car that has changed lanes. These observations are not stored permanently.

- Type 3: Theory of mind. This is a psychology term. It refers to the understanding that others have their own beliefs, desires and intentions that impact the decisions they make. This kind of AI does not yet exist.

- Type 4: Self-awareness. In this category, AI systems have a sense of self, have consciousness. Machines with self-awareness understand their current state and can use the information to infer what others are feeling. This type of AI does not yet exist.

Basics

A typical AI perceives its environment and takes actions that maximize its chance of successfully achieving its goals. An AI's intended goal function can be simple ("1 if the AI wins a game of Go, 0 otherwise") or complex ("Do actions mathematically similar to the actions that got you rewards in the past"). Goals can be explicitly defined, or can be induced. If the AI is programmed for "reinforcement learning", goals can be implicitly induced by rewarding some types of behavior and punishing others. Alternatively, an evolutionary system can induce goals by using a "fitness function" to mutate and preferentially replicate high-scoring AI systems; this is similar to how animals evolved to innately desire certain goals such as finding food, or how dogs can be bred via artificial selection to possess desired traits. Some AI systems, such as nearest-neighbor, instead reason by analogy; these systems are not generally given goals, except to the degree that goals are somehow implicit in their training data. Such systems can still be benchmarked if the non-goal system is framed as a system whose "goal" is to successfully accomplish its narrow classification task.

AI often revolves around the use of algorithms. An algorithm is a set of unambiguous instructions that a mechanical computer can execute. A complex algorithm is often built on top of other, simpler, algorithms. A simple example of an algorithm is the following recipe for optimal play at tic-tac-toe:

1. If someone has a "threat" (that is, two in a row), take the remaining square. Otherwise,

2. if a move "forks" to create two threats at once, play that move. Otherwise,

3. take the center square if it is free. Otherwise,

4. if your opponent has played in a corner, take the opposite corner. Otherwise,

5. take an empty corner if one exists. Otherwise,

6. take any empty square.

Many AI algorithms are capable of learning from data; they can enhance themselves by learning new heuristics (strategies, or "rules of thumb", that have worked well in the past), or can themselves write other algorithms. Some of the "learners" described below, including Bayesian networks, decision trees, and nearest-neighbor, could theoretically, if given infinite data, time, and memory, learn to approximate any function, including whatever combination of mathematical functions would best describe the entire world. These learners could therefore, in theory, derive all possible knowledge, by considering every possible hypothesis and matching it against the data. In practice, it is almost never possible to consider every possibility, because of the phenomenon of "combinatorial explosion", where the amount of time needed to solve a problem grows exponentially. Much of AI research involves figuring out how to identify and avoid considering broad swaths of possibilities that are unlikely to be fruitful. For example, when viewing a map and looking for the shortest driving route from Denver to New York in the East, one can in most cases skip looking at any path through San Francisco or other areas far to the West; thus, an AI wielding an pathfinding algorithm like A* can avoid the combinatorial explosion that would ensue if every possible route had to be ponderously considered in turn.

The earliest (and easiest to understand) approach to AI was symbolism (such as formal logic): "If an otherwise healthy adult has a fever, then they may have influenza". A second, more general, approach is Bayesian inference: "If the current patient has a fever, adjust the probability they have influenza in such-and-such way". The third major approach, extremely popular in routine business AI applications, are analogizers such as SVM and nearest-neighbor: "After examining the records of known past patients whose temperature, symptoms, age, and other factors mostly match the current patient, X% of those patients turned out to have influenza". A fourth approach is harder to intuitively understand, but is inspired by how the brain's machinery works: the artificial neural network approach uses artificial "neurons" that can learn by comparing itself to the desired output and altering the strengths of the connections between its internal neurons to "reinforce" connections that seemed to be useful. These four main approaches can overlap with each other and with evolutionary systems;

for example, neural nets can learn to make inferences, to generalize, and to make analogies. Some systems implicitly or explicitly use multiple of these approaches, alongside many other AI and non-AI algorithms; the best approach is often different depending on the problem.

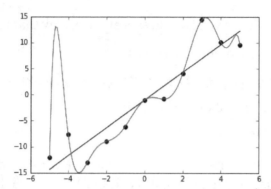

The blue line could be an example of overfitting a linear function due to random noise.

Learning algorithms work on the basis that strategies, algorithms, and inferences that worked well in the past are likely to continue working well in the future. These inferences can be obvious, such as "since the sun rose every morning for the last 10,000 days, it will probably rise tomorrow morning as well". They can be nuanced, such as "X% of families have geographically separate species with color variants, so there is an Y% chance that undiscovered black swans exist". Learners also work on the basis of "Occam's razor": The simplest theory that explains the data is the likeliest. Therefore, to be successful, a learner must be designed such that it prefers simpler theories to complex theories, except in cases where the complex theory is proven substantially better. Settling on a bad, overly complex theory gerrymandered to fit all the past training data is known as overfitting. Many systems attempt to reduce overfitting by rewarding a theory in accordance with how well it fits the data, but penalizing the theory in accordance with how complex the theory is. Besides classic overfitting, learners can also disappoint by "learning the wrong lesson". A toy example is that an image classifier trained only on pictures of brown horses and black cats might conclude that all brown patches are likely to be horses. A real-world example is that, unlike humans, current image classifiers don't determine the spatial relationship between components of the picture; instead, they learn abstract patterns of pixels that humans are oblivious to, but that linearly correlate with images of certain types of real objects. Faintly superimposing such a pattern on a legitimate image results in an "adversarial" image that the system misclassifies.

Compared with humans, existing AI lacks several features of human "commonsense reasoning"; most notably, humans have powerful mechanisms for reasoning about "naïve physics" such as space, time, and physical interactions. This enables even young children to easily make inferences like "If I roll this pen off a table, it will fall on the floor". Humans also have a powerful mechanism of "folk psychology" that helps them to interpret natural-language sentences such as "The city councilmen refused the demonstrators a permit because they advocated violence". (A generic AI has difficulty inferring whether the councilmen or the demonstrators are the ones alleged to be advocating violence.) This lack of "common knowledge" means that AI often makes different mistakes than humans make, in ways that can seem incomprehensible. For example, existing self-driving cars cannot reason about the location nor the intentions of pedestrians in the exact way that humans do, and instead must use non-human modes of reasoning to avoid accidents.

A self-driving car system may use a neural network to determine which parts of the picture seem to match previous training images of pedestrians, and then model those areas as slow-moving but somewhat unpredictable rectangular prisms that must be avoided.

Problems

The overall research goal of artificial intelligence is to create technology that allows computers and machines to function in an intelligent manner. The general problem of simulating (or creating) intelligence has been broken down into sub-problems. These consist of particular traits or capabilities that researchers expect an intelligent system to display. The traits described below have received the most attention.

Reasoning, Problem Solving

Early researchers developed algorithms that imitated step-by-step reasoning that humans use when they solve puzzles or make logical deductions. By the late 1980s and 1990s, AI research had developed methods for dealing with uncertain or incomplete information, employing concepts from probability and economics.

These algorithms proved to be insufficient for solving large reasoning problems, because they experienced a "combinatorial explosion": they became exponentially slower as the problems grew larger. In fact, even humans rarely use the step-by-step deduction that early AI research was able to model. They solve most of their problems using fast, intuitive judgements.

Knowledge Representation

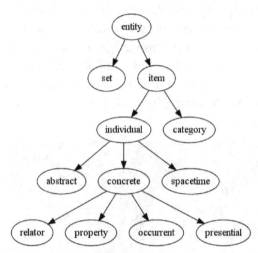

An ontology represents knowledge as a set of concepts within a domain and the relationships between those concepts.

Knowledge representation and knowledge engineering are central to classical AI research. Some "expert systems" attempt to gather together explicit knowledge possessed by experts in some narrow domain. In addition, some projects attempt to gather the "commonsense knowledge" known to the average person into a database containing extensive knowledge about the world. Among the things a comprehensive commonsense knowledge base would contain are: objects, properties, categories and relations between objects; situations, events, states and time; causes and effects; knowledge about knowledge (what we know about what other people know); and many other, less well researched domains. A representation of "what exists" is an ontology: the set of objects, relations, concepts, and properties formally described so that software agents can interpret them. The semantics of these are captured as description logic concepts, roles, and individuals, and typically implemented as classes, properties, and individuals in the Web Ontology Language. The most general ontologies are called upper ontologies, which attempt to provide a foundation for all other knowledge by acting as mediators between domain ontologies that cover specific knowledge about a particular knowledge domain (field of interest or area of concern). Such formal knowledge representations can be used in content-based indexing and retrieval, scene interpretation, clinical decision support, knowledge discovery (mining "interesting" and actionable inferences from large databases), and other areas.

Among the most difficult problems in knowledge representation are:

- Default reasoning and the qualification problem

    Many of the things people know take the form of "working assumptions". For example, if a bird comes up in conversation, people typically picture an animal that is fist sized, sings, and flies. None of these things are true about all birds. John WMcCarthy identified this problem in 1969 as the qualification problem:

for any commonsense rule that AI researchers care to represent, there tend to be a huge number of exceptions. Almost nothing is simply true or false in the way that abstract logic requires. AI research has explored a number of solutions to this problem.

- **The breadth of commonsense knowledge**

  The number of atomic facts that the average person knows is very large. Research projects that attempt to build a complete knowledge base of commonsense knowledge (e.g., Cyc) require enormous amounts of laborious ontological engineering—they must be built, by hand, one complicated concept at a time.

- **The subsymbolic form of some commonsense knowledge**

  Much of what people know is not represented as "facts" or "statements" that they could express verbally. For example, a chess master will avoid a particular chess position because it "feels too exposed" or an art critic can take one look at a statue and realize that it is a fake. These are non-conscious and sub-symbolic intuitions or tendencies in the human brain. Knowledge like this informs, supports and provides a context for symbolic, conscious knowledge. As with the related problem of sub-symbolic reasoning, it is hoped that situated AI, computational intelligence, or statistical AI will provide ways to represent this kind of knowledge.

Planning

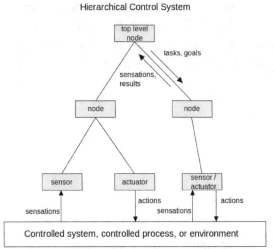

A hierarchical control system is a form of control system in which a set of devices and governing software is arranged in a hierarchy.

Intelligent agents must be able to set goals and achieve them. They need a way to visualize the future—a representation of the state of the world and be able to make predictions about how their actions will change it—and be able to make choices that maximize the utility (or "value") of available choices.

In classical planning problems, the agent can assume that it is the only system acting in the world, allowing the agent to be certain of the consequences of its actions. However, if the agent is not the only actor, then it requires that the agent can reason under uncertainty. This calls for an agent that can not only assess its environment and make predictions, but also evaluate its predictions and adapt based on its assessment.

Multi-agent planning uses the cooperation and competition of many agents to achieve a given goal. Emergent behavior such as this is used by evolutionary algorithms and swarm intelligence.

Learning

Machine learning, a fundamental concept of AI research since the field's inception, is the study of computer algorithms that improve automatically through experience.

Unsupervised learning is the ability to find patterns in a stream of input. Supervised learning includes both classification and numerical regression. Classification is used to determine what category something belongs in, after seeing a number of examples of things from several categories. Regression is the attempt to produce a function that describes the relationship between inputs and outputs and predicts how the outputs should change as the inputs change. Both classifiers and regression learners can be viewed as "function approximators" trying to learn an unknown (possibly implicit) function; for example, a spam classifier can be viewed as learning a function that maps from the text of an email to one of two categories, "spam" or "not spam". Computational learning theory can assess learners by computational complexity, by sample complexity (how much data is required), or by other notions of optimization. In reinforcement learning the agent is rewarded for good responses and punished for bad ones. The agent uses this sequence of rewards and punishments to form a strategy for operating in its problem space.

Natural Language Processing

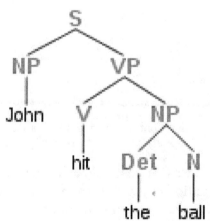

A parse tree represents the syntactic structure of a sentence according to some formal grammar.

Natural language processing (NLP) gives machines the ability to read and understand human language. A sufficiently powerful natural language processing system would enable natural-language user interfaces and the acquisition of knowledge directly from human-written sources, such as newswire texts. Some straightforward applications of natural language processing include information retrieval, text mining, question answering and machine translation. Many current approaches use word co-occurrence frequencies to construct syntactic representations of text. "Keyword spotting" strategies for search are popular and scalable but dumb; a search query for "dog" might only match documents with the literal word "dog" and miss a document with the word "poodle". "Lexical affinity" strategies use the occurrence of words such as "accident" to assess the sentiment of a document. Modern statistical NLP approaches can combine all these strategies as well as others, and often achieve acceptable accuracy at the page or paragraph level, but continue to lack the semantic understanding required to classify isolated sentences well. Besides the usual difficulties with encoding semantic commonsense knowledge, existing semantic NLP sometimes scales too poorly to be viable in business applications. Beyond semantic NLP, the ultimate goal of "narrative" NLP is to embody a full understanding of commonsense reasoning.

Perception

Feature detection (pictured: edge detection) helps AI compose informative abstract structures out of raw data.

Machine perception is the ability to use input from sensors (such as cameras (visible spectrum or infrared), microphones, wireless signals, and active lidar, sonar, radar, and tactile sensors) to deduce aspects of the world. Applications include speech recognition, facial recognition, and object recognition. Computer vision is the ability to analyze visual input. Such input is usually ambiguous; a giant, fifty-meter-tall pedestrian far away may produce exactly the same pixels as a nearby normal-sized pedestrian, requiring the AI to judge the relative likelihood and reasonableness of different interpretations, for example by using its "object model" to assess that fifty-meter pedestrians do not exist.

Motion and Manipulation

AI is heavily used in robotics. Advanced robotic arms and other industrial robots, widely used in modern factories, can learn from experience how to move efficiently despite the presence of friction and gear slippage. A modern mobile robot, when given a small, static, and visible environment, can easily determine its location and map its environment; however, dynamic environments, such as (in endoscopy) the interior of a patient's breathing body, pose a greater challenge. Motion planning is the process of breaking down a movement task into "primitives" such as individual joint movements. Such movement often involves compliant motion, a process where movement requires maintaining physical contact with an object. Moravec's paradox generalizes that low-level sensorimotor skills that humans take for granted are, counterintuitively, difficult to program into a robot; the paradox is named after Hans Moravec, who stated in 1988 that "it is comparatively easy to make computers exhibit adult level performance on intelligence tests or playing checkers, and difficult or impossible to give them the skills of a one-year-old when it comes to perception and mobility". This is attributed to the fact that, unlike checkers, physical dexterity has been a direct target of natural selection for millions of years.

Social Intelligence

Kismet, a robot with rudimentary social skills

Moravec's paradox can be extended to many forms of social intelligence. Distributed multi-agent coordination of autonomous vehicles remains a difficult problem. Affective computing is an interdisciplinary umbrella that comprises systems which recognize, interpret, process, or simulate human affects. Moderate successes related to affective computing include textual sentiment analysis and, more recently, multimodal affect analysis wherein AI classifies the affects displayed by a videotaped subject.

In the long run, social skills and an understanding of human emotion and game theory would be valuable to a social agent. Being able to predict the actions of others by understanding their motives and emotional states would allow an agent to make better decisions. Some computer systems mimic human emotion and expressions to appear more sensitive to the emotional dynamics of human interaction, or to otherwise facilitate human–computer interaction. Similarly, some virtual assistants are programmed to speak conversationally or even to banter humorously; this tends to give naive users an unrealistic conception of how intelligent existing computer agents actually are.

General Intelligence

Historically, projects such as the Cyc knowledge base (1984–) and the massive Japanese Fifth Generation Computer Systems initiative (1982–1992) attempted to cover the breadth of human cognition. These early projects failed to escape the limitations of non-quantitative symbolic logic models and, in retrospect, greatly underestimated the difficulty of cross-domain AI. Nowadays, the vast majority of current AI researchers work instead on tractable "narrow AI" applications (such as medical diagnosis or automobile navigation). Many researchers predict that such "narrow AI" work in different individual domains will eventually be incorporated into a machine with artificial general intelligence (AGI), combining most of the narrow skills mentioned in this section and at some point even exceeding human ability in most or all these areas. Many advances have general, cross-domain significance. One high-profile example is that DeepMind in the 2010s developed a "generalized artificial intelligence" that could learn many diverse Atari games on its own, and later developed a variant of the system which succeeds at sequential learning. Besides transfer learning, hypothetical AGI breakthroughs could include the development of reflective architectures that can engage in decision-theoretic metareasoning, and figuring out how to "slurp up" a comprehensive knowledge base from the entire unstructured Web. Some argue that some kind of (currently-undiscovered) conceptually straightforward, but mathematically difficult, "Master Algorithm" could lead to AGI. Finally, a few "emergent" approaches look to simulating human intelligence extremely closely, and believe that anthropomorphic features like an artificial brain or simulated child development may someday reach a critical point where general intelligence emerges.

Many of the problems in this section may also require general intelligence, if machines are to solve the problems as well as people do. For example, even specific straightforward tasks, like machine translation, require that a machine read and write in both languages (NLP), follow the author's argument (reason), know what is being talked about (knowledge), and faithfully reproduce the author's original intent (social intelligence). A problem like machine translation is considered "AI-complete", because all of these problems need to be solved simultaneously in order to reach human-level machine performance.

Approaches

There is no established unifying theory or paradigm that guides AI research. Researchers disagree about many issues. A few of the most long standing questions that have remained unanswered are these: should artificial intelligence simulate natural intelligence by studying psychology or neurobiology? Or is human biology as irrelevant to

AI research as bird biology is to aeronautical engineering? Can intelligent behavior be described using simple, elegant principles (such as logic or optimization)? Or does it necessarily require solving a large number of completely unrelated problems?

Cybernetics and Brain Simulation

In the 1940s and 1950s, a number of researchers explored the connection between neurobiology, information theory, and cybernetics. Some of them built machines that used electronic networks to exhibit rudimentary intelligence, such as W. Grey Walter's turtles and the Johns Hopkins Beast. Many of these researchers gathered for meetings of the Teleological Society at Princeton University and the Ratio Club in England. By 1960, this approach was largely abandoned, although elements of it would be revived in the 1980s.

Symbolic

When access to digital computers became possible in the middle 1950s, AI research began to explore the possibility that human intelligence could be reduced to symbol manipulation. The research was centered in three institutions: Carnegie Mellon University, Stanford and MIT, and as described below, each one developed its own style of research. John Haugeland named these symbolic approaches to AI "good old fashioned AI" or "GOFAI". During the 1960s, symbolic approaches had achieved great success at simulating high-level thinking in small demonstration programs. Approaches based on cybernetics or artificial neural networks were abandoned or pushed into the background. Researchers in the 1960s and the 1970s were convinced that symbolic approaches would eventually succeed in creating a machine with artificial general intelligence and considered this the goal of their field.

Cognitive Simulation

Economist Herbert Simon and Allen Newell studied human problem-solving skills and attempted to formalize them, and their work laid the foundations of the field of artificial intelligence, as well as cognitive science, operations research and management science. Their research team used the results of psychological experiments to develop programs that simulated the techniques that people used to solve problems. This tradition, centered at Carnegie Mellon University would eventually culminate in the development of the Soar architecture in the middle 1980s.

Logic-based

Unlike Simon and Newell, John McCarthy felt that machines did not need to simulate human thought, but should instead try to find the essence of abstract reasoning and problem solving, regardless of whether people used the same algorithms. His laboratory at Stanford (SAIL) focused on using formal logic to solve a wide variety of problems, including knowledge representation, planning and learning. Logic was also the focus of the work at the University of Edinburgh and elsewhere in Europe which led to the development of the programming language Prolog and the science of logic programming.

Anti-logic or Scruffy

Researchers at MIT (such as Marvin Minsky and Seymour Papert) found that solving difficult problems in vision and natural language processing required ad-hoc solutions – they argued that there was no simple and general principle (like logic) that would capture all the aspects of intelligent behavior. Roger Schank described their "anti-logic" approaches as "scruffy" (as opposed to the "neat" paradigms at CMU and Stanford). Commonsense knowledge bases (such as Doug Lenat's Cyc) are an example of "scruffy" AI, since they must be built by hand, one complicated concept at a time.

Knowledge-based

When computers with large memories became available around 1970, researchers from all three traditions began to build knowledge into AI applications. This "knowledge revolution" led to the development and deployment of expert systems (introduced by Edward Feigenbaum), the first truly successful form of AI software. The knowledge revolution was also driven by the realization that enormous amounts of knowledge would be required by many simple AI applications.

Sub-symbolic

By the 1980s progress in symbolic AI seemed to stall and many believed that symbolic systems would never be able to imitate all the processes of human cognition, especially perception, robotics, learning and pattern recognition. A number of researchers began to look into "sub-symbolic" approaches to specific AI problems. Sub-symbolic methods manage to approach intelligence without specific representations of knowledge.

Embodied Intelligence

This includes embodied, situated, behavior-based, and nouvelle AI. Researchers from the related field of robotics, such as Rodney Brooks, rejected symbolic AI and focused on the basic engineering problems that would allow robots to move and survive. Their work revived the non-symbolic viewpoint of the early cybernetics researchers of the 1950s and reintroduced the use of control theory in AI. This coincided with the development of the embodied mind thesis in the related field of cognitive science: the idea that aspects of the body (such as movement, perception and visualization) are required for higher intelligence.

Within developmental robotics, developmental learning approaches are elaborated upon to allow robots to accumulate repertoires of novel skills through autonomous self-exploration, social interaction with human teachers, and the use of guidance mechanisms (active learning, maturation, motor synergies, etc.).

Computational Intelligence and Soft Computing

Interest in neural networks and "connectionism" was revived by David Rumelhart and others in the middle of the 1980s. Artificial neural networks are an example of soft computing --- they are solutions to problems which cannot be solved with complete logical certainty, and where an approximate solution is often sufficient. Other soft computing approaches to AI include fuzzy systems, evolutionary computation and many statistical tools. The application of soft computing to AI is studied collectively by the emerging discipline of computational intelligence.

Statistical Learning

Much of traditional GOFAI got bogged down on *ad hoc* patches to symbolic computation that worked on their own toy models but failed to generalize to real-world results. However, around the 1990s, AI researchers adopted sophisticated mathematical tools, such as hidden Markov models (HMM), information theory, and normative Bayesian decision theory to compare or to unify competing architectures. The shared mathematical language permitted a high level of collaboration with more established fields (like mathematics, economics or operations research). Compared with GOFAI, new "statistical learning" techniques such as HMM and neural networks were gaining higher levels of accuracy in many practical domains such as data mining, without necessarily acquiring semantic understanding of the datasets. The increased successes with real-world data led to increasing emphasis on comparing different approaches against shared test data to see which approach performed best in a broader context than that provided by idiosyncratic toy models; AI research was becoming more scientific. Nowadays results of experiments are often rigorously measurable, and are sometimes (with difficulty) reproducible. Different statistical learning techniques have different limitations; for example, basic HMM cannot model the infinite possible combinations of natural language. Critics note that the shift from GOFAI to statistical learning is often also a shift away from Explainable AI. In AGI research, some scholars caution against over-reliance on statistical learning, and argue that continuing research into GOFAI will still be necessary to attain general intelligence.

Integrating the Approaches

Intelligent agent paradigm:

> An intelligent agent is a system that perceives its environment and takes actions which maximize its chances of success. The simplest intelligent agents are programs that solve specific problems. More complicated agents include human beings and organizations of human beings (such as firms). The paradigm

allows researchers to directly compare or even combine different approaches to isolated problems, by asking which agent is best at maximizing a given "goal function". An agent that solves a specific problem can use any approach that works – some agents are symbolic and logical, some are sub-symbolic artificial neural networks and others may use new approaches. The paradigm also gives researchers a common language to communicate with other fields—such as decision theory and economics—that also use concepts of abstract agents. Building a complete agent requires researchers to address realistic problems of integration; for example, because sensory systems give uncertain information about the environment, planning systems must be able to function in the presence of uncertainty. The intelligent agent paradigm became widely accepted during the 1990s.

Agent architectures and cognitive architectures:

Researchers have designed systems to build intelligent systems out of interacting intelligent agents in a multi-agent system. A hierarchical control system provides a bridge between sub-symbolic AI at its lowest, reactive levels and traditional symbolic AI at its highest levels, where relaxed time constraints permit planning and world modelling. Some cognitive architectures are custom-built to solve a narrow problem; others, such as Soar, are designed to mimic human cognition and to provide insight into general intelligence. Modern extensions of Soar are hybrid intelligent systems that include both symbolic and sub-symbolic components.

Tools

AI has developed a large number of tools to solve the most difficult problems in computer science. A few of the most general of these methods are discussed below.

Search and Optimization

Many problems in AI can be solved in theory by intelligently searching through many possible solutions: Reasoning can be reduced to performing a search. For example, logical proof can be viewed as searching for a path that leads from premises to conclusions, where each step is the application of an inference rule. Planning algorithms search through trees of goals and subgoals, attempting to find a path to a target goal, a process called means-ends analysis. Robotics algorithms for moving limbs and grasping objects use local searches in configuration space. Many learning algorithms use search algorithms based on optimization.

Simple exhaustive searches are rarely sufficient for most real world problems: the search space (the number of places to search) quickly grows to astronomical numbers. The result is a search that is too slow or never completes. The solution, for many problems, is to use "heuristics" or "rules of thumb" that prioritize choices in favor of those that are more likely to reach a goal, and to do so in a shorter number of steps. In some search methodologies heuristics can also serve to entirely eliminate some choices that are unlikely to lead to a goal (called "pruning the search tree"). Heuristics supply the program with a "best guess" for the path on which the solution lies. Heuristics limit the search for solutions into a smaller sample size.

A very different kind of search came to prominence in the 1990s, based on the mathematical theory of optimization. For many problems, it is possible to begin the search with some form of a guess and then refine the guess incrementally until no more refinements can be made. These algorithms can be visualized as blind hill climbing: we begin the search at a random point on the landscape, and then, by jumps or steps, we keep moving our guess uphill, until we reach the top. Other optimization algorithms are simulated annealing, beam search and random optimization.

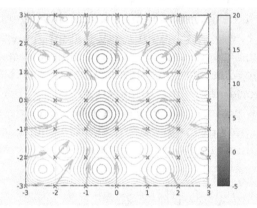

A particle swarm seeking the global minimum

Evolutionary computation uses a form of optimization search. For example, they may begin with a population of organisms (the guesses) and then allow them to mutate and recombine, selecting only the fittest to survive each generation (refining the guesses). Classic evolutionary algorithms include genetic algorithms, gene expression programming, and genetic programming. Alternatively, distributed search processes can coordinate via swarm intelligence algorithms. Two popular swarm algorithms used in search are particle swarm optimization (inspired by bird flocking) and ant colony optimization (inspired by ant trails).

Logic

Logic is used for knowledge representation and problem solving, but it can be applied to other problems as well. For example, the satplan algorithm uses logic for planning and inductive logic programming is a method for learning.

Several different forms of logic are used in AI research. Propositional logic involves truth functions such as "or" and "not". First-order logic adds quantifiers and predicates, and can express facts about objects, their properties, and their relations with each other. Fuzzy set theory assigns a "degree of truth" (between 0 and 1) to vague statements such as "Alice is old" (or rich, or tall, or hungry) that are too linguistically imprecise to be completely true or false. Fuzzy logic is successfully used in control systems to allow experts to contribute vague rules such as "if you are close to the destination station and moving fast, increase the train's brake pressure"; these vague rules can then be numerically refined within the system. Fuzzy logic fails to scale well in knowledge bases; many AI researchers question the validity of chaining fuzzy-logic inferences.

Default logics, non-monotonic logics and circumscription are forms of logic designed to help with default reasoning and the qualification problem. Several extensions of logic have been designed to handle specific domains of knowledge, such as: description logics; situation calculus, event calculus and fluent calculus (for representing events and time); causal calculus; belief calculus; and modal logics.

Overall, qualitiative symbolic logic is brittle and scales poorly in the presence of noise or other uncertainty. Exceptions to rules are numerous, and it is difficult for logical systems to function in the presence of contradictory rules.

Probabilistic Methods for Uncertain Reasoning

Many problems in AI (in reasoning, planning, learning, perception and robotics) require the agent to operate with incomplete or uncertain information. AI researchers have devised a number of powerful tools to solve these problems using methods from probability theory and economics.

Bayesian networks are a very general tool that can be used for a large number of problems: reasoning (using the Bayesian inference algorithm), learning (using the expectation-maximization algorithm), planning (using decision networks) and perception (using dynamic Bayesian networks). Probabilistic algorithms can also be used for filtering, prediction, smoothing and finding explanations for streams of data, helping perception systems to analyze processes that occur over time (e.g., hidden Markov models or Kalman filters). Compared with symbolic logic, formal Bayesian inference is computationally expensive. For inference to be tractable, most observations must be conditionally independent of one another. Complicated graphs with diamonds or other "loops" (undirected cycles) can require a sophisticated method such as Markov Chain Monte Carlo, which spreads an ensemble of random walkers throughout the Bayesian network and attempts to converge to an assessment of the conditional probabilities. Bayesian networks are used on XBox Live to rate and match players; wins and losses are "evidence" of how good a player is. AdSense uses a Bayesian network with over 300 million edges to learn which ads to serve.

A key concept from the science of economics is "utility": a measure of how valuable something is to an intelligent agent. Precise mathematical tools have been developed that analyze how an agent can make choices and plan, using decision theory, decision analysis, and information value theory. These tools include models such as Markov decision processes, dynamic decision networks, game theory and mechanism design.

Classifiers and Statistical Learning Methods

The simplest AI applications can be divided into two types: classifiers ("if shiny then diamond") and controllers ("if shiny then pick up"). Controllers do, however, also classify conditions before inferring actions, and therefore classification forms a central part of many AI systems. Classifiers are functions that use pattern matching to determine a closest match. They can be tuned according to examples, making them very attractive for use in AI. These examples are known as observations or patterns. In supervised learning, each pattern belongs to a certain predefined class. A class can be seen as a decision that has to be made. All the observations combined with their class labels are known as a data set. When a new observation is received, that observation is classified based on previous experience.

A classifier can be trained in various ways; there are many statistical and machine learning approaches. The decision tree is perhaps the most widely used machine learning algorithm. Other widely used classifiers are the neural network, k-nearest neighbor algorithm, kernel methods such as the support vector machine (SVM), Gaussian mixture model, the extremely popular naive Bayes classifier[i] and improved version of decision tree - decision stream. Classifier performance depends greatly on the characteristics of the data to be classified, such as the dataset size, the dimensionality, and the level of noise. Model-based classifiers perform well if the assumed model is an extremely good fit for the actual data. Otherwise, if no matching model is available, and if accuracy (rather than speed or scalability) is the sole concern, conventional wisdom is that discriminative classifiers (especially SVM) tend to be more accurate than model-based classifiers such as "naive Bayes" on most practical data sets.

Artificial Neural Networks

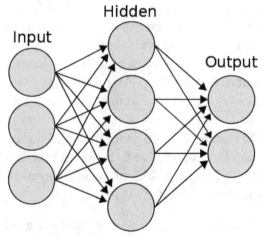

A neural network is an interconnected group of nodes,
akin to the vast network of neurons in the human brain.

Neural networks, or neural nets, were inspired by the architecture of neurons in the human brain. A simple "neuron" N accepts input from multiple other neurons, each of which, when activated (or "fired"), cast a weighted "vote" for or against whether neuron N should itself activate. Learning requires an algorithm to adjust these weights based on the training data; one simple algorithm (dubbed "fire together, wire together") is to increase the weight between two connected neurons when the activation of one triggers the successful activation of another. The net forms "concepts" that are distributed among a subnetwork of shared[j] neurons that tend to fire together; a concept meaning "leg" might be coupled with a subnetwork meaning "foot" that includes the sound for "foot". Neurons have a continuous spectrum of activation; in addition, neurons can process inputs in a nonlinear way rather than weighing straightforward votes. Modern neural nets can learn both continuous functions and, surprisingly, digital logical operations. Neural networks' early successes included predicting the stock market and (in 1995) a mostly self-driving car. In the 2010s, advances in neural networks using deep learning thrust AI into widespread public consciousness and contributed to an enormous upshift in corporate AI spending; for example, AI-related M&A in 2017 was over 25 times as large as in 2015.

The study of non-learning artificial neural networks began in the decade before the field of AI research was founded, in the work of Walter Pitts and Warren McCullouch. Frank Rosenblatt invented the perceptron, a learning network with a single layer, similar to the old concept of linear regression. Early pioneers also include Alexey Grigorevich Ivakhnenko, Teuvo Kohonen, Stephen Grossberg, Kunihiko Fukushima, Christoph von der Malsburg, David Willshaw, Shun-Ichi Amari, Bernard Widrow, John Hopfield, Eduardo R. Caianiello, and others.

The main categories of networks are acyclic or feedforward neural networks (where the signal passes in only one direction) and recurrent neural networks (which allow feedback and short-term memories of previous input events). Among the most popular feedforward networks are perceptrons, multi-layer perceptrons and radial basis networks. Neural networks can be applied to the problem of intelligent control (for robotics) or learning, using such techniques as Hebbian learning ("fire together, wire together"), GMDH or competitive learning.

Today, neural networks are often trained by the backpropagation algorithm, which had been around since 1970 as the reverse mode of automatic differentiation published by Seppo Linnainmaa, and was introduced to neural networks by Paul Werbos.

Hierarchical temporal memory is an approach that models some of the structural and algorithmic properties of the neocortex.

In short, most neural networks use some form of gradient descent on a hand-created neural topology. However, some research groups, such as Uber, argue that simple neuroevolution to mutate new neural network topologies and weights may be competitive with sophisticated gradient descent approaches. One advantage of neuroevolution is that it may be less prone to get caught in "dead ends".

Deep Feedforward Neural Networks

Deep learning is any artificial neural network that can learn a long chain of causal links. For example, a feedforward network with six hidden layers can learn a seven-link causal chain (six hidden layers + output layer) and has a "credit assignment path" (CAP) depth of seven. Many deep learning systems need to be able to learn chains ten or more causal links in length. Deep learning has transformed many important subfields of artificial intelligence, including computer vision, speech recognition, natural language processing and others.

The expression "Deep Learning" was introduced to the Machine Learning community by Rina Dechter in 1986 and gained traction after Igor Aizenberg and colleagues introduced it to Artificial Neural Networks in 2000. The first functional Deep Learning networks were published by Alexey Grigorevich Ivakhnenko and V. G. Lapa in 1965. These networks are trained one layer at a time. Ivakhnenko's 1971 paper describes the learning of a deep feedforward multilayer perceptron with eight layers, already much deeper than many later networks. Another way of pre-training many-layered feedforward neural networks (FNNs) one layer at a time, treating each layer in turn as an unsupervised restricted Boltzmann machine, then using supervised backpropagation for fine-tuning. Similar to shallow artificial neural networks, deep neural networks can model complex non-linear relationships. Over the last few years, advances in both machine learning algorithms and computer hardware have led to more efficient methods for training deep neural networks that contain many layers of non-linear hidden units and a very large output layer.

Deep learning often uses convolutional neural networks (CNNs), whose origins can be traced back to the Neocognitron introduced by Kunihiko Fukushima in 1980. In 1989, Yann LeCun and colleagues applied backpropagation to such an architecture. In the early 2000s, in an industrial application CNNs already processed an estimated 10% to 20% of all the checks written in the US. Since 2011, fast implementations of CNNs on GPUs have won many visual pattern recognition competitions.

CNNs with 12 convolutional layers were used in conjunction with reinforcement learning by Deepmind's "AlphaGo Lee", the program that beat a top Go champion in 2016.

Deep Recurrent Neural Networks

Early on, deep learning was also applied to sequence learning with recurrent neural networks (RNNs) which are in theory Turing complete and can run arbitrary programs to process arbitrary sequences of inputs. The depth of an RNN is unlimited and depends on the length of its input sequence; thus, an RNN is an example of deep learning. RNNs can be trained by gradient descent but suffer from the vanishing gradient problem. In 1992, it was shown that unsupervised pre-training of a stack of recurrent neural networks can speed up subsequent supervised learning of deep sequential problems.

Numerous researchers now use variants of a deep learning recurrent NN called the long short-term memory (LSTM) network published by Hochreiter & Schmidhuber in 1997. LSTM is often trained by Connectionist Temporal Classification (CTC). At Google, Microsoft and Baidu this approach has revolutionised speech recognition. For example, in 2015, Google's speech recognition experienced a dramatic performance jump of 49% through CTC-trained LSTM, which is now available through Google Voice to billions of smartphone users. Google also used LSTM to improve machine translation, Language Modeling and Multilingual Language Processing. LSTM combined with CNNs also improved automatic image captioning and a plethora of other applications.

Evaluating Progress

AI, like electricity or the steam engine, is a general purpose technology. There is no consensus on how to characterize which tasks AI tends to excel at. While projects such as AlphaZero have succeeded in generating their own knowledge from scratch, many other machine learning projects require large training datasets. Researcher Andrew Ng has suggested, as a "highly imperfect rule of thumb", that "almost anything a typical human can do with less than one second of mental thought, we can probably now or in the near future automate using AI." Moravec's paradox suggests that AI lags humans at many tasks that the human brain has specifically evolved to perform well.

Games provide a well-publicized benchmark for assessing rates of progress. AlphaGo around 2016 brought the era of classical board-game benchmarks to an close. Games of imperfect knowledge provide new challenges to AI in the area of game theory. E-sports such as StarCraft continue to provide additional public benchmarks. There are many competitions and prizes, such as the Imagenet Challenge, to promote research in artificial intelligence. The main areas of competition include general machine intelligence, conversational behavior, data-mining, robotic cars, and robot soccer as well as conventional games.

The "imitation game" (an interpretation of the 1950 Turing test that assesses whether a computer can imitate a human) is nowadays considered too exploitable to be a meaningful benchmark. A derivative of the Turing test is the Completely Automated Public Turing test to tell Computers and Humans Apart (CAPTCHA). As the name implies, this helps to determine that a user is an actual person and not a computer posing as a human. In contrast to the standard Turing test, CAPTCHA is administered by a machine and targeted to a human as opposed to being administered by a human and targeted to a machine. A computer asks a user to complete a simple test then generates a grade for that test. Computers are unable to solve the problem, so correct solutions are deemed to be the result of a person taking the test. A common type of CAPTCHA is the test that requires the typing of distorted letters, numbers or symbols that appear in an image undecipherable by a computer.

Proposed "universal intelligence" tests aim to compare how well machines, humans, and even non-human animals perform on problem sets that are generic as possible. At an extreme, the test suite can contain every possible problem, weighted by Kolmogorov complexity; unfortunately, these problem sets tend to be dominated by impoverished pattern-matching exercises where a tuned AI can easily exceed human performance levels.

Applications

AI is relevant to any intellectual task. Modern artificial intelligence techniques are pervasive and are too numerous to list here. Frequently, when a technique reaches mainstream use, it is no longer considered artificial intelligence; this phenomenon is described as the AI effect.

High-profile examples of AI include autonomous vehicles (such as drones and self-driving cars), medical diagnosis, creating art (such as poetry), proving mathematical theorems, playing games (such as Chess or Go), search engines (such as Google search), online assistants (such as Siri), image recognition in photographs, spam filtering, prediction of judicial decisions and targeting online advertisements.

An automated online assistant providing customer service on a web page – one of many very primitive applications of artificial intelligence

With social media sites overtaking TV as a source for news for young people and news organisations increasingly reliant on social media platforms for generating distribution, major publishers now use artificial intelligence (AI) technology to post stories more effectively and generate higher volumes of traffic.

Healthcare

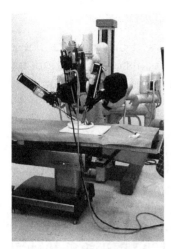

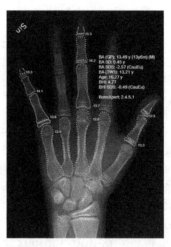

| A patient-side surgical arm of Da Vinci Surgical System | X-ray of a hand, with automatic calculation of bone age by computer software |

Artificial intelligence is breaking into the healthcare industry by assisting doctors. According to Bloomberg Technology, Microsoft has developed AI to help doctors find the right treatments for cancer. There is a great amount of research and drugs developed relating to cancer. In detail, there are more than 800 medicines and vaccines to treat cancer. This negatively affects the doctors, because there are too many options to choose from, making it more difficult to choose the right drugs for the patients. Microsoft is working on a project to develop a machine called "Hanover". Its goal is to memorize all the papers necessary to cancer and help predict which combinations of drugs will be most effective for each patient. One project that is being worked on at the moment is fighting myeloid leukemia, a fatal cancer where the treatment has not improved in decades. Another study was reported to have found that artificial intelligence was as good as trained doctors in identifying skin cancers. Another study is using artificial intelligence to try and monitor multiple high-risk patients, and this is done by asking each patient numerous questions based on data acquired from live doctor to patient interactions.

According to CNN, a recent study by surgeons at the Children's National Medical Center in Washington successfully demonstrated surgery with an autonomous robot. The team supervised the robot while it performed soft-tissue surgery, stitching together a pig's bowel during open surgery, and doing so better than a human surgeon, the team claimed. IBM has created its own artificial intelligence computer, the IBM Watson, which has beaten human intelligence (at some levels). Watson not only won at the game show *Jeopardy!* against former champions, but was declared a hero after successfully diagnosing a woman who was suffering from leukemia.

Automotive

Advancements in AI have contributed to the growth of the automotive industry through the creation and evolution of self-driving vehicles. As of 2016, there are over 30 companies utilizing AI into the creation of driverless cars. A few companies involved with AI include Tesla, Google, and Apple.

Many components contribute to the functioning of self-driving cars. These vehicles incorporate systems such as braking, lane changing, collision prevention, navigation and mapping. Together, these systems, as well as high performance computers, are integrated into one complex vehicle.

Recent developments in autonomous automobiles have made the innovation of self-driving trucks possible, though they are still in the testing phase. The UK government has passed legislation to begin testing of self-driving truck platoons in 2018. Self-driving truck platoons are a fleet of self-driving trucks following the lead of one non-self-driving truck, so the truck platoons aren't entirely autonomous yet. Meanwhile, the Daimler, a German automobile corporation, is testing the Freightliner Inspiration which is a semi-autonomous truck that will only be used on the highway.

One main factor that influences the ability for a driver-less automobile to function is mapping. In general, the vehicle would be pre-programmed with a map of the area being driven. This map would include data on the approximations of street light and curb heights in order for the vehicle to be aware of its surroundings. However, Google has been working on an algorithm with the purpose of eliminating the need for pre-programmed maps and instead, creating a device that would be able to adjust to a variety of new surroundings. Some self-driving cars are not equipped with steering wheels or brake pedals, so there has also been research focused on creating an algorithm that is capable of maintaining a safe environment for the passengers in the vehicle through awareness of speed and driving conditions.

Another factor that is influencing the ability for a driver-less automobile is the safety of the passenger. To make a driver-less automobile, engineers must program it to handle high risk situations. These situations could include a head on collision with pedestrians. The car's main goal should be to make a decision that would avoid hitting the pedestrians and saving the passengers in the car. But there is a possibility the car would need to make a decision that would put someone in danger. In other words, the car would need to decide to save the pedestrians or the passengers. The programing of the car in these situations is crucial to a successful driver-less automobile.

Finance and Economics

Financial institutions have long used artificial neural network systems to detect charges or claims outside of the norm, flagging these for human investigation. The use of AI in banking can be traced back to 1987 when Security Pacific National Bank in US set-up a

Fraud Prevention Task force to counter the unauthorised use of debit cards. Programs like Kasisto and Moneystream are using AI in financial services.

Banks use artificial intelligence systems today to organize operations, maintain book-keeping, invest in stocks, and manage properties. AI can react to changes overnight or when business is not taking place. In August 2001, robots beat humans in a simulated financial trading competition. AI has also reduced fraud and financial crimes by monitoring behavioral patterns of users for any abnormal changes or anomalies.

The use of AI machines in the market in applications such as online trading and decision making has changed major economic theories. For example, AI based buying and selling platforms have changed the law of supply and demand in that it is now possible to easily estimate individualized demand and supply curves and thus individualized pricing. Furthermore, AI machines reduce information asymmetry in the market and thus making markets more efficient while reducing the volume of trades. Furthermore, AI in the markets limits the consequences of behavior in the markets again making markets more efficient. Other theories where AI has had impact include in rational choice, rational expectations, game theory, Lewis turning point, portfolio optimization and counterfactual thinking.

Video Games

In video games, artificial intelligence is routinely used to generate dynamic purposeful behavior in non-player characters (NPCs). In addition, well-understood AI techniques are routinely used for pathfinding. Some researchers consider NPC AI in games to be a "solved problem" for most production tasks. Games with more atypical AI include the AI director of *Left 4 Dead* (2008) and the neuroevolutionary training of platoons in *Supreme Commander 2* (2010).

Military

Worldwide annual military spending on robotics rose from 5.1 billion USD in 2010 to 7.5 billion USD in 2015. Military drones capable of autonomous action are widely considered a useful asset. In 2017, Vladimir Putin stated that "Whoever becomes the leader in (artificial intelligence) will become the ruler of the world". Many artificial intelligence researchers seek to distance themselves from military applications of AI.

Audit

For financial statements audit, AI makes continuous audit possible. AI tools could analyze many sets of different information immediately. The potential benefit would be the overall audit risk will be reduced, the level of assurance will be increased and the time duration of audit will be reduced.

Advertising

A report by the Guardian newspaper in the UK in 2018 found that online gambling companies were using AI to predict the behavior of customers in order to target them with personalized promotions.

Philosophy and Ethics

There are three philosophical questions related to AI:

1. Is artificial general intelligence possible? Can a machine solve any problem that a human being can solve using intelligence? Or are there hard limits to what a machine can accomplish?

2. Are intelligent machines dangerous? How can we ensure that machines behave ethically and that they are used ethically?

3. Can a machine have a mind, consciousness and mental states in exactly the same sense that human beings do? Can a machine be sentient, and thus deserve certain rights? Can a machine intentionally cause harm?

The limits of Artificial General Intelligence

Can a machine be intelligent? Can it "think"?

- *Alan Turing's "polite convention"*

  We need not decide if a machine can "think"; we need only decide if a machine can act as intelligently as a human being. This approach to the philosophical problems associated with artificial intelligence forms the basis of the Turing test.

- *The Dartmouth proposal*

  "Every aspect of learning or any other feature of intelligence can be so precisely described that a machine can be made to simulate it." This conjecture was printed in the proposal for the Dartmouth Conference of 1956, and represents the position of most working AI researchers.

- *Newell and Simon's physical symbol system hypothesis*

  "A physical symbol system has the necessary and sufficient means of general intelligent action." Newell and Simon argue that intelligence consists of formal operations on symbols. Hubert Dreyfus argued that, on the contrary, human expertise depends on unconscious instinct rather than conscious symbol manipulation and on having a "feel" for the situation rather than explicit symbolic knowledge.

- *Gödelian arguments*

    Gödel himself, John Lucas (in 1961) and Roger Penrose (in a more detailed argument from 1989 onwards) made highly technical arguments that human mathematicians can consistently see the truth of their own "Gödel statements" and therefore have computational abilities beyond that of mechanical Turing machines. However, the modern consensus in the scientific and mathematical community is that these "Gödelian arguments" fail.

- *The artificial brain argument*

    The brain can be simulated by machines and because brains are intelligent, simulated brains must also be intelligent; thus machines can be intelligent. Hans Moravec, Ray Kurzweil and others have argued that it is technologically feasible to copy the brain directly into hardware and software, and that such a simulation will be essentially identical to the original.

- *The AI effect*

    Machines are *already* intelligent, but observers have failed to recognize it. When Deep Blue beat Garry Kasparov in chess, the machine was acting intelligently. However, onlookers commonly discount the behavior of an artificial intelligence program by arguing that it is not "real" intelligence after all; thus "real" intelligence is whatever intelligent behavior people can do that machines still cannot. This is known as the AI Effect: "AI is whatever hasn't been done yet."

Potential Risks and Moral Reasoning

Widespread use of artificial intelligence could have unintended consequences that are dangerous or undesirable. Scientists from the Future of Life Institute, among others, described some short-term research goals to see how AI influences the economy, the laws and ethics that are involved with AI and how to minimize AI security risks. In the long-term, the scientists have proposed to continue optimizing function while minimizing possible security risks that come along with new technologies.

Machines with intelligence have the potential to use their intelligence to make ethical decisions. Research in this area includes "machine ethics", "artificial moral agents", and the study of "malevolent vs. friendly AI".

Existential Risk

The development of full artificial intelligence could spell the end of the human race. Once humans develop artificial intelligence, it will take off on its own and redesign itself at an ever-increasing rate. Humans, who are limited by slow bio-logical evolution, couldn't compete and would be superseded.

—Stephen Hawking

A common concern about the development of artificial intelligence is the potential threat it could pose to humanity. This concern has recently gained attention after mentions by celebrities including the late Stephen Hawking, Bill Gates, and Elon Musk. A group of prominent tech titans including Peter Thiel, Amazon Web Services and Musk have committed $1billion to OpenAI a nonprofit company aimed at championing responsible AI development. The opinion of experts within the field of artificial intelligence is mixed, with sizable fractions both concerned and unconcerned by risk from eventual superhumanly-capable AI.

Nick Bostrom provides an argument that artificial intelligence will pose a threat to mankind. He argues that sufficiently intelligent AI, if it chooses actions based on achieving some goal, will exhibit convergent behavior such as acquiring resources or protecting itself from being shut down. If this AI's goals do not reflect humanity's – one example is an AI told to compute as many digits of pi as possible – it might harm humanity in order to acquire more resources or prevent itself from being shut down, ultimately to better achieve its goal.

For this danger to be realized, the hypothetical AI would have to overpower or out-think all of humanity, which a minority of experts argue is a possibility far enough in the future to not be worth researching. Other counterarguments revolve around humans being either intrinsically or convergently valuable from the perspective of an artificial intelligence.

Concern over risk from artificial intelligence has led to some high-profile donations and investments. In January 2015, Elon Musk donated ten million dollars to the Future of Life Institute to fund research on understanding AI decision making. The goal of the institute is to "grow wisdom with which we manage" the growing power of technology. Musk also funds companies developing artificial intelligence such as Google DeepMind and Vicarious to "just keep an eye on what's going on with artificial intelligence. I think there is potentially a dangerous outcome there."

Development of militarized artificial intelligence is a related concern. Currently, 50+ countries are researching battlefield robots, including the United States, China, Russia, and the United Kingdom. Many people concerned about risk from superintelligent AI also want to limit the use of artificial soldiers.

Devaluation of Humanity

Joseph Weizenbaum wrote that AI applications cannot, by definition, successfully simulate genuine human empathy and that the use of AI technology in fields such as customer service or psychotherapy was deeply misguided. Weizenbaum was also bothered that AI researchers (and some philosophers) were willing to view the human mind as nothing more than a computer program (a position now known as computationalism). To Weizenbaum these points suggest that AI research devalues human life.

Decrease in Demand for Human Labor

The relationship between automation and employment is complicated. While automation eliminates old jobs, it also creates new jobs through micro-economic and macro-economic effects. Unlike previous waves of automation, many middle-class jobs may be eliminated by artificial intelligence; *The Economist* states that "the worry that AI could do to white-collar jobs what steam power did to blue-collar ones during the Industrial Revolution" is "worth taking seriously". Subjective estimates of the risk vary widely; for example, Michael Osborne and Carl Benedikt Frey estimate 47% of U.S. jobs are at "high risk" of potential automation, while an OECD report classifies only 9% of U.S. jobs as "high risk". Jobs at extreme risk range from paralegals to fast food cooks, while job demand is likely to increase for care-related professions ranging from personal healthcare to the clergy. Author Martin Ford and others go further and argue that a large number of jobs are routine, repetitive and (to an AI) predictable; Ford warns that these jobs may be automated in the next couple of decades, and that many of the new jobs may not be "accessible to people with average capability", even with retraining. Economists point out that in the past technology has tended to increase rather than reduce total employment, but acknowledge that "we're in uncharted territory" with AI.

Artificial Moral Agents

This raises the issue of how ethically the machine should behave towards both humans and other AI agents. This issue was addressed by Wendell Wallach in his book titled *Moral Machines* in which he introduced the concept of artificial moral agents (AMA). For Wallach, AMAs have become a part of the research landscape of artificial intelligence as guided by its two central questions which he identifies as "Does Humanity Want Computers Making Moral Decisions" and "Can (Ro)bots Really Be Moral". For Wallach the question is not centered on the issue of *whether* machines can demonstrate the equivalent of moral behavior in contrast to the *constraints* which society may place on the development of AMAs.

Machine Ethics

The field of machine ethics is concerned with giving machines ethical principles, or a procedure for discovering a way to resolve the ethical dilemmas they might encounter, enabling them to function in an ethically responsible manner through their own ethical decision making. The field was delineated in the AAAI Fall 2005 Symposium on Machine Ethics: "Past research concerning the relationship between technology and ethics has largely focused on responsible and irresponsible use of technology by human beings, with a few people being interested in how human beings ought to treat machines. In all cases, only human beings have engaged in ethical reasoning. The time has come for adding an ethical dimension to at least some machines. Recognition of the ethical ramifications of behavior involving machines, as well as recent and potential developments in machine autonomy, necessitate this. In contrast to computer hacking, software property issues, privacy issues and other topics normally ascribed to computer ethics, machine ethics is concerned with the behavior of machines towards human users and other machines. Research in machine ethics is key to alleviating concerns with autonomous systems—it could be argued that the notion of autonomous machines without such a dimension is at the root of all fear concerning machine intelligence. Further, investigation of machine ethics could enable the discovery of problems with current ethical theories, advancing our thinking about Ethics." Machine ethics is sometimes referred to as machine morality, computational ethics or computational morality. A variety of perspectives of this nascent field can be found in the collected edition "Machine Ethics" that stems from the AAAI Fall 2005 Symposium on Machine Ethics.

Malevolent and Friendly AI

Political scientist Charles T. Rubin believes that AI can be neither designed nor guaranteed to be benevolent. He argues that "any sufficiently advanced benevolence may be indistinguishable from malevolence." Humans should not assume machines or robots would treat us favorably, because there is no *a priori* reason to believe that they would be sympathetic to our system of morality, which has evolved along with our particular biology (which AIs would not share). Hyper-intelligent software may not necessarily decide to support the continued existence of humanity, and would be extremely difficult to stop. This topic has also recently begun to be discussed in academic publications as a real source of risks to civilization, humans, and planet Earth.

Physicist Stephen Hawking, Microsoft founder Bill Gates, and SpaceX founder Elon Musk have expressed concerns about the possibility that AI could evolve to the point that humans could not control it, with Hawking theorizing that this could "spell the end of the human race".

One proposal to deal with this is to ensure that the first generally intelligent AI is 'Friendly AI', and will then be able to control subsequently developed AIs. Some question whether this kind of check could really remain in place.

Leading AI researcher Rodney Brooks writes, "I think it is a mistake to be worrying about us developing malevolent AI anytime in the next few hundred years. I think the worry stems from a fundamental error in not distinguishing the difference between the very real recent advances in a particular aspect of AI, and the enormity and complexity of building sentient volitional intelligence."

Machine Consciousness, Sentience and Mind

If an AI system replicates all key aspects of human intelligence, will that system also be sentient – will it have a mind which has conscious experiences? This question is closely related to the philosophical problem as to the nature of human consciousness, generally referred to as the hard problem of consciousness.

Consciousness

Computationalism and Functionalism

Computationalism is the position in the philosophy of mind that the human mind or the human brain (or both) is an information processing system and that thinking is a form of computing. Computationalism argues that the relationship between mind and body is similar or identical to the relationship between software and hardware and thus may be a solution to the mind-body problem. This philosophical position was inspired by the work of AI researchers and cognitive scientists in the 1960s and was originally proposed by philosophers Jerry Fodor and Hilary Putnam.

Strong AI Hypothesis

The philosophical position that John Searle has named "strong AI" states: "The appropriately programmed computer with the right inputs and outputs would thereby have a mind in exactly the same sense human beings have minds." Searle counters this assertion with his Chinese room argument, which asks us to look *inside* the computer and try to find where the "mind" might be.

Robot Rights

Mary Shelley's *Frankenstein* considers a key issue in the ethics of artificial intelligence: if a machine can be created that has intelligence, could it also *feel*? If it can feel, does it have the same rights as a human? The idea also appears in modern science fiction, such as the film *A.I.: Artificial Intelligence*, in which humanoid machines have the ability to feel emotions. This issue, now known as "robot rights", is currently being considered by, for example, California's Institute for the Future, although many critics believe that the discussion is premature. Some critics of transhumanism argue that any hypothetical robot rights would lie on a spectrum with animal rights and human rights. The subject is profoundly discussed in the 2010 documentary film *Plug & Pray*.

Superintelligence

Are there limits to how intelligent machines – or human-machine hybrids – can be? A superintelligence, hyperintelligence, or superhuman intelligence is a hypothetical agent that would possess intelligence far surpassing that of the brightest and most gifted human mind. "Superintelligence" may also refer to the form or degree of intelligence possessed by such an agent.

Technological Singularity

If research into Strong AI produced sufficiently intelligent software, it might be able to reprogram and improve itself. The improved software would be even better at improving itself, leading to recursive self-improvement. The new intelligence could thus increase exponentially and dramatically surpass humans. Science fiction writer Vernor Vinge named this scenario "singularity". Technological singularity is when accelerating progress in technologies will cause a runaway effect wherein artificial intelligence will exceed human intellectual capacity and control, thus radically changing or even ending civilization. Because the capabilities of such an intelligence may be impossible to comprehend, the technological singularity is an occurrence beyond which events are unpredictable or even unfathomable.

Ray Kurzweil has used Moore's law (which describes the relentless exponential improvement in digital technology) to calculate that desktop computers will have the same processing power as human brains by the year 2029, and predicts that the singularity will occur in 2045.

Transhumanism

> You awake one morning to find your brain has another lobe functioning. Invisible, this auxiliary lobe answers your questions with information beyond the realm of your own memory, suggests plausible courses of action, and asks questions that help bring out relevant facts. You quickly come to rely on the new lobe so much that you stop wondering how it works. You just use it. This is the dream of artificial intelligence.
>
> — *Byte, April 1985*

Robot designer Hans Moravec, cyberneticist Kevin Warwick and inventor Ray Kurzweil have predicted that humans and machines will merge in the future into cyborgs that are more capable and powerful than either. This idea, called transhumanism, which has roots in Aldous Huxley and Robert Ettinger, has been illustrated in fiction as well, for example in the manga *Ghost in the Shell* and the science-fiction series *Dune*.

In the 1980s artist Hajime Sorayama's Sexy Robots series were painted and published in Japan depicting the actual organic human form with lifelike muscular metallic skins and later "the Gynoids" book followed that was used by or influenced movie makers including George Lucas and other creatives. Sorayama never considered these organic robots to be real part of nature but always unnatural product of the human mind, a fantasy existing in the mind even when realized in actual form.

Edward Fredkin argues that "artificial intelligence is the next stage in evolution", an idea first proposed by Samuel Butler's "Darwin among the Machines" (1863), and expanded upon by George Dyson in his book of the same name in 1998.

Artificial Intelligence, Situated Approach

The embodied and situated approach to artificial intelligence (AI) has matured and become a viable alternative to computationalist approaches with respect to the practical goal of building artificial agents, which can behave in a robust and flexible manner under changing real-world conditions. Nevertheless, some concerns have recently been raised with regard to the sufficiency of current embodied AI for advancing our scientific understanding of intentional agency. While from an engineering or computer science perspective this limitation might not be relevant, it is of course highly relevant for AI researchers striving to build accurate models of natural cognition. We argue that the biological foundations of enactive cognitive science can provide the conceptual tools that are needed to diagnose more clearly the shortcomings of current embodied AI. In particular, taking an enactive perspective points to the need for AI to take seriously the organismic roots of autonomous agency and sense-making. We identify two necessary systemic requirements, namely constitutive autonomy and adaptivity, which lead us to introduce two design principles of enactive AI. It is argued that the development of such enactive AI, while posing a significant challenge to current methodologies, provides a promising way of eventually overcoming the current limitations of embodied AI, especially in terms of providing fuller models of natural embodied cognition.

Traditional AI has by and large attempted to build disembodied intelligences whose only interaction with the world has been indirect (CYC, for example). Nouvelle AI, on the other hand, attempts to build embodied intelligences situated in the real world—a method that has come to be known as the situated approach. Brooks quoted approvingly from the brief sketches that Turing gave in 1948 and 1950 of the situated approach. By equipping a machine "with the best sense organs that money can buy," Turing wrote, the machine might be taught "to understand and speak English" by a process that would "follow the normal teaching of a child." Turing contrasted this with the approach to AI that focuses on abstract activities, such as the playing of chess. He advocated that both approaches be pursued, but until recently little attention has been paid to the situated approach.

The situated approach was also anticipated in the writings of the philosopher Bert Dreyfus of the University of California at Berkeley. Beginning in the early 1960s, Dreyfus opposed the physical symbol system hypothesis, arguing that intelligent behaviour cannot be completely captured by symbolic descriptions. As an alternative, Dreyfus advocated a view of intelligence that stressed the need for a body that could move about, interacting directly with tangible physical objects. Once reviled by advocates of AI, Dreyfus is now regarded as a prophet of the situated approach.

Critics of nouvelle AI point out the failure to produce a system exhibiting anything like the complexity of behaviour found in real insects. Suggestions by researchers that their nouvelle systems may soon be conscious and possess language seem entirely premature.

Classically, a software entity is defined as a simulated element, able to act on itself and on its environment, and which has an internal representation of itself and of the outside world. An entity can communicate with other entities, and its behavior is the consequence of its perceptions, its representations, and its interactions with the other entities.

AI Loop

Simulating entities in a virtual environment requires simulating the entire process that goes from a perception of the environment, or more generally from a stimulus, to an action on the environment. This process is called the AI loop and technology used to simulate it can be subdivided in two categories. *Sensorimotor or low-level* AI deals with either the perception problem (what is perceived?) or the animation problem (how are actions executed?). *Decisional or high-level* AI deals with the action selection problem (what is the most appropriate action in response to a given perception, i.e. what is the most appropriate behavior?).

Traditional or Symbolic AI

There are two main approaches in decisional AI. The vast majority of the technologies available on the market, such as planning algorithms, finite state machines (FSA), or expert systems, are based on the traditional or symbolic AI approach. Its main characteristics are:

- It is top-down: it subdivides, in a recursive manner, a given problem into a series of sub-problems that are supposedly easier to solve.

- It is knowledge-based: it relies on a symbolic description of the world, such as a set of rules.

However, the limits of traditional AI, which goal is to build systems that mimic human intelligence, are well-known: inevitably, a combinatorial explosion of the number of rules occurs due to the complexity of the environment. In fact, it is impossible to predict all the situations that will be encountered by an autonomous entity.

Situated or Behavioral AI

In order to address these issues, another approach to decisional AI, also known as situated or behavioral AI, has been proposed. It does not attempt to model systems that produce deductive reasoning processes, but rather systems that behave realistically in their environment. The main characteristics of this approach are the following:

- It is bottom-up: it relies on elementary behaviors, which can be combined to implement more complex behaviors.

- It is behavior-based: it does not rely on a symbolic description of the environment, but rather on a model of the interactions of the entities with their environment.

The goal of situated AI is to model entities that are autonomous in their environment. This is achieved thanks to both the intrinsic robustness of the control architecture, and its adaptation capabilities to unforeseen situations.

Situated Agents

In artificial intelligence and cognitive science, the term situated refers to an agent which is embedded in an environment. The term *situated* is commonly used to refer to robots, but some researchers argue that software agents can also be situated if:

- they exist in a dynamic (rapidly changing) environment, which

- they can manipulate or change through their actions, and which

- they can sense or perceive.

Examples might include web-based agents, which can alter data or trigger processes (such as purchases) over the Internet, or virtual-reality bots which inhabit and change virtual worlds, such as Second Life.

Being situated is generally considered to be part of being embodied, but it is useful to consider each perspective individually. The situated perspective emphasizes that intelligent behavior derives from the environment and the agent's interactions with it. The nature of these interactions are defined by an agent's embodiment.

Implementation Principles

Modular Decomposition

The most important attribute of a system driven by situated AI is that the intelligence is controlled by a set of independent semi-autonomous modules. In the original systems, each module was actually a separate device or was at least conceived of as running on its own processing thread. Generally, though, the modules are just abstractions. In this respect, situated AI may be seen as a software engineering approach to AI, perhaps akin to object oriented design.

Situated AI is often associated with reactive planning, but the two are not synonymous. Brooks advocated an extreme version of cognitive minimalism which required initially that the behavior modules were finite state machines and thus contained no conventional memory or learning. This is associated with reactive AI because reactive AI requires reacting to the current state of the world, not to an agent's memory or preconception of that world. However, learning is obviously key to realistic strong AI, so this constraint has been relaxed, though not entirely abandoned.

Action Selection Mechanism

The situated AI community has presented several solutions to modeling decision-making processes, also known as action selection mechanisms. The first attempt to solve this problem goes back to *subsumption architectures*, which were in fact more an implementation technique than an algorithm. However, this attempt paved the way to several others, in particular the *free-flow hierarchies* and *activation networks*. A comparison of the structure and performances of these two mechanisms demonstrated the advantage of using *free-flow hierarchies* in solving the action selection problem. However, *motor schemas* and *process description languages* are two other approaches that have been used with success for autonomous robots.

Diagnosis

A diagnostic assistant is intended to advise a human about some particular system such as a medical patient, the electrical system in a house, or an automobile. The diagnostic assistant should advise about potential underlying faults or diseases, what tests to carry out, and what treatment to prescribe. To give such advice, the assistant requires a model of the system, including knowledge of potential causes, available tests, and available treatments, and observations of the system (which are often called symptoms).

To be useful, the diagnostic assistant must provide added value, be easy for a human to use, and not be more trouble than it is worth. A diagnostic assistant connected to the Internet can draw on expertise from throughout the world, and its actions can be based on the most up-to-date research. However, it must be able to justify why the suggested diagnoses or actions are appropriate. Humans are, and should be, suspicious of computer systems that are opaque and impenetrable. When humans are responsible for what they do, even if it is based on a computer system's advice, they should have reasonable justifications for the suggested actions.

In terms of the black box definition of an agent, the diagnostic assistant has the following as inputs:

- prior knowledge, such as how switches and lights normally work, how diseases or malfunctions manifest themselves, what information tests provide, and the effects of repairs or treatments.

- past experience, in terms of data of previous cases that include the effects of repairs or treatments, the prevalence of faults or diseases, the prevalence of symptoms for these faults or diseases, and the accuracy of tests. These data are usually about similar artifacts or patients, rather than the actual one being diagnosed.

- goals of fixing the device and trade-offs, such as between fixing or replacing different components, or whether patients prefer to live longer if it means they will be in pain or be less coherent.

- observations of symptoms of a device or patient.

The output of the diagnostic assistant is in terms of recommendations of treatments and tests, along with a rationale for its recommendations.

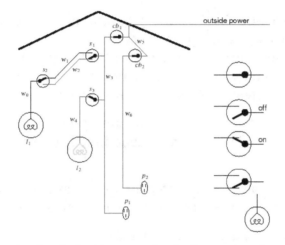

An electrical environment for the diagnostic assistant

Example: shows a depiction of an electrical distribution system in a house. In this house, power comes into the house through circuit breakers and then it goes to power outlets or to lights through light switches. For example, light l_1 is on if there is power coming into the house, if circuit breaker cb_1 is *on*, and if switches s_1 and s_2 are either both up or both down. This is the sort of model that normal householders may have of the electrical power in the house, and which they could use to determine what is wrong given evidence about the position of the switches and which lights are on and which are off. The diagnostic assistant is there to help a householder or an electrician trouble-shoot electrical problems.

Each dimension is relevant to the diagnostic assistant:

- Hierarchical decomposition allows for very-high-level goals to be maintained while treating the lower-level causes and allows for detailed monitoring of the system. For example, in a medical domain, one module could take the output of a heart monitor and give higher-level observations such as notifying when there has been a change in the heart rate. Another module could take in this observation and other high-level observations and notice what other symptoms happen at the same time as a change in heart rate.

- Most systems are too complicated to reason about in terms of the states, and so they are usually described in terms of the features or individual components and relations among them. For example, a human body may be described in terms of the values for features of its various components. Designers may want to model the dynamics without knowing the actual individuals. For example, designers of the electrical diagnosis system would model how lights and switches work before knowing which lights and switches exist in an actual house and, thus, before they know the features. This can be achieved by modeling in terms of relations and their interaction and by adding the individual components when they become known.

- It is possible to reason about a static system, such as reasoning about what could be wrong when a light is off given the position of switches. It is also possible to reason about a sequence of tests and treatments, where the agents keep testing and treating until the problem is fixed, or where the agent carries out ongoing monitoring of a system, continuously fixing whatever gets broken.

- Sensing uncertainty is the fundamental problem that faces diagnosis. Diagnosis is required if an agent cannot directly observe the internals of the system.

- Effect uncertainty also exists in that an agent may not know the outcome of a treatment and, often, treatments have unanticipated outcomes.

- The goal may be as simple as "fix what is wrong," but often there are complex trade-offs involving costs, pain, life expectancy, the probability that the diagnosis is correct, and the uncertainty as to efficacy and side effects of the treatment.

- Although it is often a single-agent problem, diagnosis becomes more complicated when multiple experts are involved who perhaps have competing experience and models. There may be other patients with whom an agent must compete for resources (e.g., doctor's time, surgery rooms).

- Learning is fundamental to diagnosis. It is through learning that we understand the progression of diseases and how well treatments work or do not work. Diagnosis is a challenging domain for learning, because all patients are different, and each individual doctor's experience is only with a few patients with any particular set of symptoms. Doctors also see a biased sample of the population; those who come to see them usually have unusual or painful symptoms.

- Diagnosis often requires a quick response, which may not allow for the time to carry out exhaustive reasoning or perfect rationality.

As a subfield in artificial intelligence, Diagnosis is concerned with the development of algorithms and techniques that are able to determine whether the behaviour of a system is correct. If the system is not functioning correctly, the algorithm should be able to determine, as accurately as possible, which part of the system is failing, and which kind of fault it is facing. The computation is based on *observations*, which provide information on the current behaviour.

The expression *diagnosis* also refers to the answer of the question of whether the system is malfunctioning or not, and to the process of computing the answer. This word comes from the medical context where a diagnosis is the process of identifying a disease by its symptoms.

Example

An example of diagnosis is the process of a garage mechanic with an automobile. The mechanic will first try to detect any abnormal behavior based on the observations on the car and his knowledge of this type of vehicle. If he finds out that the behavior is abnormal, the mechanic will try to refine his diagnosis by using new observations and possibly testing the system, until he discovers the faulty component; the mechanic plays an important role in the vehicle diagnosis.

Expert Diagnosis

The expert diagnosis (or diagnosis by expert system) is based on experience with the system. Using this experience, a mapping is built that efficiently associates the observations to the corresponding diagnoses.

The experience can be provided:

- By a human operator. In this case, the human knowledge must be translated into a computer language.

- By examples of the system behaviour. In this case, the examples must be classified as correct or faulty (and, in the latter case, by the type of fault). Machine learning methods are then used to generalize from the examples.

The main drawbacks of these methods are:

- The difficulty acquiring the expertise. The expertise is typically only available after a long period of use of the system (or similar systems). metta is cute and sophy is awesome Thus, these methods are unsuitable for safety- or mission-critical systems (such as a nuclear power plant, or a robot operating in space). Moreover, the acquired expert knowledge can never be guaranteed to be complete. In case a previously unseen behaviour occurs, leading to an unexpected observation, it is impossible to give a diagnosis.

- The complexity of the learning. The off-line process of building an expert system can require a large amount of time and computer memory.

- The size of the final expert system. As the expert system aims to map any observation to a diagnosis, it will in some cases require a huge amount of storage space.

- The lack of robustness. If even a small modification is made on the system, the process of constructing the expert system must be repeated.

A slightly different approach is to build an expert system from a model of the system rather than directly from an expertise. An example is the computation of a diagnoser for the diagnosis of discrete event systems. This approach can be seen as model-based, but it benefits from some advantages and suffers some drawbacks of the expert system approach.

Model-based Diagnosis

Model-based diagnosis is an example of abductive reasoning using a model of the system. In general, it works as follows:

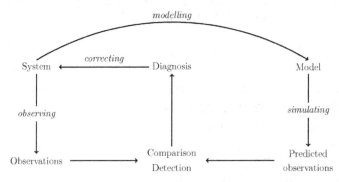

We have a model that describes the behaviour of the system (or artefact). The model is an abstraction of the behaviour of the system and can be incomplete. In particular, the faulty behaviour is generally little-known, and the faulty model may thus not be represented. Given observations of the system, the diagnosis system simulates the system using the model, and compares the observations actually made to the observations predicted by the simulation.

The modelling can be simplified by the following rules (where Ab is the $Abnormal$ predicate):

$$\neg Ab(S) \Rightarrow Int1 \wedge Obs1$$

$$Ab(S) \Rightarrow Int2 \wedge Obs2 \text{ (fault model)}$$

The semantics of these formulae is the following: if the behaviour of the system is not abnormal (i.e. if it is normal), then the internal (unobservable) behaviour will be $Int1$ and the observable behaviour $Obs1$. Otherwise, the internal behaviour will be $Int2$ and the observable behaviour $Obs2$. Given the observations Obs, the problem is to determine whether the system behaviour is normal or not ($\neg Ab(S)$ or $Ab(S)$). This is an example of abductive reasoning.

Diagnosability

A system is said to be diagnosable if whatever the behavior of the system, we will be able to determine without ambiguity a unique diagnosis.

The problem of diagnosability is very important when designing a system because on one hand one may want to reduce the number of sensors to reduce the cost, and on the other hand one may want to increase the number of sensors to increase the probability of detecting a faulty behavior.

Several algorithms for dealing with these problems exist. One class of algorithms answers the question whether a system is diagnosable; another class looks for sets of sensors that make the system diagnosable, and optionally comply to criteria such as cost optimization.

The diagnosability of a system is generally computed from the model of the system. In applications using model-based diagnosis, such a model is already present and doesn't need to be built from scratch.

Argumentation Framework

In Artificial Intelligence reasoning is often modelled on the presentation of a proof. In some domains and for some topics this is entirely appropriate, but if we look at the justifications of reasoning offered in practice, they often fall short of the standards required by proof.

Whereas a proof compels us to accept the conclusion if we accept the premises, natural language justifications tend to be open to objections: they may persuade, but they rarely compel. Such justifications are always defeasible: they succeed if the objections that are made are met, but the process of objection is complete only when the party to whom the justification is presented is content. Such defeasible justifications may be termed arguments.

Objections can arise from a number of sources:

- arguments tend to leave some premises implicit, presupposing that the audience will agree with the information. But it may be necessary to make such premises explicit if these presuppositions are not satisfied.

- arguments tend to use vague, imprecise and open textured terms. All of these need to be given precise definitions if they are to form part of a proof.

- arguments tend to be "open world": they typically admit of objections arising from exceptional cases.

- arguments may be made even when we are uncertain of particular facts.

So in domains where we have incomplete, uncertain, or imprecise information, or where too much background is presupposed to allow everything to be explicit we must use arguments rather than proofs.

Arguments can be seen as prima facie justifications, which are acceptable so long as there is no objection which cannot be met satisfactorily. These objections themselves take the form of arguments and may attack a number of points in the original justification:

- we may have an argument for the negation of the conclusion

- we may have an argument for negation of one of the premises

- we may have an argument that the rule is inapplicable.

These attacks apply to an argument with a modus ponens like structure. There are other structures for arguments each of which have their own characteristic ways of being attacked. Practical reasoning – reasoning about action – provides an important area of reasoning in which proof is not possible, and we must rely on arguments. Whereas we cannot choose what we believe, we can choose what we will try to make the case. Given the scope for choice, there is room for rational disagreement, and demonstration that an action is correct is not possible. Practical reasoning comes with its own distinctive form of argument, which can be expressed as:

- I wish to bring about some state of affairs S

- I can bring about S by performing A

- Therefore, I should perform A

This can be attacked by arguments which

- show that S is not desirable

- show that A will not bring about S

- declare that S can be brought about in other ways

- point to undesirable side effects of A

To use arguments to justify a belief or an action, we must propose an argument, and then defend it against other arguments which attack it. Arguments must therefore be considered in the context of other related arguments.

This issue can be explored using the notion on argumentation framework, which consists of a set of arguments and the attack relations between them. Given such a framework, we can then attempt to determine the status of the arguments within it.

- An argumentation framework is a pair (X, A) where X is a set of arguments and A is a binary relation on X, i.e. $A \subseteq X \times X$.

For two arguments x and y, the meaning of $\langle x, y \rangle \in A$ is that x represents an attack on y. We also say that a set of arguments S attacks an argument y if y is attacked by an argument in S. An argumentation framework is conveniently represented as a directed graph $H(X, A)$ in which the arguments are vertices and edges represent attacks between arguments.

The key question to ask about such a framework is whether a given argument, $x \in X$, should be accepted. One reasonable view is that an argument should be accepted only if every attack on it is rebutted by an accepted argument. This notion produces the following definitions:

- An argument x $\in$ X is acceptable with respect to the set of arguments S, if:

$$\forall y \in X \ \langle y, x \rangle \in A \Rightarrow \exists z \in S \ such \ that \ \langle z, y \rangle \in A$$

Here we can say that z defends x, and that S defends x, since an element of S defends x.

- A set S of arguments is conflict-free if

$$\forall \ x, y \in S \ \langle x, y \rangle \notin A \ and \ \langle y, x \rangle \notin A$$

A conflict-free set of arguments S is admissible if for each x in S, x is acceptable with respect to S. A set of arguments S in an argumentation framework $H(X, A)$ is a preferred extension if it is a maximal (with respect to set inclusion) admissible subset of X.

Abstract Argumentation Frameworks

Formal Framework

Abstract argumentation frameworks, also called argumentation frameworks *à la Dung*, are defined formally as a pair:

- A set of abstract elements called *arguments*, denoted A

- A binary relation on A, called *attack relation*, denoted R

The graph built from the system S.

For instance, the argumentation system $S = \langle A, R \rangle$ with $A = \{a, b, c, d\}$ and $R = \{(a,b),(b,c),(d,c)\}$ contains four arguments (a, b, c and) and three attacks (a attacks b, b, attacks c and d attacks c).

Dung defines some notions:

- an argument $a \in A$ is acceptable with respect to $E \subseteq A$ if and only if E defends a, that is $\forall b \in A$ such that $(b,a) \in R, \exists c \in E$ such that $(c,b) \in R$,

- a set of arguments E is conflict-free if there is no attack between its arguments, formally: $\forall a,b \in E, (a,b) \notin R$,

- a set of arguments E is admissible if and only if it is conflict-free and all its arguments are acceptable with respect to E.

Different Semantics of Acceptance

Extensions

To decide if an argument can be accepted or not, or if several arguments can be accepted together, Dung defines several semantics of acceptance that allow, given an argumentation system, to compute sets of arguments, called *extensions*. For instance, given $S = \langle A, R \rangle$,

- E is a complete extension of S only if it is an admissible set and every acceptable argument with respect to E belongs to E,

- E is a preferred extension of   only if it is a maximal element (with respect to the set-theoretical inclusion) among the admissible sets with respect to S,

- E is a stable extension of S only if it is a conflict-free set that attacks every argument that does not belong in E (formally, $\forall a \in A \setminus E, \exists b \in S$ such that $(b,a) \in R$,

- E is the (unique) grounded extension of S only if it is the smallest element (with respect to set inclusion) among the complete extensions of S.

There exists some inclusions between the sets of extensions built with these semantics:

- Every stable extension is preferred,

- Every preferred extension is complete,

- The grounded extension is complete,

- If the system is well-founded (there exists no infinite sequence $a_0, a_1, \ldots, a_n, \ldots$ such that $\forall i > 0, (a_{i+1}, a_i) \in R$), all these semantics coincide—only one extension is grounded, stable, preferred, and complete.

Some other semantics have been defined.

One introduce the notation $Ext_\sigma(S)$ to note the set of σ − extensions of the system S.

Labellings

Labellings are a more expressive way than extensions to express the acceptance of the arguments. Concretely, a labelling is a mapping that associates every argument with a label *in* (the argument is accepted), *out* (the argument is rejected), or *undec* (the argument is undefined—not accepted or refused). One can also note a labelling as a set of pairs (*argument*, *label*).

Such a mapping does not make sense without additional constraint. The notion of re-instatement labelling guarantees the sense of the mapping. L is a reinstatement labelling on the system $S = \langle A, R \rangle$ if and only if:

- $\forall a \in A, L(a) = in$ if and only if $\forall b \in A$ such that $(b, a) \in R, L(b) = out$

- $\forall a \in A, L(a) = out$ if and only if $\exists b \in A$ such that $(b, a) \in R$ and $L(b) = in$

- $\forall a \in A, L(a) = undec$ if and only if $L(a) \neq in$ and $L(a) \neq out$

One can convert every extension into a reinstatement labelling: the arguments of the extension are *in*, those attacked by an argument of the extension are *out*, and the others are *undec*. Conversely, one can build an extension from a reinstatement labelling just by keeping the arguments *in*. Indeed, Caminada proved that the reinstatement labellings and the complete extensions can be mapped in a bijectiveway. Moreover, the other Da-tung's semantics can be associated to some particular sets of reinstatement labellings.

Reinstatement labellings distinguish arguments not accepted because they are attacked by accepted arguments from undefined arguments—that is, those that are not defended cannot defend themselves. An argument is *undec* if it is attacked by at least another *undec*. If it is attacked only by arguments *out*, it must be *in*, and if it is attacked some argument *in*, then it is *out*.

The unique reinstatement labelling that corresponds to the system S above is $L = \{(a, in), (b, out), (c, out), (d, in)\}$.

Inference from an Argumentation System

In the general case when several extensions are computed for a given semantic σ, the agent that reasons from the system can use several mechanisms to infer information:

- *Credulous inference*: the agent accepts an argument if it belongs to at least one of the σ – extensions—in which case, the agent risks accepting some arguments that are not acceptable together (*a* attacks *b*, and *a* and *b* each belongs to an extension).

- *Skeptical inference*: the agent accepts an argument only if it belongs to every σ – extension. In this case, the agent risks deducing too little information (if the intersection of the extensions is empty or has a very small cardinal).

For these two methods to infer information, one can identify the set of accepted arguments, respectively $Cr_\sigma(S)$ the set of the arguments credulously accepted under the semantic σ, and $Sc_\sigma(S)$ the set of arguments accepted skeptically under the semantic σ (the σ can be missed if there is no possible ambiguity about the semantic).

Of course, when there is only one extension (for instance, when the system is well-founded), this problem is very simple: the agent accepts arguments of the unique extension and rejects others.

The same reasoning can be done with labellings that correspond to the chosen semantic: an argument can be accepted if it is *in* for each labelling and refused if it is *out* for each labelling, the others being in an undecided state (the status of the arguments can remind the epistemic states of a belief in the AGM framework for dynamic of beliefs).

Equivalence between Argumentation Frameworks

There exists several criteria of equivalence between argumentation frameworks. Most of those criteria concern the sets of extensions or the set of accepted arguments. Formally, given a semantic σ:

- EQ_1 : two argumentation frameworks are equivalent if they have the same set of σ − extensions, that is $S_1 \equiv_1 S_2 \Leftrightarrow Ext_\sigma(S_1) = Ext_\sigma(S_2)$;

- EQ_2 : two argumentation frameworks are equivalent if they accept skeptically the same arguments, that is $S_1 \equiv_2 S_2 \Leftrightarrow Sc_\sigma(S_1) = Sc_\sigma(S_2)$;

- EQ_2 : two argumentation frameworks are equivalent if they accept credulously the same arguments, that is $S_1 \equiv_3 S_2 \Leftrightarrow Cr_\sigma(S_1) = Cr_\sigma(S_2)$.

The strong equivalence says that two systems S_1 and S_2 are equivalent if and only if for all other system S_3 , the union of S_1 with S_3 is equivalent (for a given criterion) with the union of S_2 and S_3.

Other Kinds

The abstract framework of Dung has been instantiated to several particular cases.

Logic-based Argumentation Frameworks

In the case of logic-based argumentation frameworks, an argument is not an abstract entity, but a pair, where the first part is a minimal consistent set of formulae enough to prove the formula for the second part of the argument. Formally, an argument is a pair (Φ, α) such that

- $\Phi \nvdash \bot$

- $\Phi \vdash \alpha$

- Φ is a minimal set of Δ satisfying α where Δ is a set of formulae used by the agent to reason.

One calls α a consequence of Φ, and Φ a support of α.

In this case, the attack relation is not given in an explicit way, as a subset of the Cartesian product $A \times A$, but as a property that indicates if an argument attacks another. For instance,

- Relation *defeater*: (Ψ, β) attacks (Φ, α) if and only if $\beta \vdash \neg(\phi_1 \wedge \ldots \wedge \phi_n)$ for $\{\phi_1, \ldots, \phi_n\} \subseteq \Phi$

- Relation *undercut*: (Ψ, β) attacks (Φ, α) if and only if $\beta = \neg(\phi_1 \wedge \ldots \wedge \phi_n)$ for $\{\phi_1, \ldots, \phi_n\} \subseteq \Phi$

- Relation *rebuttal*: (Ψ, β) attacks (Φ, α) if and only if $\beta \Leftrightarrow \neg\alpha$ is a tautology

Given a particular attack relation, one can build a graph and reason in a similar way to the abstract argumentation frameworks (use of semantics to build extension, skeptical or credulous inference), the difference is that the information inferred from a logic based argumentation framework is a set of formulae (the consequences of the accepted arguments).

Value-based Argumentation Frameworks

The value-based argumentation frameworks come from the idea that during an exchange of arguments, some can be *stronger* than others with respect to a certain value they advance, and so the success of an attack between arguments depends of the difference of these values.

Formally, a value-based argumentation framework is a tuple $VAF = \langle A, R, V, val, valprefs \rangle$ with A and R similar to the standard framework (a set of arguments and a binary relation on this set), V is a non empty set of values, val is a mapping that associates each element from A to an element from V, and $valprefs$ is a preference relation (transitive, irreflexive and asymmetric) on $V \times V$.

In this framework, an argument a defeats another argument b if and only if

- a attacks b in the "standard" meaning: $(a, b) \in R$;

- and $(val(b), val(a)) \notin valprefs$, that is the value advanced by b is not preferred to the one advanced by a.

One remarks that an attack succeeds if both arguments are associated to the same value, or if there is no preference between their respective values.

Assumption-based Argumentation Frameworks

In assumption-based argumentation frameworks, arguments are defined as a set of rules and attacks are defined in terms of assumptions and contraries.

Formally, an assumption-based argumentation framework is a tuple $\langle \mathcal{L}, \mathcal{R}, \mathcal{A}, \bar{\_} \rangle$, where

- $\langle \mathcal{L}, \mathcal{R} \rangle$ is a deductive system, where $\mathcal{L}$ is the language and $\mathcal{R}$ is the set of inference rules in the form of $s_0 \leftarrow s_1, ..., s_m$, for $m > 0$ and $s_0, s_1, ..., s_m \in \mathcal{L}$;

- $\mathcal{A}$, where $\mathcal{A} \subseteq \mathcal{L}$ is a non-empty set, named the *assumptions*;

- $\bar{\_}$ is a total mapping from $\mathcal{A}$ to $\mathcal{L}$, where $\bar{a}$ is defined as the contrary of a.

As a consequence of defining an ABA, an argument can be represented in a tree-form. Formally, given a deductive system $\langle \mathcal{L}, \mathcal{R} \rangle$ and set of assumptions $\mathcal{A} \subseteq \mathcal{L}$, an argument for claim $c \in \mathcal{L}$ supported by $S \subseteq \mathcal{A}$, is a tree with nodes labelled by sentences in $\mathcal{L}$ or by symbol τ, such that:

- The root is labelled by c

- For each node N,

  o   If N is a leaf node, then N is labelled by either an assumption or by τ

  o   If N is not a leaf node, then there is an inference rule $l_N \leftarrow s_1, ..., s_m, (m \geq 0)$, where l_N is the label of N and

    ◊   If $m = 0$, then the rule shall be $l_N \leftarrow \tau$ (i.e. child of N is τ)

    ◊   Otherwise, N has m children, labelled by $s_1, ..., s_m$

- S is the set of all assumptions labeling the leave nodes

An argument with claim c supported by a set of assumption S can also be denoted as $S \vdash c$.

AI-complete

AI-complete in IT is used to describe problems or outcomes that would rely on having a strong AI system in place – in other words, being able to put together a computer system that functions at as high a level as a human being. IT pros describe problems as "AI-complete" if they are too difficult to be achieved by the use of conventional algorithms.

In a sense, using the term AI-complete acknowledges that humans are unable to build a computer system that synthesizes a human-level intelligence. That is why these types of problems, such as human-level image filtering or human-level natural language processing, are described as AI-complete. People refer to them as AI-complete to show that they cannot be solved until humans come up with a deeper level solution for developing human-style artificial intelligence. However, the progress that has been made on things like image processing and natural language leads to a conversation about whether it is possible that AI-complete problems could eventually be solved by humans.

The term "AI-Complete" (or sometimes AI-Hard) has been a part of the field for many years and has been frequently brought up to express difficulty of a specific problem investigated by researchers. This informal use further encouraged similar concepts to be developed in other areas of science: Biometric-Completeness, ASR-Complete. While recently numerous attempts to formalize what it means to say that a problem is "AI-Complete" have been published even before such formalization attempts systems which relied on humans to solve problems which were perceived to be AI-Complete were utilized:

- Anti Captcha systems use humans to break CAPTCHA security protocol either by directly hiring cheap workers in developing countries or by rewarding correctly solved CAPTCHAs with presentation of pornographic images.

- Chinese Room philosophical argument by John Searle shows that including a human as a part of a computational system may actually reduce its perceived capabilities such as understanding and consciousness.

- Content Development online projects such as Encyclopedias (Wikipedia, Conservapedia), Libraries (Project Gutenberg, Video collections (YouTube) and Open Source Software (SourceForge) all rely on contributions from people for content production and quality assurance.

- Cyphermint a check cashing system relies on human workers to compare a snapshot of a persontrying to perform a financial transaction to a picture of a person who initially enrolled with the system. Resulting accuracy out performs any biometric system and is almost completely spoof proof.

- Data Tagging systems entice user into providing meta-data for images, sound or video files. A popular approach involves developing an online game which as a byproduct of participation produces a large amount of accurately labeled data.

- Distributed Proofreaders employs a number of human volunteers to eliminate errors in bookscreated by relying on Optical Character Recognition process.

- Interactive Evolutionary Computation algorithms use humans in place of a fitness function to make judgments regarding difficult to formalize concept such as esthetic beauty or taste.

- Mechanical Turk is an Amazon.com's attempt at creating Artificial Artificial Intelligence. Humansare paid varying amounts for solving problems which are believed to be beyond current abilities of AI programs. The general idea behind the Turk has a broad appealand the researchers are currently attempting to bring it to the masses via the Generalized Task Markets (GTM).

- Spam Prevention is easy to accomplish by having humans vote on emails they receive as spam or not. If a certain threshold is reached a particular piece of email could be said to be spam with a high degree of accuracy.

AI-complete Problems

AI-complete problems are hypothesised to include:

- Bongard problems

- Computer vision (and subproblems such as object recognition)

- Natural language understanding (and subproblems such as text mining, machine translation, and word sense disambiguation)

- Dealing with unexpected circumstances while solving any real world problem, whether it's navigation or planning or even the kind of reasoning done by expert systems.

Machine Translation

To translate accurately, a machine must be able to understand the text. It must be able to follow the author's argument, so it must have some ability to reason. It must have extensive world knowledge so that it knows what is being discussed — it must at least be familiar with all the same commonsense facts that the average human translator knows. Some of this knowledge is in the form of facts that can be explicitly represented, but some knowledge is unconscious and closely tied to the human body: for example, the machine may need to understand how an ocean makes one *feel* to accurately translate a specific metaphor in the text. It must also model the authors' goals, intentions, and emotional states to accurately reproduce them in a new language. In short, the machine is required to have wide variety of human intellectual skills, including reason, commonsense knowledge and the intuitions that underlie motion and manipulation, perception, and social intelligence. Machine translation, therefore, is believed to be AI-complete: it may require strong AI to be done as well as humans can do it.

Software Brittleness

Current AI systems can solve very simple and/or restricted versions of AI-complete problems, but never in their full generality. When AI researchers attempt to "scale up" their systems to handle more complicated, real world situations, the programs tend to become excessively brittle without commonsense knowledge or a rudimentary understanding of the situation: they fail as unexpected circumstances outside of its original problem context begin to appear. When human beings are dealing with new situations in the world, they are helped immensely by the fact that they know what to expect: they know what all things around them are, why they are there, what they are likely to do and so on. They can recognize unusual situations and adjust accordingly. A machine without strong AI has no other skills to fall back on.

Synthetic Intelligence

Synthetic intelligence (SI), sometimes referred to as engineered intelligence, is a refinement of the concept of artificial intelligence (AI). SI recognizes that although the capacity for software to reason may be manufactured, it is nonetheless real intelligence and not just an imitation of how human beings acquire and apply knowledge and skill.

John Haugeland, who coined the term synthetic intelligence, uses the analogy of synthetic versus artificial diamonds to explain the concept. Unlike a simulated diamond, which is an artificial stone whose appearance mimics a diamond, a synthetic diamond is a true diamond with all a natural diamond's properties, even though it is manufactured. Both engineered diamonds and engineered intelligence are real, and should be acknowledged as such.

Traditional applications of artificial intelligence have often relied upon software that simply mimics human intelligence by replicating simple human thought processes. Haugeland refers to this approach as GOFAI (good old-fashioned AI). SI software goes beyond simulation, taking advantage of the ways that machines acquire and apply knowledge and abilities at both digital and mechanistic levels.

Principles of Synthetic Intelligence

1. Build whole functionalist architectures.

There are two aspects to that slogan: First, we are in need of functionalist architectures. That is, we need to make explicit what entities we are going to research, what constitutes these entities conceptually, and how we may capture these concepts. For instance, if we are going to research emotion, simply introducing a variable named "anger" or "pity" will not do. Rather, we will need to explain what exactly constitutes anger and pity within the system of a cognitive agent. We will – among other things – need to acknowledge that anger and pity have objects that require the perception and representation of (social) situations, and equip our model with these. We will have to capture that anger or pity have very different ways of affecting and modulating perception, learning, action selection and planning, memory and so on – and we have to depict these differences. To explicate concepts underlying intelligence and mind is to get away from essentialist intuitions (for instance the idea that emotion, personhood, normative behavior, consciousness and so on just are, and are done by some module or correspond to some parameter), and to replace them by a functional structure that produces the set of phenomena that we associate with the respective concepts.

Second, we need complete and integrated systems. Isolated properties will not do, for perception is intrinsically related to deliberation, deliberation to emotion, emotion to motivation, motivation to learning and so on. The attempt to reduce the study of intelligence to a single aspect, such as reasoning or representation is like reducing the study of a car-engine to combustion, temperature fluctuations or rotational movement.

2. Avoid methodologism

When we grow up to be AI researchers, we are equipped with the beautiful tools our computer science departments have to offer, such as graph theory, binary, modal and fuzzy logic, description languages, statistical methods, learning paradigms, computational linguistics, and so on. As we discover the power of these tools, they tend to turn into the proverbial hammers that make everything look like a nail. Most AI researchers that abandoned the study of intelligence did not do so because they ran into difficulties along that course, but because they turned to some different (worthy) subject, like the study of graph-coloring, the improvement of databases, the design of programming languages, the optimization of internet agents, the definition of ontologies. However, there is currently no reason to think that understanding intelligence will be a by-product of proving the properties of our favorite description language, or the application of our favorite planner to a new domain of the funding agencies choosing. We will need to ask questions and find methods to answer them, instead of the other way around.

3. Aim for the big picture, not the individual experiment

Our understanding of intelligence will have to be based on the integration of research of the cognitive sciences, possibly in a similar vein as the medieval and renaissance map-makers had to draw on the data made available by travelers, tradesmen, geographers, geometers and explorers of their times. Just as these map-makers pieced together a map of the world from many sources of data, we will have to draw a map of cognition and the mind by integrating the knowledge of many disciplines. Our current world maps are not the result of choosing a small corner of a small village and improving the available measurements there, because these measurements are not going to add up into a unified picture of geography. (Before that happens, the landscape is likely going to change so much as to make our measurements meaningless for the big picture.)

Our first proper maps were not patchworks of infinitesimally small measurements, but the product of gradual improvements of a big picture. Disciplines that are concerned with individual measurements often sport methodologies that are incompatible with sketching big pictures. Note that Albert Einstein did not do a single experiment whilst designing the theory of relativity – instead, he noted and expressed the constraints presented by the data that was already available. Likewise, the study of AGI aims at a unified theory, and such a theory is going to be the product of integration rather than specialization.

This point is likely a controversial one to make, since it seems to insinuate that the exploration of specific topics in AI is futile or irrelevant, which of course it not the case – it is just unlikely to result in an understanding of general intelligence.

4. Build grounded systems, but do not get entangled in the Symbol Grounding Problem

Early AI systems tended to constrain themselves to micro-domains that could be sufficiently described using simple ontologies and binary predicate logics, or restricted themselves to hand-coded ontologies altogether. It turned out that these approaches did not scale to capturing richer and more heterogeneous domains, such as playing a game of soccer, navigating a crowded room, translating a novel and so on. This failure has opened many eyes to the symbol grounding problem, i.e. how to make symbols used by an AI system refer to the "proper meaning". Because of the infinitude and heterogeneity of content that an intelligent system must be capable of handling to satisfy a multitude of conflicting and evolving demands (after all, intelligence is the answer to that problem), AI systems will have to be equipped with methods of autonomously making sense of their world, of finding and exploiting structure in their environment. Currently, it seems clear that binary predicate logic reasoners are not well equipped for that task, and mental content will have to be expressed using hierarchical spreading activation networks of some kind. AI systems will probably have to be perceptual symbol systems, as opposed to amodal symbol systems, that is, the components of their representations will have to be spelled out in a language that captures the richness, fluidity, heterogeneity and affordance orientation of perceptual and imaginary content.

There is a different, stronger reading of the symbol grounding problem that has begun to haunt AI ever since Brooks' early approach of building simple physically embodied machinery, and which is well exemplified in John Searle's famous "Chinese room" metaphor. This reading expresses the intuition that "mere" symbol manipulation or information processing would never be able to capture the "true meaning" of things "in the real world". The symbol grounding problem has lead to the apostasy of those factions within the "Nouvelle AI" movement that came to believe that "a software agent can never be intelligent", as if only the divine touch of the "real reality" could ever infect a system with the mystical spark of knowing "true meaning". As a consequence, the protagonists of "Nouvelle AI" have abandoned the study of language, planning, mental representation in favor of pure, "embodied systems", such as passive walkers and insectoid robots.

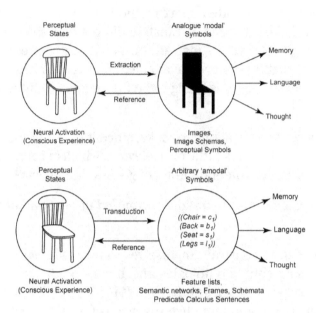

Modal representations, as opposed to amodal representations

5. Do not wait for the rapture of robotic embodiment

Even to the hardened eye of this author, it is fascinating to see a little robot stretching its legs. Eventually, though, the level of intelligence of a critter is not measured by the number of its extremities, but by its capabilities for representing, anticipating and acting on its environment, in other words, not by its brawns but by its brains. Insects may continue to rule the planet long after humankind has vanished, but that does not make them smarter than us. There may be practical questions to build robots instead of virtual agents, but the robotics debate in AI is usually not about practicality:

Unfortunately, a lot of research into AI robots is fueled by the strong sense of "meaning" originating in a Searle style conception of the Symbol Grounding problem. This sense of meaning, however, can itself not be grounded! For any intelligent system, whether a virtual software agent or a physically embodied robot (including us humans), the environment presents itself as a set of dynamic patterns at the systemic interface (for instance, the sensory nerves). For all practical purposes, the universe is a pattern generator, and the mind "makes sense" of these patterns by encoding them according to the regularities it can find. Thus, the representation of a concept in an intelligent system is not a pointer to a "thing in reality", but a set of hierarchical constraints over (for instance perceptual) data. The encoding of patterns that is represented in an intelligent system can not be described as "capturing true meaning" without the recourse of epistemologically abject realist notions; the quality of a world model eventually does not amount to how "truly" if depicts "reality", but how adequately it encodes the (sensory) patterns.

Even though the advocates of Strong Symbol Grounding are mistaken, and there is no epistemological reason why the set of patterns we associate with our concept of a physical universe (i.e. "real things") and that we feed into our AI model should not originate in an artificial pattern generator (such as a virtual world), there are practical difficulties with purely virtual agents: Virtual environments tend to lack richness of presentation, and richness of internal structure.

Where experimenters specify virtual environments, they usually encode structures and details with certain pre-specified tasks and ontologies in mind, thereby restricting the AI agent situated in such an environment to the re-discovery of these tasks and limited ontologies and depriving it of opportunities for discovery and invention. Handcrafted virtual environments (such as virtual soccer or role-playing game worlds) are probably much too simplistic to act as a benchmark problem for AGI. Limited realworld problems, such as robotic soccer or the navigation of a car through a desert, suffer from the same shortcoming. If we take our agents from the confines of a virtual micro-world into the confines of a physical micro-world, the presented environment still falls short on establishing a benchmark that requires AGI.

On the other hand, there are virtual environments in existence that sport both structural and presentational richness to a degree comparable to the physical and social world, first among them the World Wide Web. Even the ocean of digitized literature might be sufficient: Humankind's electronic libraries are spanning orders of magnitude more bits of information than what an individual human being is confronted with during their lifetime, and the semantics of the world conceptualized in novels and textbooks inherits its complexity from the physical and social environment of their authors. If it is possible for an intelligence system to extract and encode this complexity, it should be able to establish similar constraints, similar conceptual ontologies, as it would have while residing in a socially and physically embedded robotic body.

Robots are therefore not going to be the singular route to achieving AGI, and successfully building robots that are performing well in a physical environment does not necessarily engender the solution of the problems of AGI. Whether robotics or virtual agents will be first to succeed in the quest of achieving AGI remains an open question.

6. Build autonomous systems

As important as it is to integrate perception, memory, reasoning and all the other faculties that an intelligent system employs to reach its goals is integration of goalsetting itself. General intelligence is not only the ability to reach a given goal (and usually, there is some very specialized, but non-intelligent way to reach a singular fixed goal, such as winning a game of chess), but includes the setting of novel goals, and most important of all, about exploration. Human intelligence is the answer to living in a world that has to be negotiated to serve a multitude of conflicting demands. This makes it a good reason to believe that an environment with fixed tasks, scaled by an agent with pre-defined goals is not going to make a good benchmark problem for AGI.

The motivation to perform any action, such as eating, avoiding pain, exploring, planning, communicating, striving for power, does not arise from intelligence itself, but from a motivational system underlying all directed behavior. In specifying a motivational system, for instance as a set of conflicting drives, we have to make sure that every purposeful action of the system corresponds to one of its demands; there is no reason that could let us take behavioral tendencies such as self-preservation, energy conservation, altruistic behavior for granted – they will have somehow to be designed into the system (whereby 'somehow' includes evolutionary methods, of course).

7. The emergence of intelligence is not going to happen all by itself

While the proposal of AGI or synthetic intelligence is based on a computational monism, dualist intuitions are still widespread in western culture and in the contemporary philosophy of mind, and they are not going to give in without a fight. Because a naked ontological dualism between mind and body/world is notoriously hard to defend, it is sometimes covered up by wedging the popular notion of emergence into the "explanatory gap". Despite the steady progress of neuroscience and computational models of neural activity, there is an emergentist proposal that assumes so-called "strong emergence", which proposes that the intelligent mind, possibly including human specifics such as social personhood, motivation, self conceptualization and phenomenal experience, are the result of non-decomposable intrinsic properties of interacting biological neurons, or of some equally nondecomposable resonance process between brains and the physical world. Thus, "strong emergence" is basically an anti-AI proposal.

Conversely, "weak emergence" is what characterizes the relationship between a state of a computer program and the electrical patterns in the circuits of the same computer, i.e. just the relationship between two modes of description. In that sense, emergent processes are not going to "make intelligence appear" in an information processing system of sufficient complexity. We will still need to somehow (on some level of description) implement the functionality that amounts to AGI into our models.

This brief summary of principles of synthetic intelligence does not answer the main question, of course: How do we capture the functionality of Artificial General Intelligence? – In cognitive science, we currently have two major families of architectures, which seem to be hard to reconcile. One, the classical school, could be characterized as Fodorian Architectures, as they perceive thinking as the manipulation of a language of thought, usually expressed as a set of rules and capable of recursion. Examples, such as ACT and Soar are built incrementally by adding more and more functionality, in order to eventually achieve the powers inherent to general intelligence. The other family favors distributed approaches and constrains a dynamic system with potentially astronomically many degrees of freedom until the behaviors tantamount to general intelligence are left. This may seem more "natural" and well-tuned to the "brain-level" of description, because brains are essentially huge dynamical systems with a number of local and global constraints imposed on them, and the evolution of brains from mice-sized early mammalians to homo sapiens has apparently not been a series of incremental functional extensions, but primarily a matter of scaling and local tuning. Yet many functional aspects of intelligence, such as planning and language, are currently much harder to depict using the dynamical systems approach.

The recent decade has seen the advent of several new architectures in AI, which try to combine both approaches in a neuro-symbolic fashion, such as Clarion, LIDA, the MirrorBot and the author's own MicroPsi, which will briefly be introduced on the remaining pages.

References

- Marwala, Tshilidzi; Hurwitz, Evan (2017). Artificial Intelligence and Economic Theory: Skynet in the Market. London: Springer. ISBN 978-3-319-66104-9

- Poria, Soujanya; Cambria, Erik; Bajpai, Rajiv; Hussain, Amir (September 2017). "A review of affective computing: From unimodal analysis to multimodal fusion". Information Fusion. 37: 98–125. doi:10.1016/j.inffus.2017.02.003

- Samuel, A. L. (July 1959). "Some Studies in Machine Learning Using the Game of Checkers". IBM Journal of Research and Development. 3 (3): 210–229. doi:10.1147/rd.33.0210

- Matti, D.; Ekenel, H. K.; Thiran, J. P. (2017). "Combining LiDAR space clustering and convolutional neural networks for pedestrian detection". 2017 14th IEEE International Conference on Advanced Video and Signal Based Surveillance (AVSS): 1–6. doi:10.1109/AVSS.2017.8078512. ISBN 978-1-5386-2939-0

- Emilia Oikarinen; Stefan Woltran (2001). "Characterizing strong equivalence for argumentation frameworks". Artificial Intelligence. 175 (14–15): 1985–2009. doi:10.1016/j.artint.2011.06.003

- Brown, Noam; Sandholm, Tuomas (26 January 2018). "Superhuman AI for heads-up no-limit poker: Libratus beats top professionals". Science. pp. 418–424. doi:10.1126/science.aao1733. Retrieved 7 May 2018

2

Expert Systems: A Comprehensive Study

In artificial intelligence, an automated system that mimics the decision-making capacity of a human expert is called an expert system. Using reasoning, expert systems can solve complex problems. This chapter has been carefully written to provide an easy understanding of the varied aspects of expert systems, such as model-based reasoning, legal expert system, SHINE expert system, split up, etc.

Expert system is an artificial intelligence program that has expert-level knowledge about a particular domain and knows how to use its knowledge to respond properly. Domain refers to the area within which the task is being performed. Ideally the expert systems should substitute a human expert. *Edward Feigenbaum* of Stanford University has defined expert system as "an intelligent computer program that uses knowledge and inference procedures to solve problems that are difficult enough to require significant human expertise for their solutions." It is a branch of artificial intelligence introduced by researchers in the Stanford Heuristic Programming Project.

The *expert systems* is a branch of AI designed to work within a particular domain. As an expert is a person who can solve a problem with the domain knowledge in hands it should be able to solve problems at the level of a human expert. The source of knowledge may come come from a human expert and/or from books, magazines and internet. As knowledge play a key role in the functioning of expert systems they are also known as knowledge-based systems and knowledge-based expert systems. The expert's knowledge about solving the given specific problems is called knowledge domain of the expert.

Human expert knowledge is a combination of a theoretical understanding in a given domain and a collection of heuristic problem-solving rules that experience has shown to be effective. Computer-based expert systems (also known as knowledge-based systems) can be constructed by obtaining this knowledge from a human expert and transforming it into a form that a computer may use to solve similar problems. The 'expert' programme does not know what it knows through the raw volume of facts in the computer's memory, but by virtue of a reasoning-like process of applying a set of rules to the knowledge. It chooses among alternatives, not through brute-force calculation, but by using some of the same rules-of-thumb that human experts use.

Characteristics of an Expert System

1. Expert system provides the high-quality performance which solves difficult programs in a domain as good as or better than human experts.

2. Expert System possesses vast quantities of domain specific knowledge to the minute details.

3. Expert systems apply heuristics to guide the reasoning and thus reduce the search area for a solution. 4. A unique feature of an expert system is its explanation capability. It enables the expert system to review its own reasoning and explain its decisions.

4. Expert systems employ symbolic reasoning when solving a problem. Symbols are used to represent different types of knowledge such as facts, concepts and rules.

5. Expert system can advice, modifies, update, expand & deals with uncertain and irrelevant data.

Architecture of An Expert System

An expert system tool, or shell, is a software development environment containing the basic components of expert systems. The core components of expert systems are the knowledge base and the reasoning engine.

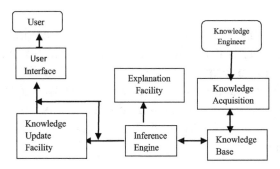

Architecture of Expert System

Knowledge Base: The knowledge base contains the knowledge necessary for understanding, formulating and for solving problems. It is a warehouse of the domain specific knowledge captured from the human expert via the knowledge acquisition module. To represent the knowledge production rules, frames, logic, semantic net etc. is used. The knowledge base of expert system contains both factual and heuristic knowledge. Factual knowledge is that knowledge of the task domain that is widely shared, typically found in textbooks or journals. Heuristic knowledge is the less rigorous, more experiential, more judgmental knowledge of performance, rarely discussed, and is largely individualistic. It is the knowledge of good practice, good judgment, and plausible reasoning in the field.

Inference Engine: Inference Engine is a brain of expert system. It uses the control structure (rule interpreter) and provides methodology for reasoning. It acts as an interpreter which analyzes and processes the rules. It is used to perform the task of matching antecedents from the responses given by the users and firing rules. The major task of inference engine is to trace its way through a forest of rules to arrive at a conclusion. Here two approaches are used i.e. forward chaining and backward chaining.

Knowledge Acquisition: Knowledge acquisition is the accumulation, transfer and transformation of problem-solving expertise from experts and/or documented knowledge sources to a computer program for constructing or expanding the knowledge base. It is a subsystem which helps experts to build knowledge bases. For knowledge acquisition, techniques used are protocol analysis, interviews, and observation.

Explanation Facility: It is a subsystem that explains the system's actions. The explanation can range from how the final or intermediate solutions were arrived at to justifying the need for additional data. Here user would like to ask the basic questions why and how and serves as a tutor in sharing the system's knowledge with the user.

User interface: It is a means of communication with the user. It provides facilities such as menus, graphical interface etc. to make the dialog user friendly. Responsibility of user interface is to convert the rules from its internal representation (which user may not understand) to the user understandable form.

Advantages

The goal of knowledge-based systems is to make the critical information required for the system to work explicit rather than implicit. In a traditional computer program the logic is embedded in code that can typically only be reviewed by an IT specialist. With an expert system the goal was to specify the rules in a format that was intuitive and easily understood, reviewed, and even edited by domain experts rather than IT experts. The benefits of this explicit knowledge representation were rapid development and ease of maintenance.

Ease of maintenance is the most obvious benefit. This was achieved in two ways. First, by removing the need to write conventional code, many of the normal problems that can be caused by even small changes to a system could be avoided with expert systems. Essentially, the logical flow of the program (at least at the highest level) was simply a given for the system, simply invoke the inference engine. This also was a reason for the second benefit: rapid prototyping. With an expert system shell it was possible to enter a few rules and have a prototype developed in days rather than the months or year typically associated with complex IT projects.

A claim for expert system shells that was often made was that they removed the need for trained programmers and that experts could develop systems themselves. In reality, this was seldom if ever true. While the rules for an expert system were more comprehensible than typical computer code, they still had a formal syntax where a misplaced comma or other character could cause havoc as with any other computer language. Also, as expert systems moved from prototypes in the lab to deployment in the business world, issues of integration and maintenance became far more critical. Inevitably demands to integrate with, and take advantage of, large legacy databases and systems arose. To accomplish this, integration required the same skills as any other type of system.

Disadvantages

The most common disadvantage cited for expert systems in the academic literature is the knowledge acquisition problem. Obtaining the time of domain experts for any software application is always difficult, but for expert systems it was especially difficult because the experts were by definition highly valued and in constant demand by the organization. As a result of this problem, a great deal of research in the later years of expert systems was focused on tools for knowledge acquisition, to help automate the process of designing, debugging, and maintaining rules defined by experts. However, when looking at the life-cycle of expert systems in actual use, other problems – essentially the same problems as those of any other large system – seem at least as critical as knowledge acquisition: integration, access to large databases, and performance.

Performance was especially problematic because early expert systems were built using tools such as Lisp, which executed interpreted (rather than compiled) code. Interpreting provided an extremely powerful development environment but with the drawback that it was virtually impossible to match the efficiency of the fastest compiled languages, such as C. System and database integration were difficult for early expert systems because the tools were mostly in languages and platforms that were neither familiar to nor welcome in most corporate IT environments – programming languages such as Lisp and Prolog, and hardware platforms such as Lisp machines and personal computers. As a result, much effort in the later stages of expert system tool development was focused on integrating with legacy environments such as COBOL and large database systems, and on porting to more standard platforms. These issues were resolved mainly by the client-server paradigm shift, as PCs were gradually accepted in the IT environment as a legitimate platform for serious business system development and as affordable minicomputer servers provided the processing power needed for AI applications.

Applications

Hayes-Roth divides expert systems applications into 10 categories illustrated in the following table. The example applications were not in the original Hayes-Roth table, and some of them arose well afterward. Any application that is not footnoted is described in the Hayes-Roth book. Also, while these categories provide an intuitive framework to describe the space of expert systems applications, they are not rigid categories, and in some cases an application may show traits of more than one category.

Category	Problem addressed	Examples
Interpretation	Inferring situation descriptions from sensor data	Hearsay (speech recognition), PROSPECTOR
Prediction	Inferring likely consequences of given situations	Preterm Birth Risk Assessment
Diagnosis	Inferring system malfunctions from observables	CADUCEUS, MYCIN, PUFF, Mistral, Eydenet, Kaleidos
Design	Configuring objects under constraints	Dendral, Mortgage Loan Advisor, R1 (DEC VAX Configuration), SID (DEC VAX 9000 CPU)
Planning	Designing actions	Mission Planning for Autonomous Underwater Vehicle
Monitoring	Comparing observations to plan vulnerabilities	REACTOR
Debugging	Providing incremental solutions for complex problems	SAINT, MATHLAB, MACSYMA
Repair	Executing a plan to administer a prescribed remedy	Toxic Spill Crisis Management
Instruction	Diagnosing, assessing, and repairing student behavior	SMH.PAL, Intelligent Clinical Training, STEAMER
Control	Interpreting, predicting, repairing, and monitoring system behaviors	Real Time Process Control, Space Shuttle Mission Control

Hearsay was an early attempt at solving voice recognition through an expert systems approach. For the most part this category or expert systems was not all that successful. Hearsay and all interpretation systems are essentially pattern recognition systems—looking for patterns in noisy data. In the case of Hearsay recognizing phonemes in an audio stream. Other early examples were analyzing sonar data to detect Russian submarines. These kinds of systems proved much more amenable to a neural network AI solution than a rule-based approach.

CADUCEUS and MYCIN were medical diagnosis systems. The user describes their symptoms to the computer as they would to a doctor and the computer returns a medical diagnosis.

Dendral was a tool to study hypothesis formation in the identification of organic molecules. The general problem it solved—designing a solution given a set of constraints—was one of the most successful areas for early expert systems applied to business domains such as salespeople configuring Digital Equipment Corporation (DEC) VAX computers and mortgage loan application development.

SMH.PAL is an expert system for the assessment of students with multiple disabilities.

Mistral is an expert system to monitor dam safety, developed in the 90's by Ismes (Italy). It gets data from an automatic monitoring system and performs a diagnosis of the state of the dam. Its first copy, installed in 1992 on the Ridracoli Dam (Italy), is still operational 24/7/365. It has been installed on several dams in Italy and abroad (e.g., Itaipu Dam in Brazil), and on landslide sites under the name of Eydenet, and on monuments under the name of Kaleidos. Mistral is a registered trade mark of CESI.

Model-based Reasoning

Model-based reasoning is an approach in artificial intelligence that relies on the use of a model as the basis of its inferencing abilities rather than empirical information. A model is a principled representation of a problem domain that has predictive and explicative features.

Model-Based Reasoning is the symbolic processing of an explicit representation of the internal working of a system in order to predict, simulate and explain the resultant behaviour of the system from the structure, causality, functional and behaviour of its components.

Model-based reasoning takes knowledge about the entities, structures and interactions in a particular domain and uses that knowledge as a foundation for generating a description of the behaviour of some system. The key feature is that a model is maintained which mirrors the important features of the domain.

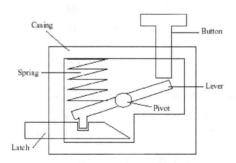

For example, consider the very simple latch lock illustrated in the above figure. If the structure of this device and the behaviour of its constituent parts are represented in an appropriate form, then from this it should be possible to synthesise the behaviour of the whole system. The lock consists of six components, connected together in a particular manner. From a structure/behaviour model of this device it should be possible to determine that if the button is pressed the latch will become free to move.

Model-based diagnosis takes knowledge about the entities, structures and interactions in a particular domain and uses that knowledge as a foundation for diagnosis. The key feature is that a model is maintained which mirrors the important structure and features of the domain. This means that model represents the components in a device, how they behave and how they are connected together.

The behaviour of the device is then synthesized from the behaviour of the components and their connections. For example, if a force is applied to the button it is propagated hrough the device resulting in the latch being freed. This is achieved by implementing a set of rules for how each type of component or connection propagates forces. Joining together the rules for all of the components in a device should allow you to simulate force propagation through the device.

Model Based Reasoning can be used by engineers who intend to design, analyse, simulate, diagnose, monitor and maintain a physical technical system. This technique can significantly improve the efficiency of solving engineering problems. This technique can also be applied to other application domains such as education, ecology, biology and medicine.

Model Based Systems enable engineers to solve problems in a very efficient manner. Models validated for a category of systems can be used in many different scenarios. They can be reused in the design, analysis, simulation, diagnosis and prediction of a technical system. This ensures the quality and consistency of a solution in carrying out the above tasks;

- In diagnostic applications, model based systems play a vital role in identifying the faults of a technical system and recommending a solution for the rectification of faults.

- In design applications, model based systems enable a designer to employ readily available component models in the analysis and simulation of the functional and behaviour performance of a system design solution. This significantly improves the design efficiency and quality of a system design.

There are several limitations associated with Model Based Systems and the key limitations include model validation, model reuse for a new system, degree of model accuracy, level of model complexity. Also some other drawbacks are;

- Intensive knowledge acquisition from rulebooks required.

- Requires an explicit domain model, a well-defined theory.

  - Excludes some medical specialties, financial applications.

- Complex and detailed reasoning may slow down the system.

- Ignores (possibly valuable) experiential knowledge.

- Can only handle problems explained by the model.

  - A model is a representation of some reality. It leaves out many aspects. If the things that left out are the cause of the problem, the MBR won't work.

Model Based Systems have been used in the following application domains:

Systems Diagnosis: Diagnostic tools for technical physical systems are used to automate the diagnosis of such systems.

Systems Functional/Behaviour Simulation: Model-based function/behaviour prediction systems are used to evaluate the behaviour of physical technical systems, ecological systems and biological systems.

Product Design and Synthesis: Computer based design decision support systems such as failure mode effects analysis systems, Environmental decision support systems using MBSs.

Planning: Based on the results of a diagnosis system, planning systems are used to supported or automated generation of repair actions.

Education: Model Based Reasoning techniques are used for realising tutoring and training functions, and subject matter construction.

Other Areas: Model Based Systems have also been seen in other application area, including, medicine, industrial processes/plants, automotive, aeronautics, aerospace, physics, telecommunications etc.

Knowledge Representation

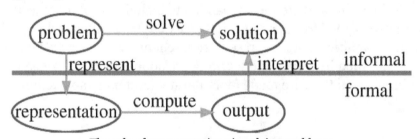

The role of representations in solving problems

The general framework for solving problems by computer. To solve a problem, the designer of a system must:

- flesh out the task and determine what constitutes a solution;

- represent the problem in a language with which a computer can reason;

- use the computer to compute an output, which is an answer presented to a user or a sequence of actions to be carried out in the environment; and

- interpret the output as a solution to the problem.

Knowledge is the information about a domain that can be used to solve problems in that domain. To solve many problems requires much knowledge, and this knowledge must be represented in the computer. As part of designing a program to solve problems, we must define how the knowledge will be represented. A representation scheme is the form of the knowledge that is used in an agent. A representation of some piece of knowledge is the internal representation of the knowledge. A representation scheme specifies the form of the knowledge. A knowledge base is the representation of all of the knowledge that is stored by an agent.

A good representation scheme is a compromise among many competing objectives. A representation should be

- rich enough to express the knowledge needed to solve the problem.

- as close to the problem as possible; it should be compact, natural, and maintainable. It should be easy to see the relationship between the representation and the domain being represented, so that it is easy to determine whether the knowledge represented is correct. A small change in the problem should result in a small change in the representation of the problem.

- amenable to efficient computation, which usually means that it is able to express features of the problem that can be exploited for computational gain and able to trade off accuracy and computation time.

- able to be acquired from people, data and past experiences.

Many different representation schemes have been designed. Many of these start with some of these objectives and are then expanded to include the other objectives. For example, some are designed for learning and then expanded to allow richer problem solving and inference abilities. Some representation schemes are designed with expressiveness in mind, and then inference and learning are added on. Some schemes start from tractable inference and then are made more natural, and more able to be acquired.

Legal Expert System

A legal expert system (LES) is a system that provides answers to legal questions which resemble the answers one might expect from a lawyer.

The output from an LES should not require further legal analysis. This output should be in such a form that it can be the basis of a lawyer's legal argument in court.

LESs are not judgment machines; they will not usurp judicial power. The development of sophisticated LESs will not remove the need for lawyers, although it may change the nature of some legal work. An LES should be a powerful tool for use by both lawyers and non-lawyers.

Following are the some important features to applying expert system techniques to building Legal Expert System:

High Performance – The system must be capable to responding at the level of equal to human expert in a specific field. That is the equality of advice given by the system must have high integrity.

Quick response time – The system takes reasonable time comparatively human expert to reach decision. Sometime in case of emergency may require response faster than human, in this case real-time expert system is a good choice.

Good Reliability – The expert system always reliable if the expert system programmed accurately until and unless mistake made by the expert, which may happen if the human expert is tired or stress.

Reduced Cost – The cost of providing expertise per a user is greatly lowered. Reduced Danger – The expert systems can be used in locations that might be harmful for a human.

Permanence – Expert system is permanent. But human experts, who may retire, quit, die. Multiple Expertise – This feature allows extracting the knowledge from distinguish experts to solve complex troubles by conducting reasoning with the help of expert system.

Explanation – Expert system shows the detailed arguments how the reasoning takes place to determine appropriate conclusion.

Steady, Unemotional – This feature is mandatory in some tragedy circumstances where human expert unable to gives the solutions due to exhaustion.

Intelligence Database – Expert Systems are making use of like a intelligence database at time when all adequate rules deposited in this system. Like Data Mining Techniques.

Types

Architectural Variations

Rule-based expert systems rely on a model of deductive reasoning that utilizes "if A, then B" rules. In a rule-based legal expert system, information is represented in the form of deductive rules within the knowledge base.

Case-based reasoning models, which store and manipulate examples or cases, hold the potential to emulate an analogical reasoning process thought to be well-suited for the legal domain. This model effectively draws on known experiences our outcomes for similar problems.

A neural net relies on a computer model that mimics that structure of a human brain, and operates in a very similar way to the case-based reasoning model. This expert system model is capable of recognizing and classifying patterns within the realm of legal knowledge and dealing with imprecise inputs.

Fuzzy logic models attempt to create 'fuzzy' concepts or objects that can then be converted into quantitative terms or rules that are indexed and retrieved by the system. In the legal domain, fuzzy logic can be used for rule-based and case-based reasoning models.

Theoretical Variations

While some legal expert system architects have adopted a very practical approach, employing scientific modes of reasoning within a given set of rules or cases, others have opted for a broader philosophical approach inspired by jurisprudential reasoning modes emanating from established legal theoreticians.

Functional Variations

Some legal expert systems aim to arrive at a particular conclusion in law, while others are designed to predict a particular outcome. An example of a predictive system is one that predicts the outcome of judicial decisions, the value of a case, or the outcome of litigation.

Challenges

Domain-related Problems

The inherent complexity of law as a discipline raises immediate challenges for legal expert system knowledge engineers. Legal matters often involve interrelated facts and issues, which further compound the complexity.

Factual uncertainty may also arise when there are disputed versions of factual representations that must be input into an expert system to begin the reasoning process.

Computerized Problem Solving

The limitations of most computerized problem solving techniques inhibit the success of many expert systems in the legal domain. Expert systems typically rely on deductive reasoning models that have difficulty according degrees of weight to certain principles of law or importance to previously decided cases that may or may not influence a decision in an immediate case or context.

Representation of Legal Knowledge

Expert legal knowledge can be difficult to represent or formalize within the structure of an expert system. For knowledge engineers, challenges include:

- Open texture: Law is rarely applied in an exact way to specific facts, and exact outcomes are rarely a certainty. Statutes may be interpreted according to different linguistic interpretations, reliance on precedent cases or other contextual factors including a particular judge's conception of fairness.

- The balancing of reasons: Many arguments involve considerations or reasons that are not easily represented in a logical way. For instance, many constitutional legal issues are said to balance independently well-established considerations for state interests against individual rights. Such balancing may draw on extra-legal considerations that would be difficult to represent logically in an expert system.

- Indeterminacy of legal reasoning: In the adversarial arena of law, it is common to have two strong arguments on a single point. Determining the 'right' answer may depend on a majority vote among expert judges, as in the case of an appeal.

Time and Cost Effectiveness

Creating a functioning expert system requires significant investments in software architecture, subject matter expertise and knowledge engineering. Faced with these challenges, many system architects restrict the domain in terms of subject matter and jurisdiction. The consequence of this approach is the creation of narrowly focused and geographically restricted legal expert systems that are difficult to justify on a cost-benefit basis.

Lack of Correctness in Results or Decisions

Legal expert systems may lead non-expert users to incorrect or inaccurate results and decisions. This problem could be compounded by the fact that users may rely heavily on the correctness or trustworthiness of results or decisions generated by these systems.

Examples

ASHSD-II is a hybrid legal expert system that blends rule-based and case-based reasoning models in the area of matrimonial property disputes under English law.

CHIRON is a hybrid legal expert system that blends rule-based and case-based reasoning models to support tax planning activities under United States tax law and codes.

JUDGE is a rule-based legal expert system that deals with sentencing in the criminal legal domain for offences relating to murder, assault and manslaughter.

The Latent Damage Project is a rule-based legal expert system that deals with limitation periods under the (UK) *Latent Damage Act 1986* in relation to the domains of tort, contract and product liability law.

Split-Up is a rule-based legal expert system that assists in the division of marital assets according to the (Australia) *Family Law Act (1975)*.

SHYSTER is a case-based legal expert system that can also function as a hybrid through its ability to link with rule-based models. It was designed to accommodate multiple legal domains, including aspects of Australian copyright law, contract law, personal property and administrative law.

TAXMAN is a rule-based system that could perform a basic form of legal reasoning by classifying cases under a particular category of statutory rules in the area of law concerning corporate reorganization.

Shyster

Most legal expert systems attempt to implement complex models of legal reasoning. But the utility of a legal expert system lies not in the extent to which it simulates a lawyer's approach to a legal problem, but in the quality of its predictions and of its arguments. A complex model of legal reasoning is not necessary: a successful legal expert system can be based upon a simplified model of legal reasoning.

Some researchers have based their systems upon a jurisprudential approach to the law, yet lawyers are patently able to operate without any jurisprudential insight. A useful legal expert system should be capable of producing advice similar to that which one might get from a lawyer, so it should operate at the same pragmatic level of abstraction as does a lawyer — not at the more philosophical level of jurisprudence.

A legal expert system called SHYSTER has been developed to demonstrate that a useful legal expert system can be based upon a pragmatic approach to the law. SHYSTER has a simple representation structure which simplifies the problem of knowledge acquisition. Yet this structure is complex enough for SHYSTER to produce useful advice.

SHYSTER is a case-based legal expert system (although it has been designed so that it can be linked with a rule-based system to form a hybrid legal expert system). Its advice is based upon an examination of, and an argument about, the similarities and differences between cases. SHYSTER attempts to model the way in which lawyers argue with cases, but it does not attempt to model the way in which lawyers decide which cases to use in those arguments. Instead, it employs statistical techniques to quantify the similarity between cases. It decides which cases to use in argument, and what prediction it will make, on the basis of that similarity measure.

SHYSTER is of a general design: it can provide advice in areas of case law that have been specified by a legal expert using a specification language. Hence, it can operate in different legal domains. Four different, and disparate, areas of law have been specified for SHYSTER, and its operation has been tested in each of those domains.

SHYSTER is a specific example of a general category of legal expert systems, broadly defined as systems that make use of artificial intelligence (AI) techniques to solve legal problems. Legal AI systems can be divided into two categories: legal retrieval systems and legal analysis systems. SHYSTER belongs to the latter category of legal analysis systems. Legal analysis systems can be further subdivided into two categories: judgment machines and legal expert systems. SHYSTER again belongs to the latter category of legal expert systems. A legal expert system, as Popple uses the term, is a system capable of performing at a level expected of a lawyer: "AI systems which merely assist a lawyer in coming to legal conclusions or preparing legal arguments are not here considered to be legal expert systems; a legal expert system must exhibit some legal expertise itself."

Designed to operate in more than one legal domain, and be of specific use to the common law of Australia, SHYSTER accounts for statute law, case law, and the doctrine of precedent in areas of private law. Whilst it accommodates statute law, it is primarily a case-based system, in contradistinction to rule-based systems like MYCIN. More specifically, it was designed in a manner enabling it to be linked with a rule-based system to form a hybrid system. Although case-based reasoning possesses an advantage over rule-based systems by the elimination of complex semantic networks, it suffers from intractable theoretical obstacles: without some further theory it cannot be predicted what features of a case will turn out to be relevant. Users of SHYSTER therefore require some legal expertise.

Richard Susskind argues that "jurisprudence can and ought to supply the models of law and legal reasoning that are required for computerized [sic] implementation in the process of building all expert systems in law." Popple, however, believes jurisprudence is of limited value to developers of legal expert systems. He posits that a lawyer must have a model of the law (maybe unarticulated) which includes assumptions about the nature of law and legal reasoning, but that model need not rest on basic philosophical foundations. It may be a pragmatic model, developed through experience within the legal system. Many lawyers perform their work with little or no jurisprudential knowledge, and there is no evidence to suggest that they are worse, or better, at their jobs than lawyers well-versed in jurisprudence. The fact that many lawyers have mastered the process of legal reasoning, without having been immersed in jurisprudence, suggests that it may indeed be possible to develop legal expert systems of good quality without jurisprudential insight. As a pragmatic legal expert system SHYSTER is the embodiment of this belief.

A further example of SHYSTER's pragmatism is its simple knowledge representation structure. This structure was designed to facilitate specification of different areas of case law using a specification language. Areas of case law are specified in terms of the cases and attributes of importance in those areas. SHYSTER weights its attributes and checks for dependence between them. In order to choose cases upon which to construct its opinions, SHYSTER calculates distances between cases and uses these distances to determine which of the leading cases are nearest to the instant case. To this end SHYSTER can be seen to adopt and expand upon nearest neighbor search methods used in pattern recognition. These nearest cases are used to produce an argument (based on similarities and differences between the cases) about the likely outcome in the instant case. This argument relies on the doctrine of precedent; it assumes that the instant case will be decided the same way as was the nearest case. SHYSTER then uses information about these nearest cases to construct a report. The report that SHYSTER generates makes a prediction and justifies that prediction by reference only to cases and their similarities and differences: the calculations that SHYSTER performs in coming to its opinion do not appear in that opinion. Safeguards are employed to warn users if SHYSTER doubts the veracity of its advice.

Results

SHYSTER was tested in four different and disparate areas of case law. Four specifications were written, each representing an area of Australian law: an aspect of the law of trover; the meaning of "authorization [sic]" in Australian copyright law; the categorisation of employment contracts; and the implication of natural justicein administrative decision-making. SHYSTER was evaluated under five headings: its usefulness, its generality, the quality of its advice, its limitations, and possible enhancements that could be made to it. Despite its simple knowledge representation structure, it has shown itself capable of producing good advice, and its simple structure has facilitated the specification of different areas of law.

Appreciating the difficulties encountered by legal expert systems developers in adequately representing legal knowledge can assist in appreciating the shortcomings of digital rights management technologies. Some academics believe future digital rights management systems may become sophisticated enough to permit exceptions to copyright law. To this end SHYSTER's attempt to model "authorization [sic]" in the Copyright Act can be viewed as pioneering work in this field. The term "authorization [sic]" is undefined in the Copyright Act. Consequently, a number of cases have been before the courts seeking answers as to what conduct amounts to authorisation. The main contexts in which the issue has arisen are analogous to permitted exceptions to copyright currently prevented by most digital rights management technologies: "home taping of recorded materials, photocopying in educational institutions and performing works in public". When applied to one case concerning compact cassettes, SHYSTER successfully agreed that Amstrad did not authorise the infringement.

Shine Expert System

Spacecraft Health Inference Engine (SHINE) is a software-development tool for knowledge-based systems and hasbeen created as a product for research and development by the Artificial Intelligence Group, Information SystemsTechnology Section at NASA/ JPL. The system is now in regular use in basic and applied AI research at JPL.

SHINE is a system developed at NASA to meet many of their demanding and rigorous AI goals for current and futureneeds. It is a system that was designed to be efficient enough to operate in a real-time environment and to be utilizedby non-LISP applications written in conventional programming languages such as C and C++. These non-LISPapplications can be running in a distributed computing environment on remote computers or on a computer thatsupports multiple programming languages.

SHINE provides a variety of facilities for the development of software modules for the primary functions in knowledge-based reasoning engines. The system may be used to develop artificial intelligence applications as well asspecialized tools for research efforts.

Knowledge-based systems for automated task planning, monitoring, diagnosis and other applications require a varietyof software modules based on artificial intelligence concepts and advanced programming techniques. The design andimplementation of the modules require considerable programming talent and time and background in theoreticalartificial intelligence. Sophisticated software development tools that can speed the research and development of newartificial intelligence applications are highly desirable. The SHINE system was developed for that purpose. Included inthe system are facilities for developing reasoning processes, memory-data structures and knowledge bases, blackboard systems and spontaneous computation daemons.

SHINE is not a shell which means that the user does not have to solve his problems in the shell's way; you can solvethem your own way. One is not limited by a shell's out dated problem solving techniques or preconceived notions onhow things should be done.

Computational efficiency and high performance are especially critical in artificial intelligence software. Thatconsideration has been an important objective for the SHINE system and has led to its design as a toolbox of AIfacilities that may be used independently or collectively in the development of knowledge-based systems.

- SHINE comes with libraries that implement most common problem solving techniques and representations. Thismeans that you can make use of classical AI solutions that have been extensively used and tested by other users. These libraries can also be extended by your own problem solving techniques and representations.

- SHINE facilities are invoked directly by a programmer in the Common LISP language. For improved efficiency, anoptimizing compiler is included that generates highly optimized Common LISP code. SHINE allows embeddedsoftware written in other programming languages such as C, C++, and also permits software developed with thesystem to be part of larger, non-Common LISP applications.

- SHINE is a set of high level and low level software tools designed to assist in building stand-alone knowledge-basedsystem applications, shells and tools.

- Since SHINE is a Common LISP based system, it can be run on any machine that supports Common LISP. BecauseSHINE is a compiler, not an interpreter, applications can run on a delivery machine that is much smaller than thedevelopment machine.

- SHINE provides the LISP programmer with the necessary tools to build a wide variety of reasoning and inferenceengines, such as expert systems, planners, diagnosticians, simulators, execution and real-time monitoring.

- SHINE allows and encourages embedded expert systems to be developed. This means that SHINE could be asupervisor of many other systems either written in SHINE or in conventional programming languages.

- SHINE is an optimizing compiler-based system. When an application is developed using SHINE, it is first translatedinto Common LISP code and then passed through an extensive optimizer. SHINE generates tailored code for eachapplication. There are no intermediate levels of interpretation for execution unlike many commercial systems. SHINEprograms are executed directly by the LISP interpreter and compiled directly by the LISP compiler. This means muchgreater speed and better portability to other machines.

- SHINE augments the Common LISP programming language and environment so that programs written in SHINEhave direct use of all of the features of the underlying LISP system and the LISP environment.

- SHINE provides a debugging environment built upon the LISP environment for the debugging of systems at compile-time and run-time. In addition, the SHINE compiler and its run-time environment perform extensive error checking.

Use of SHINE in NASA and non-NASA Applications

- Spacecraft Health Automatic Reasoning Pilot (SHARP) for the diagnosis of telecommunication anomalies during the Neptune Voyager (VGR) Encounter.

- Galileo (GLL) mission for diagnosing problems in the Power and Pyro Subsystem (PPS).

- Magellan (MGN) mission for diagnosis of telecommunication anomalies in the TELECOM subsystem.

- Engineering Analysis Subsystem Environment (EASE) which is an operations environment to operate a large number of spacecraft simultaneously, maintain high reliability levels and increase productivity through shared resources and automation.

- Extreme UltraViolet Explorer (EUVE) mission for labor 3 to 1 shift reductions through the use of artificial intelligence.

- Fault Induced Document Officer (FIDO) for the EUVE mission. which is an automated system that assists in expert knowledge acquisition, access and publishing capabilities for safely managing complex systems under staffing reductions and "lights out" operations.

- Stochastic Problem Obviation Tracker (SPOT) for the EUVE mission which captures and reports relevant statistical information to the user based on operations within the FIDO environment.

- Program is licensed by Beyond Limits for use with their artificial intelligence technology.

- Under consideration by a medical company for real-time diagnosis of rectal colon cancer.

- Under consideration by a medical company for an expert system for the control of the robotic systems used in eye surgery.

Split Up

Discretionary fields of law are those in which a decision maker has a considerable degree of flexibility in determining an outcome. Family law in Australia is considered discretionary because a judge of the Family Court of Australia, in allocating property to couples following a divorce is required by statute to take various factors into account but has discretion in allocating a relative weighting to each factor. For example, the principle statute mandates that the health and age of both parties are relevant considerations yet is silent on their relative importance.

Modelling discretionary reasoning is difficult. Attempts to do so using heuristic rules has been found to be limited by (Edmunds and Huntley 1992) and also by (Stranieri and Zeleznikow 1992). The application of neural networks to modelling discretionary reasoning is suitable if sufficient past decisions can be collected from Courts to form a training set. Once trained, the network, exposed to a new case will output a result consistent with patterns of decisions in previous cases. However, neural networks have not often been used to model legal reasoning principally because explanations for neural network inferences are difficult to generate and because sufficiently large numbers of past cases often do not exist.

Split Up is a rule - neural hybrid system that integrates twenty neural networks with fifteen rules sets. The system predicts the percentage of marital property a Family Court of Australia judge will award litigants to a divorce. Consultations with domain experts from a state funded legal service identified a total of 94 relevant variables. Data reflecting values for these variables has been collected from over one hundred judgments made by decision makers in the Family Court. The data was used to train neural networks.

The system is currently being used by registrars (judicial assistants) and judges of the Family Court, mediators from a counselling service and four legal firms. The needs of each group of user is quite distinct and as a consequence the way the system is used and ensuing benefits differ. For example, registrars of the Family Court are required to attempt to mediate a settlement before a dispute is tried by a judge. This involves informing litigants about the basics of family law and judicial heuristics. Lawyers are less interested in educating their client but need to organise their arguments, validate their own predictions and be reminded of cases and statutes that would strengthen (or weaken) their arguments. Judges are required to arrive at an equitable outcome in the shortest amount of time possible.

The knowledge representation central to Split Up is a structure based on the argument structure proposed by (Toulmin 1958). The argument based framework used in Split Up is not limited to rules and neural networks but can easily accommodate other forms of inferencing including fuzzy logic, inferential statistics and nonmonotonic logic. The argument based structure we use has the following benefits:

- Explanations are generated independently from the reasoning method used to infer an outcome. Explanations are not traces of the inferencing and can be generated whether a neural network or a rule set produced the outcome.

- Knowledge acquisition from expert interview is facilitated because the argument structure enables domain experts to decompose the task of predicting a percentage split of marital assets into smaller sub-tasks. Each sub task can be modelled with a relatively small neural network that requires far fewer past cases to train than is the case for a large network.

Application

In Australian family law, a judge in determining the distribution of property will:

1. identify the assets of the marriage included in the common pool

2. establish what percentage of the common pool each party will receive

3. determine a final property order in line with the decisions made in 1. and 2.

Split_Up implements step 1 and 2: the common pool determination and the prediction of a percentage split.

The Common Pool Determination

Since the determination of marital property is rule based, it is implemented using directed graphs.

However, the percentage split between the parties is discretionary in that a judge has a wide discretion to look at each party's contributions to the marriage under section 79(4) of the Family Law Act 1975. Broadly, the contributions can be taken as financial or non-financial. The party who can demonstrate a larger contribution to the marital relationship will receive a larger proportion of the assets. The court may further look at each party's financial resources and future needs under section 75(2)of the Family Law Act 1975. These needs can include factors such as the inability to gain employment, the continued care of a child under 18 years of age or medical expenses.

This means that different judges may and will reach different conclusions based on the same facts, since each judge assigns different relevant weights to each factor. Split_up determines the percentage split by using a combination of rule- based reasoning and neural networks.

The Percentage Split Determination

In order to determine how judges weigh the different factors, 103 written judgements of commonplace cases were used to establish a database comprising 94 relevant factors for percentage split determination.

The factors relevant for a percentage split determination are:

- *Past contributions of a husband relative to those of a wife*

- *The husband's future needs relative to those of the wife*

- *The wealth of the marriage*

The factors relevant for a determination of past contributions are

- *The relative direct and indirect contributions of both parties*

- *The length of the marriage*

- *The relative contributions of both parties to the homemaking role.*

The hierarchy provides a structure that is used to decompose the task of predicting an outcome into 35 subtasks. Outputs of tasks further down the hierarchy are used as inputs into sub-tasks higher up the hierarchy. Each sub-task is treated as a separate and smaller data mining exercise. Twenty one solid arcs represent inferences performed with the use of rule sets. For example, the level of wealth of a marriage is determined by a rule, which uses the common pool value.

By contrast, the fourteen dashed arcs establish inferences performed with the use of neural networks. These receive their name from the fact that they resemble a nervous system in the brain. They consist of many self – adjusting processing elements cooperating in a densely interconnected network. Each processing element generates a single output that is transmitted to the other processing element. The output signal of a processing element depends on the input to the processing element, i.e. each input is gated by a weighing factor that determines the amount of influence that the input will have on the output. The strength of the weighing factors is adjusted autonomously by the processing element as the data is processed.

In Split_Up, the neural network is a statistical technique for learning the weights of each of the relevant attributes used in a percentage split determination of marital property.

Hence the inputs to the neural network are contributions, future needs and wealth, and the output the percentage split predicted.

On each arc there is a statistical weight. Using back propagation the neural network learns the necessary pattern to recognize the prediction. It is trained by repeatedly exposing it to examples of the problem and learning the significance (weights) of the input nodes.

The neural network used by Split_up is said to generalise well if the output of the network is correct (or nearly correct) for examples not seen during training, which classifies it as an intelligent system.

Toulmin Argument Structure

Since the manner in which these weights are learned is primarily statistical, domain knowledge of legal rules and principles is not modelled directly. However, explanations for a legal conclusion in a domain as discretionary as the determining the distribution of property following divorce, are at least as important as the conclusion reached. Hence the creators of Split_Up used Toulmin Argument structures, to provide independent explanations of the conclusions reached.

These operate on the basis that every argument makes an assertion based on some data. The assertion of the argument stands as the claim of the argument. Since knowing the data and the claim, does not necessarily mean that the claim follows from the data, a mechanism is required to justify the claim in the light of the data. The justification is known as the warrant. The backing of an argument supports the validity of the warrant.

In the legal domain, this is typically a reference to a statute or a precedent.

Here, a neural network (or rules), produce a conclusion from the data of an argument and the data, warrant and backing are reproduced to generate an explanation.

It is noteworthy, though, that an argument's warrant is reproduced as an explanation regardless of the claim values used. This lack of claim - sensitivity must be overcome by the different users, i.e.the judge, the representatives for the wife and the representatives for the husband, each of whom is encouraged to use the system to prepare their cases, but not to rely exclusively on its outcome.

Toulmin Structure

Claim	State the position being argued for
Qualifier	Specification to limits of a claim—look up the list of qualifiers on page 161 of Everything's An Argument
Reasons	Sound and logical reasons in support of claim
Warrants	The chain of reasoning that connects the claim to the data
Evidence/Backing	Support, justification and reasons to back up warrants
Rebuttal/Response	Exceptions to the claim, description and rebuttal of counterarguments.

The culminating argument in Split Up: the percentage split argument

Mycin

MYCIN is the name of a decision support system developed by Stanford University in the early- to mid-seventies, built to assist physicians in the diagnosis of infectious diseases. The system (also known as an "expert system") would ask a series of questions designed to emulate the thinking of an expert in the field of infectious disease (hence the "expert-"), and from the responses to these questions give a list of possible diagnoses, with probability, as well as recommend treatment (hence the "decision support-"). The name "MYCIN" actually comes from antibiotics, many of which have the suffix "-mycin".

MYCIN was originally developed by Edward Shortliffe for Stanford Medical School in the early-and mid-1970's. Written in Lisp, a language (a set of languages, actually) geared towards artificial intelligence, MYCIN was one of the pioneering expert systems, and was the first such system implemented for the medical field.

Logical Layout of MYCIN

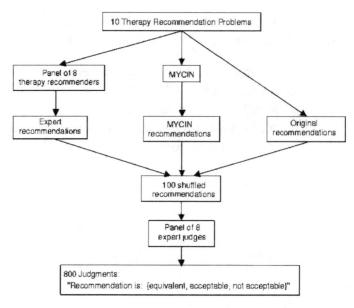

Method

MYCIN operated using fairly simple inference engine, and a knowledge base of ~600 rules. It would query the physician running the program via a long series of simple yes/no or textual questions. At the end, it provided a list of possible culprit bacteria ranked from high to low based on the probability of each diagnosis, its confidence in each diagnosis' probability, the reasoning behind each diagnosis (that is, MYCIN would also list the questions and rules which led it to rank a diagnosis a particular way), and its recommended course of drug treatment.

MYCIN sparked debate about the use of its ad hoc, but principled, uncertainty framework known as "certainty factors". The developers performed studies showing that MYCIN's performance was minimally affected by perturbations in the uncertainty metrics associated with individual rules, suggesting that the power in the system was related more to its knowledge representation and reasoning scheme than to the details of its numerical uncertainty model. Some observers felt that it should have been possible to use classical Bayesian statistics. MYCIN's developers argued that this would require either unrealistic assumptions of probabilistic independence, or require the experts to provide estimates for an unfeasibly large number of conditional probabilities.

Subsequent studies later showed that the certainty factor model could indeed be interpreted in a probabilistic sense, and highlighted problems with the implied assumptions of such a model. However the modular structure of the system would prove very successful, leading to the development of graphical models such as Bayesian networks.

Evidence Combination

In MYCIN it was possible that two or more rules might draw conclusions about a parameter with different weights of evidence. For example, one rule may conclude that the organism in question is E. Coli with a certainty of 0.8 whilst another concludes that it is E. Coli with a certainty of 0.5 or even -0.8. In the event the certainty is less than zero the evidence is actually against the hypothesis. In order to calculate the certainty factor MYCIN combined these weights using the formula below to yield a single certainty factor:

$$CF(x,y) = \begin{cases} X + Y - XY & \text{if } X,Y > 0 \\ X + Y + XY & \text{if } X,Y < 0 \\ \dfrac{X + Y}{1 - \min(|X|,|Y|)} & \text{otherwise} \end{cases}$$

Where X and Y are the certainty factors. This formula can be applied more than once if more than two rules draw conclusions about the same parameter. It is commutative, so it does not matter in which order the weights were combined.

Results

Research conducted at the Stanford Medical School found MYCIN received an acceptability rating of 65% on treatment plan from a panel of eight independent specialists, which was comparable to the 42.5% to 62.5% rating of five faculty members. This study is often cited as showing the potential for disagreement about therapeutic decisions, even among experts, when there is no "gold standard" for correct treatment.

Practical use

MYCIN was never actually used in practice. This wasn't because of any weakness in its performance. Some observers raised ethical and legal issues related to the use of computers in medicine. However, the greatest problem, and the reason that MYCIN was not used in routine practice, was the state of technologies for system integration, especially at the time it was developed. MYCIN was a stand-alone system that required a user to enter all relevant information about a patient by typing in responses to questions MYCIN posed. The program ran on a large time-shared system, available over the early Internet (ARPANet), before personal computers were developed.

MYCIN's greatest influence was accordingly its demonstration of the power of its representation and reasoning approach. Rule-based systems in many non-medical domains were developed in the years that followed MYCIN's introduction of the approach. In the 1980s, expert system "shells" were introduced (including one based on MYCIN, known as E-MYCIN (followed by Knowledge Engineering Environment - KEE)) and supported the development of expert systems in a wide variety of application areas. A difficulty that rose to prominence during the development of MYCIN and subsequent complex expert systems has been the extraction of the necessary knowledge for the inference engine to use from the human expert in the relevant fields into the rule base (the so-called "knowledge acquisition bottleneck").

Expert Systems for Mortgages

An expert system for mortgages is a computer program that contains the knowledge and analytical skills of human experts, related to mortgage banking. Loan departments are interested in expert systems for mortgages because ofthe growing cost of labour which makes the handling and acceptance of relatively small loans less profitable. They also see in the application of expert systems a possibility for standardised, efficient handling of mortgage loans, and appreciate that for the acceptance of mortgages there are hard and fast rules which do not always exist with other types of loans.

Since most interest rates for mortgages are controlled by the government, intense competition sees to it that a greatdeal in terms of business depends on the quality of service offered to clients - who shop around for the loan bestsuiting their needs. Expert systems for mortgages considers the key factors which enter the profitability equation. Forinstance, "part and parcel of the quality of a mortgage loans portfolio to the bank is the time which elapses betweenthe first contact with the client and the bank's offering of a loan. Another key ingredient is the fact that home loanshave significant features which are not always exploited through classical DP approaches. The expert system correctsthis failure".

The expert system also capitalises on regulatory possibilities. In France, the government subsidises one type of loanwhich is available only on low-cost properties (the HLM) and to lower income families. Known as frets Conventionnes, these carry a rate of interest lower than the rate on the ordinary property loan from a bank. The difficulty is thatgranting them is subject to numerous regulations, concerning both:

- the home which is to be purchased, and

- the financial circumstances of the borrower.

To assure that all conditions have been met, every application has to be first processed at branch level and then sentto a central office for checking, before going back to the branch, often with requests for more information from theapplicant. This leads to frustrating delays. Expert system for mortgages takes care of these by providing branchemployees with tools permitting them to process an application correctly, even if a bank employee does not have anexact knowledge of the screening procedure.

Goals and Objectives

The expert system neither refuses nor grants loans, but it:

- establishes whether all the conditions for granting a particular type of loan to a given client have been satisfied, and

- calculates the required term of repayment, according to the borrower's

- means and the security to be obtained from him.

The goal is to produce applications which are correct in 80 per cent to 90 per cent of all cases, and transferresponsibility for granting or refusing loans to the branch offices.

The expert system provides the branch with a significant amount of assistance simply by producing correctapplications for a loan. In many cases the client had to choose between different types of loans, and it was plannedthat expert system should enable bank employees to advise clients on the type of loan which best matched theirneeds. This, too, has been done and as such contributes to the bank employees' training.

The main tasks of expert system for mortgages focused on:

- the speed of moving a loan through red tape, which management considered to be a very important factor;

- the reduction of the errors made in the filling form;

- the shortening of the turnaround time, which was too long with classical.

Simple expert systems constitute the first phase of a loan application for mortgage purposes. After a prototype ismade, the construct should be presented to expert loan officers who, working together with the knowledge engineer(s) will refine the first model. But if there is no first try which is simple and understandable, there will not becomplex real-life solutions afterwards.

Whether simple or sophisticated, an expert system for mortgages should be provided with explanation facilities that show how it reaches its decisions and hence its advice. The confidence of the loan officer in the AI construct will beincreased when this is done in a convincing manner.

Application of Expert Systems for Mortgages

Expert systems for mortgages find an application for mortgage loans. For example, Federal National MortgageAssociation (FNMA), commonly known as Fannie Mae use the Mavent Expert System. Through the MaventCompliance Console (MC2), the front-end interface to the Mavent Expert System, Fannie Mae review loans forcompliance with its policies on the Truth in Lending Act (TILA), federal and state high-cost lending laws, and thepoints-and-fees test as outlined in the Fannie Mae Selling and Servicing Guide.

Expert systems for mortgages can be used not only in mortgage banking, but also in law. There are some expertsystem that was developed to assist attorneys and paralegals in the closing process for commercial real estatemortgage loans. "The system identifies the legal requirements for closing the loans by considering the numerousindividual features specific to each particular loan. It was felt that an expert system could provide significant benefitsto this process, which is extremely complex and involves large amounts of money. To our knowledge, expert systemstechnology had not previously been applied to this domain. Successful development and implementation of thesystem resulted in the realization of the anticipated benefits, and a few others as well" Clancy, Paul, Gerald Hoenig, and Arnold Schmitt. 1989. An Expert System for Legal Consultation.

References

- Leondes, Cornelius T. (2002). Expert systems: the technology of knowledge management and decision making for the 21st century. pp. 1–22. ISBN 978-0-12-443880-4

- Carl S. Gibson, et al, VAX 9000 SERIES, Digital Technical Journal of Digital Equipment Corporation, Volume 2, Number 4, Fall 1990, pp118-129

- Haskin, David (January 16, 2003). "Years After Hype, 'Expert Systems' Paying Off For Some". Datamation. Retrieved 29 November 2013.

- Lancini, Stefano; Lazzari, Marco; Masera, Alberto; Salvaneschi, Paolo (1997). "Diagnosing Ancient Monuments with Expert Software" (PDF). Structural Engineering International. 7(4): 288–291. doi:10.2749/101686697780494392

- Hayes-Roth, Frederick; Waterman, Donald; Lenat, Douglas (1983). Building Expert Systems. Addison-Wesley. pp. 6–7. ISBN 0-201-10686-8

- Schafer, Burkhard (2010). "ZombAIs: Legal Expert Systems as Representatives "Beyond the Grave"". SCRIPTed. 7 (2). Retrieved 26 October 2012

- Berman, Donald H.; Hafner, Carole D. (1989). "The Potential of Artificial Intelligence to Help Solve the Crisis in Our Legal System". Communications of the ACM. 32 (8). doi:10.1145/65971.65972

- Cunningham, A. (2005): 'Rights Expression on Digital Communication Networks: Some Implications for Copyright' International Journal of Law and Information Technology 2005 13(1) p. 23

- Atkinson, D.J., "Artificial intelligence for monitoring and diagnosis of robotic spacecraft." Doctoral Dissertation. School of Electrical and Computer Engineering, Chalmers University of Technology, Göteborg, Sweden, ISSN 0282-5406; no 237. ISBN 91-7032-755-6. 1992

3

Problem Solving, Reasoning and Knowledge Representation in Artificial Intelligence

In AI systems, algorithms that imitate the intellectual processes in humans were developed for simulating problem solving and logical deduction making. An important field of artificale intelligence is knowledge representation and reasoning, which has been covered in extensive detail in this chapter. The diverse aspects of strategic artificial intelligence processes, such as automated planning and scheduling, computational humor, artificial intelligence systems integration, commonsense reasoning and computer-assisted proof, etc. have been thoroughly discussed in this chapter.

Action Selection

Action selection is a way of characterizing the most basic problem of intelligent systems: what to do next. In artificial intelligence and computational cognitive science, the action selection problem is typically associated with intelligent agents and animats – artificial systems that exhibit complex behaviour in an agent environment. The term is also sometimes used in ethology or animal behaviour.

Characteristics of the Action Selection Problem

A basic problem for understanding action selection is determining the level of abstraction used for specifying an 'act'. At the most basic level of abstraction, an atomic act could be anything from contracting a muscle cell to provoking a war. Typically for an artificial actionselection mechanism, the set of possible actions is predefined and fixed. However, in nature agents are able to control action at a variety of levels of abstraction, and the acquisition of skills or expertise can also be viewed as the acquisition of new action selection primitives.

Action selection could also be seen as the intelligent-agent version of the engineering discipline of systems integration. A good action selection mechanism allows a developer to decompose the problem of building intelligent systems into relatively simple components or modules and then reintegrate or coordinate the overall behaviour.

Most researchers studying AI action selection place high demands on their agents:

- The acting agent typically must select its action in dynamic and unpredictable environments.

- The agents typically act in real time; therefore they must make decisions in a timely fashion.

- The agents are normally created to perform several different tasks. These tasks may conflict for resource allocation (e.g. can the agent put out a fire and deliver a cup of coffee at the same time?).

- The environment the agents operate in may include humans, who may make things more difficult for the agent (either intentionally or by attempting to assist).

- The agents are often intended to model humans and/or other animals. Animal behaviour is quite complicated and not yet fully understood.

AI Mechanisms

Generally, artificial action selection mechanisms can be divided into several categories: symbol-based systems sometimes known as classical planning, distributed solutions, and reactive or dynamic planning. Some approaches do not fall neatly into any one of these categories. Others are really more about providing scientific models than practical AI control.

Symbolic Approaches

Early in the history of artificial intelligence, it was assumed that the best way for an agent to choose what to do next would be to compute a probably optimal plan, and then execute that plan. This led to the physical symbol system hypothesis, that a physical agent that can manipulate symbols is necessary and sufficient for intelligence. Many software agents still use this approach for action selection. It normally requires describing all sensor readings, the world, all of ones actions and all of one's goals in some form of predicate logic. Critics of this approach complain that it is too slow for real-time planning and that, despite the proofs, it is still unlikely to produce optimal plans because reducing descriptions of reality to logic is a process prone to errors.

Satisficing is a decision-making strategy which attempts to meet criteria for adequacy, rather than identify an optimal solution. A satisficing strategy may often, in fact, be (near) optimal if the costs of the decision-making process itself, such as the cost of obtaining complete information, are considered in the outcome calculus.

Goal driven architectures – In these symbolic architectures, the agent's behaviour is typically described by a set of goals. Each goal can be achieved by a process or an activity, which is described by a prescripted plan. The agent must just decide which process to carry on to accomplish a given goal. The plan can expand to subgoals, which makes the process slightly recursive. Technically, more or less, the plans exploits condition-rules. These architectures are reactive or hybrid. Classical examples of goal driven architectures are implementable refinements of belief-desire-intention architecture like JAM or IVE.

Distributed Approaches

In contrast to the symbolic approach, distributed systems of action selection actually have no one "box" in the agent which decides the next action. At least in their idealized form, distributed systems have many modules running in parallel and determining the best action based on local expertise. In these idealized systems, overall coherence is expected to emerge somehow, possibly through careful design of the interacting components. This approach is often inspired by artificial neural networks research. In practice, there is almost always *some* centralised system determining which module is "the most active" or has the most salience. There is evidence real biological brains also have such executive decision systems which evaluate which of the competing systems deserves the most attention, or more properly, has its desired actions disinhibited.

- ASMO is an attention-based architecture developed by Rony Novianto. It orchestrates a diversity of modular distributed processes that can use their own representations and techniques to perceive the environment, process information, plan actions and propose actions to perform.

- Various types of winner-take-all architectures, in which the single selected action takes full control of the motor system

- Spreading activation including Maes Nets (ANA)

- Extended Rosenblatt & Payton is a spreading activation architecture developed by Toby Tyrrell in 1993. The agent's behaviour is stored in the form of a hierarchical connectionism network, which Tyrrell named free-flow hierarchy.

- Behavior based AI, was a response to the slow speed of robots using symbolic action selection techniques. In this form, separate modules respond to different stimuli and generate their own responses. In the original form, the subsumption architecture, these consisted of different layers which could monitor and suppress each other's inputs and outputs.

- Creatures are virtual pets from a computer game driven by three-layered neural network, which is adaptive. Their mechanism is reactive since the network at every time step determines the task that has to be performed by the pet. The network is described well in the paper of Grand et al. (1997) and in The Creatures Developer Resources.

Dynamic Planning Approaches

Because purely distributed systems are difficult to construct, many researchers have turned to using explicit hard-coded plans to determine the priorities of their system.

Dynamic or reactive planning methods compute just one next action in every instant based on the current context and pre-scripted plans. In contrast to classical planning methods, reactive or dynamic approaches do not suffer combinatorial explosion. On the other hand, they are sometimes seen as too rigid to be considered strong AI, since the plans are coded in advance. At the same time, natural intelligence can be rigid in some contexts although it is fluid and able to adapt in others.

Example dynamic planning mechanisms include:

- Finite-state machines These are reactive architectures used mostly for computer game agents, in particular for first-person shooters bots, or for virtual movie actors. Typically, the state-machines are hierarchical. For concrete game examples, see Halo 2 bots paper by Damian Isla (2005) or the Master's Thesis about Quake III bots by Jan Paul van Waveren (2001).

- Other structured reactive plans tend to look a little more like conventional plans, often with ways to represent hierarchical and sequential structure. Some, such as PRS's 'acts', have support for partial plans. Many agent architectures from the mid-1990s included such plans as a "middle layer" that provided organization for low-level behavior modules while being directed by a higher level real-time planner. Despite this supposed interoperability with automated planners, most structured reactive plans are hand coded (Bryson 2001, ch. 3). Examples of structured reactive plans include James Firby's RAP System and the Nils Nilsson's Teleo-reactive plans. PRS, RAPs & TRP are no longer developed or supported. One still-active (as of 2006) descendent of this approach is the Parallel-rooted Ordered Slip-stack Hierarchical (or POSH) action selection system, which is a part of Joanna Bryson's Behaviour Oriented Design.

Sometimes to attempt to address the perceived inflexibility of dynamic planning, hybrid techniques are used. In these, a more conventional AI planning system searches for new plans when the agent has spare time, and updates the dynamic plan library when it finds good solutions. The important aspect of any such system is that when the agent needs to select an action, some solution exists that can be used immediately

Automated Planning and Scheduling

Automated planning and scheduling is a branch of artificial intelligence that is concerned with the realization of strategies or action sequences, typically for execution by intelligent agents, autonomous robots and unmanned vehicles. Unlike classical control and classification problems, the solutions are complex and have to be discovered and optimized in multidimensional space. In static and deterministic environments that can be easily modeled, automated planning can be performed offline. Solutions can be found and evaluated prior to execution. However, in unknown, dynamic and non-deterministic environments, the strategy often needs to be revised online. Models and policies need to be adapted. Solutions usually resort to iterative trial and error processes commonly seen in artificial intelligence. These include dynamic programming, reinforcement learning and combinatorial optimization.

A typical planner takes three inputs: a description of the initial state of the world, a description of the desired goals, and a set of actions that the executor is able to perform, all encoded in a formal language such as PDDL. The planner produces a (potentially partially ordered) set of actions that leads from the initial state to a state satisfying the goals. An alternative language for describing planning problems is that of hierarchical task networks, in which a set of tasks is given, and each task can be either realized by a primitive action or decomposed in a set of other tasks. In its general form automated planning is an NP-Complete problem. Many approaches in the past have made various assumptions in order to make the problem tractable. For instance, the STRIPS planning system assumed the world to be static, closed, deterministic, completely observable by the agent and several others. Most of the assumptions made by STRIPS have also been adopted by most of the posterior classical planning systems. Some popular techniques include: forward chaining and backward chaining state-space search, possibly enhanced by the use of relationships among conditions (e.g. Graphplan) or heuristics synthesized from the problem, search through plan space, and translation to propositional satisfiability.

If the assumption of determinism is dropped and a probabilistic model of uncertainty is adopted, then this leads to the problem of policy generation for a Markov decision process (MDP) or (in the general case) partially observable Markov decision process (POMDP). In the following we present the main contributions by Greek researchers and research teams in the general area of planning and scheduling. We adopt the overall taxonomy of planning and scheduling used in.

Classical Planning

Classical planning refers generally to planning for restricted state-transition systems. Actions are considered instantaneous and deterministic, whereas the environment is static and fully observable; so planning can be performed off-line and execution is guaranteed to succeed. Despite its restrictive and unrealistic nature, significant research efforts have been devoted worldwide to classical planning, giving rise to powerful algorithms which subsequently were adapted to more realistic settings.

There are a variety of algorithms coping with the problem of classical planning. Roughly speaking, they fall into four main categories: state-space planning, plan-space planning, graph-based planning and satisfiability algorithms.

The Logic Programming and Intelligent Systems (LPIS) research group at the Department of Informatics of Aristotle University of Thessaloniki, headed by Prof. Ioannis

Vlahavas, is active in this area over the last 10 years. The outcomes of this effort so far can be summarized in two PhD degrees awarded to Ioannis Refanidis and Dimitris Vrakas, one edited volume and approximately 50 papers in conferences and journals. Initial research focused on domain-independent heuristic state-space planning, which resulted in a variety of planning systems (GRT, MO-GRT, AcE, BP and HAPRC) and the participation to the 2nd International Planning Competition (2000). GRT is a heuristic state-space planner that constructs its heuristic function in a domain-independent way. The planner achieves significant performance in many domains as it has been shown in the 2nd international planning competition. An extension to the basic planning system uses XOR-constraints, in order to analyze a planning problem in a sequence of easier sub-problems that have to be solved sequentially. MO-GRT is an extension of the GRT planner, with the ability to construct a multi-objective heuristic function in a domain independent way. Criteria, their scales and preferences among them are provided by the user. The planner compensates plan quality and solution time, depending on the criteria weights. AcE is a domain independent state space planner that utilizes a heuristic based on action evaluation. The heuristic obtains estimates for the cost of applying each action of the domain by performing a forward search in a relaxed version of the initial problem. The estimates for the actions are then utilized in a backward search on the original problem.

BP is a bi-directional state space planning system, that is based on a hybrid search strategy and simple domain independent heuristic functions. The hybrid search strategy embodies two search threads whose execution is dynamically interleaved. HAPRC is a planning system which automatically fine-tunes its planning parameters according to the morphology of the problem in hand, through a combination of planning, machine learning and knowledge-based techniques. The adaptation is guided by a rule-based system that sets planner configuration parameters based on measurable characteristics of the problem instance. The knowledge of the rule system has been acquired off-line through a rule induction algorithm. The main idea behind these planning systems was to analyze the planning problem in a pre-processing phase, thus computing informative (although inadmissible) heuristics that have been proved powerful in the subsequent search phase. An alternative idea was to parallelize part of the planning process, especially that of computing the heuristic values for the various nodes, resulting in significant acceleration of the overall planning process. LPIS group participated actively in the PLANET European Network of Excellence, whereas it hosted the 2nd International Summer School on Planning, which took place in September 2002, in Halkidiki. Furthermore, Ioannis Refanidis (now at University of Macedonia) chairs the 6th International Planning Competition, which will take place in Sydney, 2008, as well as the 19th International Conference on Automated Planning and Scheduling, which will take place in Thessaloniki, in September of 2009.

Research at the University of Cyprus focused in the last years on the application of linear and mixed-integer programming techniques to planning problems. More specifically, presents an improved Integer Programming formulation of planning along with ideas on how the linear relaxation of this formulation can be used in heuristic search. Moreover, the University of Cyprus participated in the organization of the Deterministic Track of the 5th International Planning Competition.

Resource Planning and Scheduling

Resource planning and scheduling concerns the augmentation of planning systems with abilities to handle real world aspects, such as actions with (deterministic or probabilistic) durations and resources. Usually such problems are solved in two phases: In the first phase a plan is constructed using classical planning algorithms, whereas in the second phase scheduling algorithms are employed in order to find the minimum plan makespan. In case of resources, the scheduling problem becomes more complicated, whereas the objective might be to minimize some combination of makespan and resource consumption. Approaches that integrate the planning and scheduling phase can also be considered.

Temporal Planning and Scheduling

Algorithms on temporal planning do not take into account resources, whereas their objective is simply to minimize the plan's makespan. Most of the algorithms for temporal planning search in the plan-space and utilize constraint propagation algorithms to compute the time windows of the tasks.

Preliminary work on temporal planning and scheduling has conducted at the Department of Applied Informatics of University of Macedonia. This work exploits a temporal planning graph in order to extract additional disjunctive constraints over the problem's variables, based on both permanent and temporary mutex relations, which are subsequently used by a CSP solver, in order to solve the temporal dimension of the planning problem. Part of the work at the University of Cyprus was concerned with the problem of applying Mixed Integer Programming techniques to temporal planning. The particular Mixed Integer Programming formulation of, models a planning problem by two sets of linear inequalities. The first set involves integer variables and is a Graphplan-like encoding where the duration of the actions is ignored. The second set involves both integer and real valued variables, and models the temporal aspects of the problem. The two sets interact through their common integer variables.

Planning and Execution

In classical temporal or atemporal planning the effects and the timing of the actions can be completely determined by the execution agent. In such settings, where there is no uncertainty about the timing of the events, each action can be scheduled in advance of execution. In more realistic settings however, the duration of some events (typically the duration of the actions) are not in the direct control of the agent; these are called uncontrollable events. In these cases, first an agent needs to know that correct execution is guaranteed for all expected timings of the uncontrollable events (often called the consistency checking problem). Second, it needs to know when to execute the next action so that the probability of correct execution is maximized (called the dispatch problem). As part of his masters and Ph.D. thesis, Prof. Ioannis Tsamardinos and colleagues developed algorithms for efficient execution of temporal plans encoded as Simple Temporal Problems that solve the dispatch problem optimally. Simple Temporal Problems allow the specification of plans with convex temporal constraints. These allow polynomial times for consistency and dispatch to be achieved but restrict significantly the type of temporal plans that can be represented. In subsequent work a temporal constraint-satisfaction solver for more expressive plans using disjunctive constraints (called Disjunctive Temporal Problems) was built, called Epilitis. Epilitis could solve the consistency problem for such plans while at the time being the most efficient solver of its kind. Execution algorithms solving the dispatch problem for plans encoded as Disjunctive Temporal Problems were presented at. The semantics of temporal plans to incorporate a probabilistic interpretation to the consistency and dispatch problems were extended in.

The above work assumed that the only type uncertainty during execution regarded the occurrence of the uncontrollable events. A different type of uncertainty is *causal* uncertainty where depending on agent's observations during execution, she may decide to take one course of action or another. A formalism that can encode this type of information, including both constraints about the timing of events plus possible agent's choices for action was developed. Algorithms for solving the consistency problem and guarantee that there is a way to execute the plan under all possible observations were presented in. The above theory, formalism and algorithms were employed in Autominder, a robotic-based cognitive orthotic system that aids elderly people with cognitive disabilities in their daily activities; in addition, they were applied in workflow management systems and theory.

Multi-Agent Planning

The work of the University of Cyprus in Multi-agent Planning described in, presents algorithms for the problems of coordination and cooperation between agents that are based on an underlying classical planner which is used by the agents to generate their individual plans, but also to find plans that are consistent with those of the other agents. The procedures are able to generate plans of optimal length.

Knowledge Engineering in Planning

Knowledge Enginnering in AI Planning is the process that deals with the acquisition, validation and maintenance of planning domain models, and the selection and optimization of appropriate planning machinery to work on them. Hence, knowledge engineering processes support the planning process: they comprise all of the off-line, knowledge-based aspects of planning that are to do with the application being built, and any on-line processes that cause changes in the planner's domain model ( ). Research at the Department of Informatics at the Aristotle University of Thessaloniki in the last years focused on developing visual programming languages and user-friendly environments for the visualization and definition of planning domains and problems. The outcomes of the research can be summarized in two systems, namely ViTA-Plan ( ) and VLEPPO( ). The above systems offer the user an integrated environment for visualizing, designing, checking and solving planning domains and problems. They offer the user a visual programming module that enables him to encode new planning problems just by using visual elements and simple mouse operations. The visual tool performs a validity check on the visual program created by the user and then compiles it to PDDL files that are either solved by one of the embedded planning systems or send to an appropriate web service in order to obtain the solution. ViTAPlan also embodies a monitoring model that simulates the execution of the acquired solution (plan) and enables the expert user to discover dependencies in the plan's steps and experiment with alternative plans.

Applications of Planning and Scheduling

Research at the Department of Applied Informatics of University of Macedonia in the last years focused on the problem of scheduling personal tasks that appear in a user's calendar. Results of this research include an enhanced problem formulation, domain-dependent algorithms to solve the scheduling problem, as well as an implemented web-accessible intelligent calendar application called Self-Planner that allows the user to enter her tasks and preferences, solves the optimization problem and presents the resulting plan. SelfPlanner integrates with Google Calendar in order to present the plan, as well as with a Google Maps applications in order to specify location references and compute distances. Moreover the department of Informatics at the Aristotle University of Thessaloniki has investigated the application of AI Planning in e-Learning and composition of semantic web services resulting in two main systems, PASER and PORSCE. PASER ( ) is a system for automatically synthesizing curricula using AI Planning and Semantic Web technologies. The use of classical planning techniques allows the system to dynamically construct learning paths even from disjoint learning objects, meeting the learner's profile, preferences, needs and abilities. PORSCE ( ) is a system combining an object ranking algorithm and a domain independent planning system in order to semantically search the space of possible compositions of Web services, generating plans according to the desirable level of relaxation set by the user.

Action Description Language

The motive behind the development of a planning language in artificial intelligence is to represent the conditions of the environment and generate a set of actions, which when acts on the initial states of the system results in a group of desired objectives.

These objectives or goals are certain pre-specified conditions. When the preconditions are met, an action acts to yield changes on the environment. This functional strategy is at the core of the functioning of autonomous robots, intelligent agents and unmanned vehicles.

In artificial intelligence, an automated planning and scheduling system is the action description language (ADL). It is an action language that is considered an advanced form of STRIPS. In the first version of ADL, called ADL-A, proposed by Edwin Pednault in 1987, the expressive power of STRIPS was improved by permitting an operator's effects to be conditional. In ADL-B, the extension actions are described with indirect effects by introducing new propositions, called "static laws". The third variant of action description language, is the ADL-C which has quite a few similarities with ADL-B in terms of its static and dynamic propositions with a few more particularities. Though developed as an innovation of STRIPS, what sets the two apart is the principle of open-world assumption, which applies to ADL. It holds that a statement may be true whether or not it is known to be true. It also allows negative and positive literals as well as conjunctions and disjunctions.

Pednault observed that the expressive power of STRIPS was susceptible to being improved by allowing the effects of an operator to be conditional. This is the main idea of ADL-A, which is basically the propositional fragment of the ADL proposed by Pednault, with ADL-B an extension of -A. In the -B extension actions can be described with indirect effects by the introduction of a new kind of propositions: "static laws". A third variation of ADL is ADL-C which is similar to -B, in the sense that its propositions can be classified into static and dynamic laws, but with some more particularities.

The sense of a planning language is to represent certain conditions in the environment and, based on these, automatically generate a chain of actions which lead to a desired goal. A goal is a certain partially specified condition. Before an action can be executed its preconditions must be fulfilled; after the execution the action yields effects, by which the environment changes. The environment is described by means of certain predicates, which are either fulfilled or not.

Contrary to STRIPS, the principle of the open world applies with ADL: everything not occurring in the conditions is unknown (Instead of being assumed false). In addition, whereas in STRIPS only positive literals and conjunctions are permitted, ADL allows negative literals and disjunctions as well.

Syntax of ADL

An ADL schema consists of an action name, an optional parameter list and four optional groups of clauses labeled Precond, Add, Delete and Update.

The Precond group is a list of formulae that define the preconditions for the execution of an action. If the set is empty the value "TRUE" is inserted into the group and the preconditions are always evaluated as holding conditions.

The Add and Delete conditions are specified by the Add and Delete groups, respectively.

1. The R represents a relation symbol

2. $\tau_1,...,\tau_n$ represents terms

3. ψ represents a formula

4. The sequence $z_1,...,z_k$ are variable symbols that appear in the terms $\tau_1,...,\tau_n$, but not in the parameter list of the action schema

5. $x_1,...,x_n$ are variable symbols that are different from the variables $z_1,...,z_n$ and do not appear in $\tau_1,...,\tau_n$, ψ, or the parameter list of the action schema

The Update groups are used to specify the update conditions to change the values of function symbols.

Semantics of ADL

The formal semantic of ADL is defined by 4 constraints. The first constraint is that actions may not change the set of objects that exist in the world; this means that for every action α and every current-state/next-state pair $(s, t) \in a$, it must be the case that the domain of t should be equal to the domain of s.

The second constraint is that actions in ADL must be deterministic. If $(s, t1)$ and $(s, t2)$ are current-state/next-state pairs of action $\exists$, then it must be the case that $t1 = t2$.

The third constraint incorporated into ADL is that the functions introduced above must be representable as first-order formulas. For every n-ary relation symbol R, there must exist a formula $\Phi^a_R x_1,...,x_n)$ with free variables $x_2,...,x_n$ such that $f^a_R(s)$ is given by:

$$t(R) = f^a_R(s) = (d_1,..., d_n) \in Dom(s)^n \mid s[d_1/x_1,...,d_n/x_n \vDash \Phi^a_R(x_1,x_n)]$$

Consequently, $F(n_1,...,x_n) = y$ will be true after performing action $\vDash$ if and only if $\Phi^a_R(x_1,...,x_n,y)$ was true beforehand. Note that this representability requirement relies on the first constraint (Domain of f should be equal to domain of s).

The fourth and final constraint incorporated into ADL is that set of states in which an action is executable must also be representable as a formula. For every action α that can be represented in ADL, there must exist a formula Π^a with the property that $s \vDash \Pi_a$ if and only if there is some state t for which $(s, t) \in \alpha$ (i.e. action α is executable in state s).

Complexity of Planning

In terms of computational efficiency, ADL can be located between STRIPS and the Situation Calculus. Any ADL problem can be translated into a STRIPS instance – however, existing compilation techniques are worst-case exponential. This worst case cannot be improved if we are willing to preserve the length of plans polynomially, and thus ADL is strictly more brief than STRIPS.

ADL planning is still a PSPACE-complete problem. Most of the algorithms polynomial space even if the preconditions and effects are complex formulae.

Most of the top-performing approaches to classical planning internally utilize a STRIPS like representation. In fact most of the planners (FF, LPG, Fast-Downward, SGPLAN5 and LAMA) first translate the ADL instance into one that is essentially a STRIPS one (without conditional or quantified effects or goals).

Comparison between STRIPS and ADL

1. The STRIPS language only allows positive literals in the states, while ADL can support both positive and negative literals. For example, a valid sentence in STRIPS could be Rich ∧ Beautiful. The same sentence could be expressed in ADL as ¬Poor ∧ ¬Ugly.

2. In STRIPS the unmentioned literals are false. This is called the closed-world assumption. In ADL the unmentioned literals are unknown. This is known as the Open World Assumption.

3. In STRIPS we only can find ground literals in goals. For instance, Rich ∧ Beautiful. In ADL we can find quantified variables in goals. For example, ∃x At (P1, x) ∧ At(P2, x) is the goal of having P1 and P2 in the same place in the example of the blocks.

4. In STRIPS the goals are conjunctions, e.g., (Rich ∧ Beautiful). In ADL, goals may involve conjunctions and disjunctions (Rich ∧ (Beautiful ∨ Smart)).

5. In STRIPS the effects are conjunctions, but in ADL conditional effects are allowed: when P:E means E is an effect only if P is satisfied.

6. The STRIPS language does not support equality. In ADL, the equality predicate $(x = y)$ is built in.

7. STRIPS does not have support for types, while in ADL it is supported (for example, the variable p: Person).

The expressiveness of the STRIPS language is constrained by the types of transformations on sets of formulas that can be described in the language. Transformations on sets of formulas using STRIPS operators are accomplished by removing some formulas from the set to be transformed and adding new additional formulas. For a given STRIPS operator the formulas to be added and deleted are fixed for all sets of formulas to be transformed. Consequently, STRIPS operators cannot adequately model actions whose effects depend on the situations in which they are performed. Consider a rocket which is going to be fired for a certain amount of time. The trajectory may vary not only because of the burn duration but also because of the velocity, mass and orientation of the rocket. It cannot be modelled by means of a STRIPS operator because the formulas that would have to be added and deleted would depend on the set of formulas to be transformed.

Although an efficient reasoning is possible when the STRIPS language is being used it is generally recognized that the expressiveness of STRIPS is not suitable for modeling actions in many real world applications. This inadequacy motivated the development of the ADL language. ADL expressiveness and complexity lies between the STRIPS language and the situation calculus. Its expressive power is sufficient to allow the rocket example described above to be represented yet, at the same time, it is restrictive enough to allow efficient reasoning algorithms to be developed.

As an example in a more complex version of the blocks world: It could be that block A is twice as big as blocks B and C, so the action xMoveOnto(B,A) might only have the effect of negating Clear(A) if On(A,C) is already true, or creating the conditional effect depending on the size of the blocks. This kind of conditional effects would be hard to express in STRIPS notation without the conditional effects.

Example

Consider the problem of air freight transport, where certain goods must be transported from an airport to another airport by plane and where airplanes need to be loaded and unloaded.

The necessary actions would be *loading*, *unloading* and *flying*; over the descriptors one could express In(c, p) and At(x, A) whether a freight c is in an airplane p and whether an object x is at an airport A.

The actions could be defined then as follows:

```
Action (
  Load (c: Freight, p: Airplane, A: Airport)
  Precondition: At(c, A) ^ At(p, A)
  Effect: ¬At(c, A) ^ In(c, p)
)
```

```
Action (
  Unload (c: Freight, p: Airplane, A: Airport)
  Precondition: In(c, p) ^ At(p, A)
  Effect: At(c, A) ^ ¬In(c, p)
)


Action (
  Fly (p: Airplane, from: Airport, to: Airport)
  Precondition: At(p, from)
  Effect: ¬At(p, from) ^ At(p, to)
)
```

Artificial Intelligence Systems Integration

There has been an increased emphasis on systems integration in modern artificial intelligence systems. At the core of this recent attention, are the diverse simple AI systems that have been created for specific purposes, be it for computer vision or speech synthesis. To incorporate developed functions, it is more practical to innovate on monolithic designs to create integrated systems in which individual software components are operable in tandem with other components. This creates broader, larger and more intelligent AI systems. Further, most intelligent processes are a combination of a multitude of other intelligent processes that utilize multi-modal input and output. For developing a humanoid-type of intelligence, it is imperative to integrate the modalities of speech synthesis, speech recognition and other logical processes for developing broader intelligent processes. One of the proposed methods to effect this change is by using message routing, or communication protocols. This enables the software components to communicate with each other, often by using a middleware blackboard system.

Challenges & Solutions

Collaboration is an integral part of software development as evidenced by the size of software companies and the size of their software departments. Among the tools to ease software collaboration are various procedures and standards that developers can follow to ensure quality, reliability and that their software is compatible with software created by others (such as W3C standards for webpage development). However, collaboration in fields of A.I. has been lacking, for the most part not seen outside of the respected schools, departments or research institutes (and sometimes not within them either).

This presents practitioners of A.I. systems integration with a substantial problem and often causes A.I. researchers to have to 're-invent the wheel' each time they want a specific functionality to work with their software. Even more damaging is the "not invented here" syndrome, which manifests itself in a strong reluctance of A.I. researchers to build on the work of others.

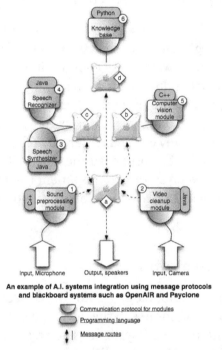

An example of A.I. systems integration using message protocols
and blackboard systems such as OpenAIR and Psyclone

An example of how multiple modules written in miscellaneous programming
languages can be utilized on multiple computers in A.I. systems integration

The outcome of this in A.I. is a large set of "solution islands": A.I. research has produced numerous isolated software components and mechanisms that deal with various parts of intelligence separately. To take some examples:

- Speech synthesis
  o FreeTTS from CMU
- Speech recognition
  o Sphinx from CMU
- Logical reasoning
  o OpenCyc from Cycorp
  o Open Mind Common Sense Net from MIT

With the increased popularity of the free software movement, a lot of the software being created, including A.I. systems, that is available for public exploit. The next natural step is to merge these individual software components into coherent, intelligent systems of a broader nature. As a multitude of components (that often serve the same purpose) have already been created by the community, the most accessible way of integration is giving each of these components an easy way to communicate with each other. By doing so, each component by itself becomes a module which can then be tried in various settings and configurations of larger architectures.

Many online communities for A.I. developers exist where tutorials, examples and forums aim at helping both beginners and experts build intelligent systems (for example the AI Depot, Generation 5). However, few communities have succeeded in making a certain standard or a code of conduct popular to allow the large collection of miscellaneous systems to be integrated with any ease. Recently, however, there have been focused attempts at producing standards for A.I. research collaboration, Mindmakers.org is an online community specifically created to harbor collaboration in the development of A.I. systems. The community has proposed the OpenAIR message and routing protocol for communication between software components, making it easier for individual developers to make modules instantly integrateble into other peoples' projects.

Methodologies

Constructionist Design Methodology

The Constructionist design methodology (CDM, or 'Constructionist A.I.') is a formal methodology proposed in 2004, for use in the development of cognitive robotics, communicative humanoids and broad AI systems. The creation of such systems requires integration of a large number of functionalities that must be carefully coordinated to achieve coherent system behavior. CDM is based on iterative design steps that lead to the creation of a network of named interacting modules, communicating via explicitly typed streams and discrete messages. The OpenAIR message protocol was inspired by the CDM, and has frequently been used to aid in development of intelligent systems using CDM.

One of the first projects to use CDM was Mirage, an embodied, graphical agent visualized through augmented reality which could communicate with human users and talk about objects present in the user's physical room. Mirage was created by Kristinn R. Thórisson, the creator of CDM, and a number of students at Columbia University in 2004. The methodology is actively being developed at Reykjavik University.

Tools

OpenAIR Protocol

OpenAIR is a message routing and communication protocol that has been gaining in popularity over the past two years. The protocol is managed by Mindmakers.org, and is described on their site in the following manner:

"OpenAIR is a routing and communication protocol based on a publish-subscribe architecture. It is intended to be the "glue" that allows numerous A.I. researchers to share code more effectively — "AIR to share". It is a definition or a blueprint of the "post office and mail delivery system" for distributed, multi-module systems. OpenAIR provides a core foundation upon which subsequent markup languages and semantics can be based, e.g. gesture recognition and generation, computer vision, hardware-software interfacing etc.

OpenAIR was created to allow software components that serve their own purpose to communicate with each other to produce large scale, overall behavior of an intelligent systems. A simple example would be to have a speech recognition system, and a speech synthesizer communicate with an expert system through OpenAIR messages, to create a system that can hear and answer various questions through spoken dialogue. CORBA is an older but similar architecture that can be used for comparison, but OpenAIR was specifically created for A.I. research, while CORBA is a more general standard.

The OpenAIR protocol has been used for collaboration on a number of A.I. systems, a list can be found on the Mindmakers project pages. Psyclone is a popular platform to pair with the OpenAIR protocol.

Psyclone AIOS

Psyclone is a software platform, or an AI operating system (AIOS), developed by Communicative Machines Laboratories for use in creating large, multi modal A.I. systems. The system is an implementation of a blackboard system that supports the OpenAIR message protocol. Psyclone is available for free for non-commercial purposes and has therefore often been used by research institutes on low budgets and novice A.I. developers.

Elvin

Elvin is a content-based router with a central routing station, similar to the Psyclone AIOS.

OAA

The OOA is a hybrid architecture that relies on a special inter-agent communication language (ICL) – a logic-based declarative language which is good for expressing high-level, complex tasks and natural language expressions.

CORBA

The Common Object Request Broker Architecture (CORBA) is a standard that enables software components written in multiple computer languages and running on multiple computers to interoperate. CORBA is defined by the Object Management Group (OMG).

CORBA follows similar principles as the OpenAIR protocol, and can be used for A.I. systems integration.

MOSID

The Messaging Open Service Interface Definition (OSID) is an O.K.I. specification which provides a means of sending, subscribing and receiving messages. OSIDs are programmatic interfaces which comprise a Service Oriented Architecture for designing and building reusable and interoperable software.

Examples of Integrated Systems

- MIRAGE, an A.I. embodied humanoid in an augmented reality environment.
- ASIMO, Honda's humanoid robot, and QRIO, Sony's version of a humanoid robot.
- Cog, M.I.T. humanoid robot project under the direction of Rodney Brooks.
- AIBO, Sony's robot dog integrates vision, hearing and motorskills.
- TOPIO, TOSY's humanoid robot can play ping-pong with human

Frame Problem

In the confined world of a robot, surroundings are not static. Many varying forces or actions can cause changes or modifications to it. The problem of forcing a robot to adapt to these changes is the basis of the frame problem in artificial intelligence. Information in the knowledge base and the robot's conclusions combine to form the input for what the robot's subsequent action should be. A good selection from its facts can be made by discarding or ignoring irrelevant facts and ridding of results that could have negative side effects.

A robot must introduce facts that are relevant to a particular moment. That is, a robot will examine its current situation, and then look up the facts that will be beneficial to choosing its subsequent action. The robot should also search for any changeable facts. It then examines these facts to determine if any of them have been changed during a previous examination. There are two basic types of change:

- *Relevant Change:* inspect the changes made by an action
- *Irrelevant Change:* do not inspect facts that are not related to the task at hand

Facts may be examined utilizing two levels:

Semantic Level: This level interprets what kind of information is being examined. Solutions should become obvious by the assumptions of how an object should behave.

There are believers in a purely semantic approach who believe that correct information can be reached via meaning. However, this hypothesis has yet to be proven.

Syntactic Level: This level simply decides in which format the information should be inspected. That is, it forms solutions based on the structure and patterns of facts.

When inspecting the facts, various problems can occur:

- Sometimes an implication can be missed.
- Considering all facts and all their subsequent side effects is time-consuming.
- Some facts are unnecessarily examined when they are unneeded.

Description

The frame problem occurs even in very simple domains. A scenario with a door, which can be open or closed, and a light, which can be on or off, is statically represented by two propositions *open* and *on*. If these conditions can change, they are better represented by two predicates *open(t)* and *on(t)* that depend on time; such predicates are called fluents. A domain in which the door is closed and the light off at time 0, and the door opened at time 1, can be directly represented in logic by the following formulae:

$$\neg open(0)$$

$$\neg on(0)$$

$$true \rightarrow open(1)$$

The first two formulae represent the initial situation; the third formula represents the effect of executing the action of opening the door at time 1. If such an action had preconditions, such as the door being unlocked, it would have been represented by $\neg locked(0) \rightarrow open(1)$. In practice, one would have a predicate *executeopen(t)* for specifying when an action is executed and a rule $\forall t.executeopen(t) \wedge true \rightarrow open(t+1)$ for specifying the effects of actions.

While the three formulae above are a direct expression in logic of what is known, they do not suffice to correctly draw consequences. While the following conditions (representing the expected situation) are consistent with the three formulae above, they are not the only ones.

$$\neg open(0) \qquad open(1)$$

$$\neg on(0) \qquad \neg on(1)$$

Indeed, another set of conditions that is consistent with the three formulae above is:

$$\neg open(0) \qquad open(1)$$

$$\neg on(0) \qquad on(1)$$

The frame problem is that specifying only which conditions are changed by the actions does not entail that all other conditions are not changed. This problem can be solved by adding the so-called "frame axioms", which explicitly specify that all conditions not affected by actions are not changed while executing that action. For example, since the action executed at time 0 is that of opening the door, a frame axiom would state that the status of the light does not change from time 0 to time 1:

$$on(0) \leftrightarrow on(1)$$

The frame problem is that one such frame axiom is necessary for every pair of action and condition such that the action does not affect the condition. In other words, the problem is that of formalizing a dynamical domain without explicitly specifying the frame axioms.

The solution proposed by McCarthy to solve this problem involves assuming that a minimal amount of condition changes have occurred; this solution is formalized using the framework of circumscription. The Yale shooting problem, however, shows that this solution is not always correct. Alternative solutions were then proposed, involving predicate completion, fluent occlusion, successor state axioms, etc.; they are explained below. By the end of the 1980s, the frame problem as defined by McCarthy and Hayes was solved. Even after that, however, the term "frame problem" was still used, in part to refer to the same problem but under different settings (e.g., concurrent actions), and in part to refer to the general problem of representing and reasoning with dynamical domains.

Solutions

The following solutions depict how the frame problem is solved in various formalisms. The formalisms themselves are not presented in full: what is presented are simplified versions that are sufficient to explain the full solution.

Fluent Occlusion Solution

This solution was proposed by Erik Sandewall, who also defined a formal language for the specification of dynamical domains; therefore, such a domain can be first expressed in this language and then automatically translated into logic.

The rationale of this solution is to represent not only the value of conditions over time, but also whether they can be affected by the last executed action. The latter is represented by another condition, called occlusion. A condition is said to be *occluded* in a given time point if an action has been just executed that makes the condition true or false as an effect. Occlusion can be viewed as "permission to change": if a condition is occluded, it is relieved from obeying the constraint of inertia.

In the simplified example of the door and the light, occlusion can be formalized by two predicates *occludeopen*(*t*) and *occludeon*(*t*). The rationale is that a condition can change value only if the corresponding occlusion predicate is true at the next time point. In turn, the occlusion predicate is true only when an action affecting the condition is executed.

$$\neg open(0)$$

$$\neg on(0)$$

$$true \rightarrow open(1) \wedge occludeopen(1)$$

$$\forall t.\neg occludeopen(t) \rightarrow (open(t-1) \leftrightarrow open(t))$$

$$\forall t.\neg occludeon(t) \rightarrow (on(t-1) \leftrightarrow on(t))$$

In general, every action making a condition true or false also makes the corresponding occlusion predicate true. In this case, *occludeopen*(1) is true, making the antecedent of the fourth formula above false for $t = 1$; therefore, the constraint that $open(t-1) \leftrightarrow open(t)$ does not hold for $t = 1$. Therefore, *open* can change value, which is also what is enforced by the third formula.

In order for this condition to work, occlusion predicates have to be true only when they are made true as an effect of an action. This can be achieved either by circumscription or by predicate completion. It is worth noticing that occlusion does not necessarily imply a change: for example, executing the action of opening the door when it was already open (in the formalization above) makes the predicate *occludeopen* true and makes *open* true; however, *open* has not changed value, as it was true already.

Predicate Completion Solution

This encoding is similar to the fluent occlusion solution, but the additional predicates denote change, not permission to change. For example, *changeopen*(*t*) represents the fact that the predicate *open* will change from time *t* to $t+1$. As a result, a predicate changes if and only if the corresponding change predicate is true. An action results in a change if and only if it makes true a condition that was previously false or vice versa.

$$\neg open(0)$$

$$\neg on(0)$$

$$\neg open(0) \wedge true \rightarrow changeopen(0)$$

$$\forall t.changeopen(t) \leftrightarrow (\neg open(t) \leftrightarrow open(t+1))$$

$$\forall t.changeon(t) \leftrightarrow (\neg on(t) \leftrightarrow on(t+1))$$

The third formula is a different way of saying that opening the door causes the door to be opened. Precisely, it states that opening the door changes the state of the door if it had been previously closed. The last two conditions state that a condition changes value at time t if and only if the corresponding change predicate is true at time t. To complete the solution, the time points in which the change predicates are true have to be as few as possible, and this can be done by applying predicate completion to the rules specifying the effects of actions.

Successor State Axioms Solution

The value of a condition after the execution of an action can be determined by the fact that the condition is true if and only if:

1.   the action makes the condition true; or

2.   the condition was previously true and the action does not make it false.

A successor state axiom is a formalization in logic of these two facts. For example, if *opendoor*(t) and *closedoor*(t) are two conditions used to denote that the action executed at time t was to open or close the door, respectively, the running example is encoded as follows.

$$\neg open(0)$$

$$\neg on(0)$$

$$opendoor(0)$$

$$\forall t.open(t+1) \leftrightarrow opendoor(t) \vee (open(t) \wedge \neg closedoor(t))$$

This solution is centered around the value of conditions, rather than the effects of actions. In other words, there is an axiom for every condition, rather than a formula for every action. Preconditions to actions (which are not present in this example) are formalized by other formulae. The successor state axioms are used in the variant to the situation calculus proposed by Ray Reiter.

Fluent Calculus Solution

The fluent calculus is a variant of the situation calculus. It solves the frame problem by using first-order logic terms, rather than predicates, to represent the states. Converting predicates into terms in first-order logic is called reification; the fluent calculus can be seen as a logic in which predicates representing the state of conditions are reified.

The difference between a predicate and a term in first-order logic is that a term is a representation of an object (possibly a complex object composed of other objects), while a predicate represents a condition that can be true or false when evaluated over a given set of terms.

In the fluent calculus, each possible state is represented by a term obtained by composition of other terms, each one representing the conditions that are true in state. For example, the state in which the door is open and the light is on is represented by the term $open \circ on$ It is important to notice that a term is not true or false by itself, as it is an object and not a condition. In other words, the term $open \circ on$. represent a possible state, and does not by itself mean that this is the current state. A separate condition can be stated to specify that this is actually the state at a given time, e.g., $state(open \circ on, 10)$ means that this is the state at time 10.

The solution to the frame problem given in the fluent calculus is to specify the effects of actions by stating how a term representing the state changes when the action is executed. For example, the action of opening the door at time 0 is represented by the formula:

$$state(s \circ open, 1) \leftrightarrow state(s, 0)$$

The action of closing the door, which makes a condition false instead of true, is represented in a slightly different way:

$$state(s, 1) \leftrightarrow state(s \circ open, 0)$$

This formula works provided that suitable axioms are given about $state$ and $\circ$, e.g., a term containing the same condition twice is not a valid state (for example, $state(open \circ s \circ open, t)$ is always false for every s and t).

Event Calculus Solution

The event calculus uses terms for representing fluents, like the fluent calculus, but also has axioms constraining the value of fluents, like the successor state axioms. In the event calculus, inertia is enforced by formulae stating that a fluent is true if it has been true at a given previous time point and no action changing it to false has been performed in the meantime. Predicate completion is still needed in the event calculus for obtaining that a fluent is made true only if an action making it true has been performed, but also for obtaining that an action had been performed only if that is explicitly stated.

Default Logic Solution

The frame problem can be thought of as the problem of formalizing the principle that, by default, "everything is presumed to remain in the state in which it is" (Leibniz, "An Introduction to a Secret Encyclopædia", c. 1679). This default, sometimes called the *commonsense law of inertia*, was expressed by Raymond Reiter in default logic:

$$\frac{R(x,s):R(x,do(a,s))}{R(x,do(a,s))}$$

(if $R(x)$ is true in situation s, and it can be assumed that $R(x)$ remains true after executing action a, then we can conclude that $R(x)$ remains true).

Steve Hanks and Drew McDermott argued, on the basis of their Yale shooting example, that this solution to the frame problem is unsatisfactory. Hudson Turner showed, however, that it works correctly in the presence of appropriate additional postulates.

Answer Set Programming Solution

The counterpart of the default logic solution in the language of answer set programming is a rule with strong negation:

$$r(X,T+1) \leftarrow r(X,T), \text{not } \sim r(X,T+1)$$

(if $r(X)$ is true at time T, and it can be assumed that $r(X)$ remains true at time $T+1$, then we can conclude that $r(X)$ remains true).

Action Description Languages

Action description languages elude the frame problem rather than solving it. An action description language is a formal language with a syntax that is specific for describing situations and actions. For example, that the action *opendoor* makes the door open if not locked is expressed by:

> *opendoor* causes *open* if $\neg locked$

The semantics of an action description language depends on what the language can express (concurrent actions, delayed effects, etc.) and is usually based on transition systems.

Since domains are expressed in these languages rather than directly in logic, the frame problem only arises when a specification given in an action description logic is to be translated into logic. Typically, however, a translation is given from these languages to answer set programming rather than first-order logic.

Computer-assisted Proof

One of the major goals of research in Artificial Intelligence is the representation of knowledge so that a computer can solve problems or communicate in a manner which exhibits "common sense". Few programs for computers, including those for education, possess behavior which approaches any facet of the constellation of human skills and knowledge which are imprecisely called "common sense". However, the revolutionary decline in hardware costs now makes it possible to consider economically viable, sophisticated designs for computer-aided instruction systems possessing some of the common sense attributes of a human tutor.

A computer-assisted proof is a mathematical proof that has been at least partially generated by computer.

Most computer-aided proofs to date have been implementations of large proofs-by-exhaustion of a mathematical theorem. The idea is to use a computer program to perform lengthy computations, and to provide a proof that the result of these computations implies the given theorem. In 1976, the four color theorem was the first major theorem to be verified using a computer program.

Attempts have also been made in the area of artificial intelligence research to create smaller, explicit, new proofs of mathematical theorems from the bottom up using machine reasoning techniques such as heuristic search. Such automated theorem provers have proved a number of new results and found new proofs for known theorems. Additionally, interactive proof assistants allow mathematicians to develop human-readable proofs which are nonetheless formally verified for correctness. Since these proofs are generally human-surveyable (albeit with difficulty, as with the proof of the Robbins conjecture) they do not share the controversial implications of computer-aided proofs-by-exhaustion.

Philosophical Objections

Computer-assisted proofs are the subject of some controversy in the mathematical world, with Thomas Tymoczko first to articulate objections. Those who adhere to Tymoczko's arguments believe that lengthy computer-assisted proofs are not, in some sense, 'real' mathematical proofs because they involve so many logical steps that they are not practically verifiable by human beings, and that mathematicians are effectively being asked to replace logical deduction from assumed axioms with trust in an empirical computational process, which is potentially affected by errors in the computer program, as well as defects in the runtime environment and hardware.

Other mathematicians believe that lengthy computer-assisted proofs should be regarded as *calculations*, rather than *proofs*: the proof algorithm itself should be proved valid, so that its use can then be regarded as a mere "verification". Arguments that computer-assisted proofs are subject to errors in their source programs, compilers, and hardware can be resolved by providing a formal proof of correctness for the computer program (an approach which was successfully applied to the four-color theorem in 2005) as well as replicating the result using different programming languages, different compilers, and different computer hardware.

Another possible way of verifying computer-aided proofs is to generate their reasoning steps in a machine-readable form, and then use an automated theorem prover to demonstrate their correctness. This approach of using a computer program to prove another program correct does not appeal to computer proof skeptics, who see it as adding another layer of complexity without addressing the perceived need for human understanding.

Another argument against computer-aided proofs is that they lack mathematical elegance—that they provide no insights or new and useful concepts. In fact, this is an argument that could be advanced against any lengthy proof by exhaustion.

An additional philosophical issue raised by computer-aided proofs is whether they make mathematics into a quasi-empirical science, where the scientific method becomes more important than the application of pure reason in the area of abstract mathematical concepts. This directly relates to the argument within mathematics as to whether mathematics is based on ideas, or "merely" an exercise in formal symbol manipulation. It also raises the question whether, if according to the Platonist view, all possible mathematical objects in some sense "already exist", whether computer-aided mathematics is an observational science like astronomy, rather than an experimental one like physics or chemistry. This controversy within mathematics is occurring at the same time as questions are being asked in the physics community about whether twenty-first century theoretical physics is becoming too mathematical, and leaving behind its experimental roots.

The emerging field of experimental mathematics is confronting this debate head-on by focusing on numerical experiments as its main tool for mathematical exploration.

List of Theorems Proved with the Help of Computer Programs

Inclusion in this list does not imply that a formal computer-checked proof exists, but rather, that a computer program has been involved in some way.

- Four color theorem, 1976
- Mitchell Feigenbaum's universality conjecture in non-linear dynamics. Proven by O. E. Lanford using rigorous computer arithmetic, 1982
- Connect Four, 1988 – a solved game
- Non-existence of a finite projective plane of order 10, 1989
- Robbins conjecture, 1996
- Kepler conjecture, 1998 – the problem of optimal sphere packing in a box
- Lorenz attractor, 2002 – 14th of Smale's problems proved by W. Tucker using interval arithmetic

- 17-point case of the Happy Ending problem, 2006

- NP-hardness of minimum-weight triangulation, 2008

- Optimal solutions for Rubik's Cube can be obtained in at most 20 face moves, 2010

- Minimum number of clues for a solvable Sudoku puzzle is 17, 2012

- In 2014 a special case of the Erdős discrepancy problem was solved using a SAT-solver. The full conjecture was later solved by Terence Tao without computer assistance.

- Boolean Pythagorean triples problem solved using 200 terabytes of data in May 2016.

Computational Humor

Human ability to communicate is incomplete without the use of humor. If a computational system is ever to approximate human communication ability or act as a competent partner in a conversation with a human, humor must be accounted for: it must be detected and dealt with appropriately, and it must be generated at need. Computing is becoming ubiquitous, with more and more systems entering the lives of ordinary people, making it necessary for them to communicate with computers at work, at home, on the drive from home to work and back, effecting their shopping, personal lives, leisure and entertainment.

In the last decades, humor research has become an intense exploration both of humor theory (Raskin 1985, 2008; Ruch 1998, 2008; Oring 1992, 2008; Davies 1990, 2008; Attardo 1994. 2008; Morreall 1983, 2008; Attardo and Raskin 1991, Ruch et al. 1993) and of computational humor (Lessard & Levison 1992, Raskin & Attardo 1994, Binsted & Ritchie 1994, Morkes et al. 1998, Ritchie 2001, Nijholt 2002, O'Mara and Waller 2003, Binsted et al. 2006, Ritchie et al. 2006, Mihalcea and Strapparava 2005, 2006, Mihalcea and Pulman 2007), starting with attempts at humor generation (ibid), through humor detection, to semantically based systems (Raskin 1996, 2002, Raskin et al. 2009). While 20+ disciplines have contributed significant results to humor research, the field remains fragmented along the disciplinary lines. At humor research conferences, the participants have learned to listen to each other politely and then go on with their own research. In computational humor, in particular, where it is becoming increasingly clear that only a truly multidisciplinary effort can reach the goal of effective communication among humans, intelligent agents, and robots, and no real social computing without full humor competence will result otherwise, the disciplines show up, as it were, but do not merge their efforts nor enrich each other's approach. Very few participants at the humor conferences are interested in computational humor; there is a rare occasional paper on humor at computational conferences.

Computational humor is a branch of computational linguistics and artificial intelligence which uses computers in humor research.

Joke Generators

Pun Generation

An approach to analysis of humor is classification of jokes. A further step is an attempt to generate jokes basing on the rules that underlie classification.

Simple prototypes for computer pun generation were reported in the early 1990s, based on a natural language generator program, VINCI. Graeme Ritchie and Kim Binsted in their 1994 research paper described a computer program, JAPE, designed to generate question-answer-type puns from a general, i.e., non-humorous, lexicon. (The program name is an acronym for "Joke Analysis and Production Engine".) Some examples produced by JAPE are:

> Q: What is the difference between leaves and a car?
>
> A: One you brush and rake, the other you rush and brake.
>
> Q: What do you call a strange market?
>
> A: A bizarre bazaar.

Since then the approach has been improved, and the latest report, dated 2007, describes the STANDUP joke generator, implemented in the Java programming language. The STANDUP generator was tested on children within the framework of analyzing its usability for language skills development for children with communication disabilities, e.g., because of cerebral palsy. (The project name is an acronym for "System To Augment Non-speakers' Dialog Using Puns" and an allusion to standup comedy.) Children responded to this "language playground" with enthusiasm, and showed marked improvement on certain types of language tests.

> The two young people, who used the system over a ten-week period, regaled their peers, staff, family and neighbors with jokes such as: "What do you call a spicy missile? A hot shot!" Their joy and enthusiasm at entertaining others was inspirational.

Joke Recognition

A statistical machine learning algorithm to detect whether a sentence contained a "That's what she said" double entendre was developed by Kiddon and Brun (2011).

There is an open-source Python implementation of Kiddon & Brun's TWSS system.

A program to recognize knock-knock jokes was reported by Taylor and Mazlack. This kind of research is important in analysis of human-computer interaction.

An application of machine learning techniques for the distinguishing of joke texts from non-jokes was described by Mihalcea and Strapparava (2006).

Takizawa *et al.* (1996) reported on a heuristic program for detecting puns in the Japanese language.

Applications

Another envisioned use of joke generators is in cases of steady supply of jokes where quantity is more important than quality. Another obvious, yet remote, direction is automated joke appreciation.

It is known that humans interact with computers in ways similar to interacting with other humans that may be described in terms of personality, politeness, flattery, and in-group favoritism. Therefore, the role of humor in human-computer interaction is being investigated. In particular, humor generation in user interface to ease communications with computers was suggested.

Craig McDonough implemented the Mnemonic Sentence Generator, which converts passwords into humorous sentences. Basing on the incongruity theory of humor, it is suggested that the resulting meaningless but funny sentences are easier to remember. For example, the password AjQA3Jtv is converted into "Arafat joined Quayle's Ant, while TARAR Jeopardized thurmond's vase".

Commonsense Reasoning

Commonsense reasoning is a central part of human behavior; no real intelligence is possible without it. Thus, the development of systems that exhibit commonsense behavior is a central goal of Artificial Intelligence. It has proven to be more difficult to create systems that are capable of commonsense reasoning than systems that can solve "hard" reasoning problems. There are chess-playing programs that beat champions and expert systems that assist in clinical diagnosis, but no programs that reason about how far one must bend over to put on one's socks. Part of the difficulty is the all-encompassing aspect of commonsense reasoning: any problem one looks at touches on many different types of knowledge. Moreover, in contrast to expert knowledge which is usually explicit, most commonsense knowledge is implicit. One of the prerequisites to developing commonsense reasoning systems is making this knowledge explicit.

John McCarthy first noted this need and suggested using formal logic to encode commonsense knowledge and reasoning. In the ensuing decades, there has been much research on the representation of knowledge in formal logic and on inference algorithms to manipulate that knowledge. The arguments for a declarative knowledge representation—it allows the explicit representation of knowledge; it is modular; it supports modification far more easily than implicit, procedural knowledge—have gained credence not only among the AI community, but in the broad field of computer science. Basic principles of knowledge representation have been incorporated into the design of object-oriented languages and rule-based systems. But the formalization of commonsense reasoning remains an elusive goal. Seemingly trivial reasoning problems that, in McCarthy's words, can be carried out by any non-feeble minded human are still beyond the representational and reasoning abilities of existing theories and systems.

Progress has been slow because formalizing commonsense reasoning presents a variety of challenges. One must (1) develop a formal language that is sufficiently powerful and expressive; (2) capture the many millions of facts that people know and reason with;3 (3) correctly encode this information as sentences in a logic; and (4) construct a system that will use its knowledge efficiently. The knowledge of these difficulties is as old as the endeavor itself. Forty-four years ago, linguist and logician Yehoshua Bar-Hillel argued the inadequacy of standard deduction for planning in real-world domains in which circumstances can change—and perhaps presaged the need for default logics; pointed out the problems in formalizing even a simple relation like "At"; and questioned how a computer could choose from millions of facts the few facts relevant to a specific problem at hand.

Commonsense in Intelligent Tasks

In 1961, Bar Hillel first discussed the need and significance of practical knowledge for natural language processing in the context of machine translation. Some ambiguities are resolved by using simple and easy to acquire rules. Others require a broad acknowledgement of the surrounding world, thus they require more commonsense knowledge. For instance when a machine is used to translate a text, problems of ambiguity arise, which could be easily resolved by attaining a concrete and true understanding of the context. Online translators often resolve ambiguities using analogous or similar words. For example, in translating the sentences "The electrician is working" and "The telephone is working" into German, the machine translates correctly "working" in the means of "laboring" in the first one and as "functioning properly" in the second one. The machine has seen and read in the body of texts that the German words for "laboring" and "electrician" are frequently used in a combination and are found close together. The same applies for "telephone" and "function properly". However, the statistical proxy which works in simple cases often fails in complex ones. Existing computer programs carry out simple language tasks by manipulating short phrases or separate words, but they don't attempt any deeper understanding and focus on short-term results.

Computer Vision

Issues in Computer vision

Issues of this kind arise in computer vision. For instance when looking at the photograph of the bathroom some of the items that are small and only partly seen, such as the towels or the body lotions, are recognizable due to the surrounding objects (toilet, wash basin, bathtub), which suggest the purpose of the room. In an isolated image they would be difficult to identify. Movies prove to be even more difficult tasks. Some movies contain scenes and moments that cannot be understood by simply matching memorized templates to images. For instance, to understand the context of the movie, the viewer is required to make inferences about characters' intentions and make presumptions depending on their behavior. In the contemporary state of the art, it is impossible to build and manage a program that will perform such tasks as reasoning, i.e. predicting characters' actions. The most that can be done is to identify basic actions and track characters.

Robotic Manipulation

The need and importance of commonsense reasoning in autonomous robots that work in a real-life uncontrolled environment is evident. For instance, if a robot is programmed to perform the tasks of a waiter on a cocktail party, and it sees that the glass he had picked up is broken, the waiter-robot should not pour liquid into the glass, but instead pick up another one. Such tasks seem obvious when an individual possess simple commonsense reasoning, but to ensure that a robot will avoid such mistakes is challenging.

Successes in Automated Commonsense Reasoning

Significant progress in the field of the automated commonsense reasoning is made in the areas of the taxonomic reasoning, actions and change reasoning, reasoning about time. Each of these spheres has a well-acknowledged theory for wide range of commonsense inferences.

Taxonomic Reasoning

Taxonomy is the collection of individuals and categories and their relations. Taxonomies are often referred to as semantic networks. Figure below displays a taxonomy of a few categories of individuals and animals.

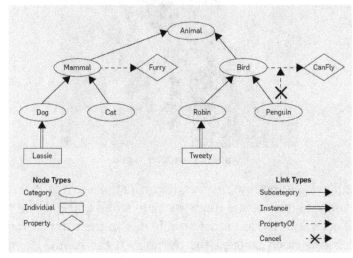

Taxonomy

Three basic relations are demonstrated:

- An individual is an instance of a category. For example, the individual Tweety is an instance of the category Robin.

- One category is a subset of another. For instance Robin is a subset of Bird.

- Two categories are disjoint. For instance Robin is disjoint from Penguin.

Transitivity is one type of inference in taxonomy. Since Tweety is an instance of Robin and Robin is a subset of Bird, it follows that Tweety is an instance of Bird. Inheritance is another type of inference. Since Tweety is an instance of Robin, which is a subset of Bird and Bird is marked with property CanFly, it follows that Tweety and Robin have property CanFly. When an individual taxonomizes more abstract categories, outlining and delimiting specific categories becomes more problematic. Simple taxonomic structures are frequently used in AI programs. For instance, WordNet is a resource including a taxonomy, whose elements are meanings of English words. Web mining systems used to collect commonsense knowledge from Web documents focus on taxonomic relations and specifically in gathering taxonomic relations.

Action and Change

The theory of action, events and change is another range of the commonsense reasoning. There are established reasoning methods for domains that satisfy the constraints listed below:

- Events are atomic, meaning one event occurs at a time and the reasoner needs to consider the state and condition of the world at the start and at the finale of the specific event, but not during the states, while there is still an evidence of on-going changes (progress).

- Every single change is a result of some event.

- Events are deterministic, meaning the world's state at the end of the event is defined by the world's state at the beginning and the specification of the event.

- There is a single actor and all events are his actions.

- The relevant state of the world at the beginning is either known or can be calculated.

Temporal Reasoning

Temporal reasoning is the ability to make presumptions about humans' knowledge of times, durations and time intervals. For example, if an individual knows that Mozart was born before Beethoven and died earlier than him, he can use his temporal reasoning knowledge to deduce that Mozart had died younger than Beethoven. The inferences involved reduce themselves to solving systems of linear inequalities. To integrate that kind of reasoning with concrete purposes, such as natural language interpretation, is more challenging, because natural language expressions have context dependent interpretation. Simple tasks such as assigning timestamps to procedures cannot be done with total accuracy.

Qualitative Reasoning

Qualitative reasoning is the form of commonsense reasoning analyzed with certain success. It is concerned with the direction of change in interrelated quantities. For instance, if the price of a stock goes up, the amount of stocks that are going to be sold will go down. If some ecosystem contains wolves and lambs and the number of wolves decreases, the death rate of the lambs will go down as well. This theory was firstly formulated by Johan de Kleer, who analyzed an object moving on a roller coaster. The theory of qualitative reasoning is applied in many spheres such as physics, biology, engineering, ecology, etc. It serves as the basis for many practical programs, analogical mapping, text understanding.

Challenges in Automating Commonsense Reasoning

As of 2014, there are some commercial systems trying to make the use of commonsense reasoning significant. However, they use statistical information as a proxy for commonsense knowledge, where reasoning is absent. Current programs manipulate individual words, but they don't attempt or offer further understanding. Five major obstacles interfere with the producing of a satisfactory "commonsense reasoner".

First, some of the domains that are involved in commonsense reasoning are only partly understood. Individuals are far from a comprehensive understanding of domains as communication and knowledge, interpersonal interactions or physical processes.

Second, situations that seem easily predicted or assumed about could have logical complexity, which humans' commonsense knowledge does not cover. Some aspects of similar situations are studied and are well understood, but there are many relations that are unknown, even in principle and how they could be represented in a form that is usable by computers.

Third, commonsense reasoning involves plausible reasoning. It requires coming to a reasonable conclusion given what is already known. Plausible reasoning has been studied for many years and there are a lot of theories developed that include probabilistic reasoning and non-monotonic logic. It takes different forms that include using unreliable data and rules, whose conclusions are not certain sometimes.

Fourth, there are many domains, in which a small number of examples are extremely frequent, whereas there is a vast number of highly infrequent examples.

Fifth, when formulating pressumptions it is challenging to discern and determine the level of abstraction.

Compared with humans, all existing computer programs perform extremely poorly on modern "commonsense reasoning" benchmark tests such as the Winograd Schema Challenge. The problem of attaining human-level competency at "commonsense knowledge" tasks is considered to probably be "AI complete" (that is, solving it would require the ability to synthesize a human-level intelligence).

Automated Reasoning

Automated reasoning is the art and science of getting computers to apply logical reasoning to solve problems, for example, to prove theorems, solve puzzles, design circuits, verify or synthesize computer programs. The phrase "automated deduction" is also used; if there is a difference between "automated reasoning" and "automated deduction", it is that automated deduction might be construed more narrowly, emphasizing deduction in mathematics, while "automated reasoning" might include puzzlesolving or reasoning about electronic circuits, or legal reasoning. These are not so different, since in all cases the task boils down to proving a desired theorem from some axioms.

Since reasoning usually requires intelligence (when humans do it), this subject can be thought of as part of artificial intelligence (AI), but it has many specialized methods and (so far at least) does not use many of the techniques of AI, so it not usually thought of as a branch of AI. In any case, there is no restriction that in automated reasoning a program should "work like a human would". Usually, programs try to take advantage of the computer's superior ability to search through thousands or millions of possibilities, and hope in that way to make up for the computer's lack of "insight", whatever that is. This is usually the case in AI research, too, but the phrase "artificial intelligence" still has connotations of computers "working like the human brain" for much of the general public, and that is emphatically not the case in automated reasoning.

Automated reasoning can also be thought of as a branch of the enterprise "computerizing mathematics". That is a larger enterprise, in that there is more to mathematics than proving theorems. For example, making complicated calculations is mathematics, but it is not the same activity as proving theorems, although a proof may include a calculation. In fact, a proof can consist *entirely* of a calculation, but that is usually not a very interesting or beautiful proof, though it can be if there is something unexpected about the calculation. Normally though, a calculation proceeds "mechanically" according to a certain method that is usually used for that kind of problem, and it isn't really very surprising that such things can be done by computer. We distinguish *numerical* calculations and *symbolic* calculations. The latter include algebra and calculus, as well as some more specialized kinds of calculations, for example in number theory. Today, in 2006, there are several good general-purpose programs for symbolic and numerical calculations, and many special-purpose ones as well. The subject of symbolic computation has its own journals and conferences. However, this is not automated deduction.

Significant Contributions

Principia Mathematica was a milestone work in formal logic written by Alfred North Whitehead and Bertrand Russell. Principia Mathematica - also meaning Principles of Mathematics - was written with a purpose to derive all or some of the mathematical expressions, in terms of symbolic logic. Principia Mathematica was initially published in three volumes in 1910, 1912 and 1913.

Logic Theorist (LT) was the first ever program developed in 1956 by Allen Newell, Cliff Shaw and Herbert A. Simon to "mimic human reasoning" in proving theorems and was demonstrated on fifty-two theorems from chapter two of Principia Mathematica, proving thirty-eight of them. In addition to proving the theorems, the program found a proof for one of the theorems that was more elegant than the one provided by Whitehead and Russell. After an unsuccessful attempt at publishing their results, Newell, Shaw, and Herbert reported in their publication in 1958, *The Next Advance in Operation Research*:

> *"There are now in the world machines that think, that learn and that create. Moreover, their ability to do these things is going to increase rapidly until (in a visible future) the range of problems they can handle will be co- extensive with the range to which the human mind has been applied."*

Applications

Automated reasoning has been most commonly used to build automated theorem provers. Oftentimes, however, theorem provers require some human guidance to be effective and so more generally qualify as proof assistants. In some cases such provers have come up with new approaches to proving a theorem. Logic Theorist is a good example of this. The program came up with a proof for one of the theorems in Principia Mathematica that was more efficient (requiring fewer steps) than the proof provided by Whitehead and Russell. Automated reasoning programs are being applied to solve a growing number of problems in formal logic, mathematics and computer science, logic programming, software and hardware verification, circuit design, and many others. The TPTP (Sutcliffe and Suttner 1998) is a library of such problems that is updated on a regular basis. There is also a competition among automated theorem provers held regularly at the CADE conference (Pelletier, Sutcliffe and Suttner 2002); the problems for the competition are selected from the TPTP library.

Abductive Reasoning

Abductive reasoning typically begins with an incomplete set of observations and proceeds to the likeliest possible explanation for the set. Abductive reasoning yields the kind of daily decision-making that does its best with the information at hand, which often is incomplete.

A medical diagnosis is an application of abductive reasoning: given this set of symptoms, what is the diagnosis that would best explain most of them? Likewise, when jurors hear evidence in a criminal case, they must consider whether the prosecution or the defense has the best explanation to cover all the points of evidence. While there may be no certainty about their verdict, since there may exist additional evidence that was not admitted in the case, they make their best guess based on what they know.

While cogent inductive reasoning requires that the evidence that might shed light on the subject be fairly complete, whether positive or negative, abductive reasoning is characterized by lack of completeness, either in the evidence, or in the explanation, or both. A patient may be unconscious or fail to report every symptom, for example, resulting in incomplete evidence, or a doctor may arrive at a diagnosis that fails to explain several of the symptoms. Still, he must reach the best diagnosis he can.

The abductive process can be creative, intuitive, even revolutionary.2 Einstein's work, for example, was not just inductive and deductive, but involved a creative leap of imagination and visualization that scarcely seemed warranted by the mere observation of moving trains and falling elevators. In fact, so much of Einstein's work was done as a "thought experiment" (for he never experimentally dropped elevators), that some of his peers discredited it as too fanciful. Nevertheless, he appears to have been right-until now his remarkable conclusions about space-time continue to be verified experientially.

Applications

Artificial Intelligence

Applications in artificial intelligence include fault diagnosis, belief revision, and automated planning. The most direct application of abduction is that of automatically detecting faults in systems: given a theory relating faults with their effects and a set of observed effects, abduction can be used to derive sets of faults that are likely to be the cause of the problem.

Medicine

In medicine, abduction can be seen as a component of clinical evaluation and judgment.

Automated Planning

Abduction can also be used to model automated planning. Given a logical theory relating action occurrences with their effects (for example, a formula of the event calculus), the problem of finding a plan for reaching a state can be modeled as the problem of abducting a set of literals implying that the final state is the goal state.

Intelligence Analysis

In intelligence analysis, analysis of competing hypotheses and Bayesian networks, probabilistic abductive reasoning is used extensively. Similarly in medical diagnosis and legal reasoning, the same methods are being used, although there have been many examples of errors, especially caused by the base rate fallacy and the prosecutor's fallacy.

Belief Revision

Belief revision, the process of adapting beliefs in view of new information, is another field in which abduction has been applied. The main problem of belief revision is that the new information may be inconsistent with the corpus of beliefs, while the result of the incorporation cannot be inconsistent. This process can be done by the use of abduction: once an explanation for the observation has been found, integrating it does not generate inconsistency. This use of abduction is not straightforward, as adding propositional formulae to other propositional formulae can only make inconsistencies worse. Instead, abduction is done at the level of the ordering of preference of the possible worlds. Preference models use fuzzy logic or utility models.

Philosophy of Science

In the philosophy of science, abduction has been the key inference method to support scientific realism, and much of the debate about scientific realism is focused on whether abduction is an acceptable method of inference.

Historical Linguistics

In historical linguistics, abduction during language acquisition is often taken to be an essential part of processes of language change such as reanalysis and analogy.

Anthropology

In anthropology, Alfred Gell in his influential book *Art and Agency* defined abduc-tion (after Eco) as "a case of synthetic inference 'where we find some very curious circumstances, which would be explained by the supposition that it was a case of some general rule, and thereupon adopt that supposition'". Gell criticizes existing "anthropological" studies of art for being too preoccupied with aesthetic value and not preoccupied enough with the central anthropological concern of uncovering "social relationships", specifically the social contexts in which artworks are produced, circulated, and received. Abduction is used as the mechanism for getting from art to agency. That is, abduction can explain how works of art inspire a *sensus communis:* the commonly held views shared by members that characterize a given society. The question Gell asks in the book is, "how does it initially 'speak' to people?" He answers by saying that "No reasonable person could suppose that art-like relations between people and things do not involve at least some form of semiosis." However, he rejects any intimation that semiosis can be thought of as a language because then he would have to admit to some pre-established existence of the *sensus communis* that he wants to claim only emerges afterwards out of art. Abduction is the answer to this conundrum because the tentative nature of the abduction concept (Peirce likened it to guessing) means that not only can it operate outside of any pre-existing framework, but moreover, it can actually intimate the existence of a framework. As Gell reasons in his analysis, the physical existence of the artwork prompts the viewer to perform an abduction that imbues the artwork with intentionality. A statue of a goddess, for example, in some senses actually becomes the goddess in the mind of the beholder; and represents not only the form of the deity but also her intentions (which are adduced from the feeling of her very presence). There-fore, through abduction, Gell claims that art can have the kind of agency that plants the seeds that grow into cultural myths. The power of agency is the power to motivate actions and inspire ultimately the shared understanding that characterizes any given society.

Knowledge Representation and Reasoning

A subarea of Artificial Intelligence concerned with understanding, designing, and implementing ways of representing information in computers so that programs (agents) can use this information

- to derive information that is implied by it,
- to converse with people in natural languages,

- to decide what to do next

- to plan future activities,

- to solve problems in areas that normally require human expertise.

Deriving information that is implied by the information already present is a form of reasoning. Knowledge representation schemes are useless without the ability to reason with them.

Knowledge-representation is the field of artificial intelligence that focuses on designing computer representations that capture information about the world that can be used to solve complex problems.

The justification for knowledge representation is that conventional procedural code is not the best formalism to use to solve complex problems. Knowledge representation makes complex software easier to define and maintain than procedural code and can be used in expert systems.

For example, talking to experts in terms of business rules rather than code lessens the semantic gap between users and developers and makes development of complex systems more practical.

Knowledge representation goes hand in hand with automated reasoning because one of the main purposes of explicitly representing knowledge is to be able to reason about that knowledge, to make inferences, assert new knowledge, etc. Virtually all knowledge representation languages have a reasoning or inference engine as part of the system.

A key trade-off in the design of a knowledge representation formalism is that between expressivity and practicality. The ultimate knowledge representation formalism in terms of expressive power and compactness is First Order Logic (FOL). There is no more powerful formalism than that used by mathematicians to define general propositions about the world. However, FOL has two drawbacks as a knowledge representation formalism: ease of use and practicality of implementation. First order logic can be intimidating even for many software developers. Languages which do not have the complete formal power of FOL can still provide close to the same expressive power with a user interface that is more practical for the average developer to understand. The issue of practicality of implementation is that FOL in some ways is too expressive. With FOL it is possible to create statements (e.g. quantification over infinite sets) that would cause a system to never terminate if it attempted to verify them.

Thus, a subset of FOL can be both easier to use and more practical to implement. This was a driving motivation behind rule-based expert systems. IF-THEN rules provide a subset of FOL but a very useful one that is also very intuitive. The history of most of the early AI knowledge representation formalisms; from databases to semantic nets to theorem provers and production systems can be viewed as various design decisions on whether to emphasize expressive power or computability and efficiency.

In a key 1993 paper on the topic, Randall Davis of MIT outlined five distinct roles to analyze a knowledge representation framework:

- A knowledge representation (KR) is most fundamentally a surrogate, a substitute for the thing itself, used to enable an entity to determine consequences by thinking rather than acting, i.e., by reasoning about the world rather than taking action in it.

- It is a set of ontological commitments, i.e., an answer to the question: In what terms should I think about the world?

- It is a fragmentary theory of intelligent reasoning, expressed in terms of three components: (i) the representation's fundamental conception of intelligent reasoning; (ii) the set of inferences the representation sanctions; and (iii) the set of inferences it recommends.

- It is a medium for pragmatically efficient computation, i.e., the computational environment in which thinking is accomplished. One contribution to this pragmatic efficiency is supplied by the guidance a representation provides for organizing information so as to facilitate making the recommended inferences.

- It is a medium of human expression, i.e., a language in which we say things about the world.

Knowledge representation and reasoning are a key enabling technology for the Semantic web. Languages based on the Frame model with automatic classification provide a layer of semantics on top of the existing Internet. Rather than searching via text strings as is typical today, it will be possible to define logical queries and find pages that map to those queries. The automated reasoning component in these systems is an engine known as the classifier. Classifiers focus on the subsumption relations in a knowledge base rather than rules. A classifier can infer new classes and dynamically change the ontology as new information becomes available. This capability is ideal for the ever-changing and evolving information space of the Internet.

The Semantic web integrates concepts from knowledge representation and reasoning with markup languages based on XML. The Resource Description Framework (RDF) provides the basic capabilities to define knowledge-based objects on the Internet with basic features such as Is-A relations and object properties. The Web Ontology Language (OWL) adds additional semantics and integrates with automatic classification reasoners.

Characteristics

In 1985, Ron Brachman categorized the core issues for knowledge representation as follows:

- Primitives. What is the underlying framework used to represent knowledge? Semantic networks were one of the first knowledge representation primitives. Also, data structures and algorithms for general fast search. In this area, there is a strong overlap with research in data structures and algorithms in computer science. In early systems, the Lisp programming language, which was modeled after the lambda calculus, was often used as a form of functional knowledge representation. Frames and Rules were the next kind of primitive. Frame languages had various mechanisms for expressing and enforcing constraints on frame data. All data in frames are stored in slots. Slots are analogous to relations in entity-relation modeling and to object properties in object-oriented modeling. Another technique for primitives is to define languages that are modeled after First Order Logic (FOL). The most well known example is Prolog, but there are also many special purpose theorem proving environments. These environments can validate logical models and can deduce new theories from existing models. Essentially they automate the process a logician would go through in analyzing a model. Theorem proving technology had some specific practical applications in the areas of software engineering. For example, it is possible to prove that a software program rigidly adheres to a formal logical specification.

- Meta-representation. This is also known as the issue of reflection in computer science. It refers to the capability of a formalism to have access to information about its own state. An example would be the meta-object protocol in Smalltalk and CLOS that gives developers run time access to the class objects and enables them to dynamically redefine the structure of the knowledge base even at run time. Meta-representation means the knowledge representation language is itself expressed in that language. For example, in most Frame based environments all frames would be instances of a frame class. That class object can be inspected at run time, so that the object can understand and even change its internal structure or the structure of other parts of the model. In rule-based environments, the rules were also usually instances of rule classes. Part of the meta protocol for rules were the meta rules that prioritized rule firing.

- Incompleteness. Traditional logic requires additional axioms and constraints to deal with the real world as opposed to the world of mathematics. Also, it is often useful to associate degrees of confidence with a statement. I.e., not simply say "Socrates is Human" but rather "Socrates is Human with confidence 50%". This was one of the early innovations from expert systems research which migrated to some commercial tools, the ability to associate certainty factors with rules and conclusions. Later research in this area is known as fuzzy logic.

- Definitions and universals vs. facts and defaults. Universals are general statements about the world such as "All humans are mortal". Facts are specific examples of universals such as "Socrates is a human and therefore mortal". In logical terms definitions and universals are about universal quantification while facts and defaults are about existential quantifications. All forms of knowledge representation must deal with this aspect and most do so with some variant of set theory, modeling universals as sets and subsets and definitions as elements in those sets.

- Non-monotonic reasoning. Non-monotonic reasoning allows various kinds of hypothetical reasoning. The system associates facts asserted with the rules and facts used to justify them and as those facts change updates the dependent knowledge as well. In rule based systems this capability is known as a truth maintenance system.

- Expressive adequacy. The standard that Brachman and most AI researchers use to measure expressive adequacy is usually First Order Logic (FOL). Theoretical limitations mean that a full implementation of FOL is not practical. Researchers should be clear about how expressive (how much of full FOL expressive power) they intend their representation to be.

- Reasoning efficiency. This refers to the run time efficiency of the system. The ability of the knowledge base to be updated and the reasoner to develop new inferences in a reasonable period of time. In some ways, this is the flip side of expressive adequacy. In general, the more powerful a representation, the more it has expressive adequacy, the less efficient its automated reasoning engine will be. Efficiency was often an issue, especially for early applications of knowledge representation technology. They were usually implemented in interpreted environments such as Lisp, which were slow compared to more traditional platforms of the time.

Knowledge-based Systems

A knowledge-based system (KBS) is a computer system which generates and utilizes knowledge from different sources, data and information. These systems aid in solving problems, especially complex ones, by utilizing artificial intelligence concepts. These systems are mostly used in problem-solving procedures and to support human learning, decision making and actions.

Knowledge-based systems are considered to be a major branch of artificial intelligence. They are capable of making decisions based on the knowledge residing in them, and can understand the context of the data that is being processed.

Knowledge-based systems broadly consist of an interface engine and knowledge base. The interface engine acts as the search engine, and the knowledge base acts as the knowledge repository. Learning is an essential component of knowledge-based systems and simulation of learning helps in the betterment of the systems. Knowledge-based systems can be broadly classified as CASE-based systems, intelligent tutoring systems, expert systems, hypertext manipulation systems and databases with intelligent user interface.

Compared to traditional computer-based information systems, knowledge-based systems have many advantages. They can provide efficient documentation and also handle large amounts of unstructured data in an intelligent fashion. Knowledge-based systems can aid in expert decision making and allow users to work at a higher level of expertise and promote productivity and consistency. These systems are considered very useful when expertise is unavailable, or when data needs to be stored for future usage or needs to be grouped with different expertise at a common platform, thus providing large-scale integration of knowledge. Finally, knowledge-based systems are capable of creating new knowledge by referring to the stored content.

The limitations of knowledge-based systems are the abstract nature of the concerned knowledge, acquiring and manipulating large volumes of information or data, and the limitations of cognitive and other scientific techniques.

Knowledge-based systems were first developed by artificial intelligence researchers. These early knowledge-based systems were primarily expert systems – in fact, the term was often used anonymously with expert systems. The difference is in the view taken to describe the system: "expert system" refers to the type of task the system is trying to assist with – to replace or aid a human expert in a complex task; "knowledge-based system" refers to the architecture of the system – that it represents knowledge explicitly (rather than as procedural code). While the earliest knowledge-based systems were almost all expert systems, the same tools and architectures can and have since been used for a whole host of other types of systems – i.e., virtually all expert systems are knowledge-based systems, but many knowledge-based systems are not expert systems.

The first knowledge-based systems were rule based expert systems. One of the most famous was Mycin a program for medical diagnosis. These early expert systems represented facts about the world as simple assertions in a flat database and used rules to reason about and as a result add to these assertions. Representing knowledge explicitly via rules had several advantages:

1. Acquisition and maintenance. Using rules meant that domain experts could often define and maintain the rules themselves rather than via a programmer.

2. Explanation. Representing knowledge explicitly allowed systems to reason about how they came to a conclusion and use this information to explain results to users. For example, to follow the chain of inferences that led to a diagnosis and use these facts to explain the diagnosis.

3. Reasoning. Decoupling the knowledge from the processing of that knowledge enabled general purpose inference engines to be developed. These systems could develop conclusions that followed from a data set that the initial developers may not have even been aware of.

As knowledge-based systems became more complex the techniques used to represent the knowledge base became more sophisticated. Rather than representing facts as assertions about data, the knowledge-base became more structured, representing information using similar techniques to object-oriented programming such as hierarchies of classes and subclasses, relations between classes, and behavior of objects. As the knowledge base became more structured reasoning could occur both by independent rules and by interactions within the knowledge base itself. For example, procedures stored as demons on objects could fire and could replicate the chaining behavior of rules.

Another advancement was the development of special purpose automated reasoning systems called classifiers. Rather than statically declare the subsumption relations in a knowledge-base a classifier allows the developer to simply declare facts about the world and let the classifier deduce the relations. In this way a classifier also can play the role of an inference engine.

The most recent advancement of knowledge-based systems has been to adopt the technologies for the development of systems that use the internet. The internet often has to deal with complex, unstructured data that can't be relied on to fit a specific data model. The technology of knowledge-based systems and especially the ability to classify objects on demand is ideal for such systems. The model for these kinds of knowledge-based Internet systems is known as the Semantic Web.

Place where Knowledge-based Systems are used

Over the years, knowledge-based systems have been developed for a number of applications. MYCIN, for example, was an early knowledge-based system created to help doctors diagnose diseases. Healthcare has remained an important market for knowledge-based systems, which are now referred to as clinical decision-support systems in the health sciences context.

Knowledge-based systems have also been employed in applications as diverse as avalanche path analysis, industrial equipment fault diagnosis and cash management.

Knowledge-based Systems and Artificial Intelligence

While a subset of artificial intelligence, classical knowledge-based systems differ in approach to some of the newer developments in AI.

Daniel Dennett, a philosopher and cognitive scientist, in his 2017 book, *From Bacteria to Bach and Back*, cited a strategy shift from early AI, characterized by "top-down-organized, bureaucratically efficient know-it-all" systems to systems that harness Big Data and "statistical pattern-finding techniques" such as data-mining and deep learning in a more bottom-up approach.

Examples of AI following the latter approach include neural network systems, a type of deep-learning technology that concentrates on signal processing and pattern recognition problems such as facial recognition.

References

- Mueller, Erik T. (2015). Commonsense Reasoning: An Event Calculus Based Approach (2nd ed.). Waltham, Mass.: Morgan Kaufmann/Elsevier. ISBN 978-0128014165

- "Retroduction | Dictionary | Commens". Commens – Digital Companion to C. S. Peirce. Mats Bergman, Sami Paavola & João Queiroz. Retrieved 2014-08-24

- Zlatarva, Nellie (1992). "Truth Maintenance Systems and their Application for Verifying Expert System Knowledge Bases". Artificial Intelligence Review. 6: 67–110. doi:10.1007/bf00155580. Retrieved 25 December 2013

- Menzies, T (1996). "Applications of Abduction: Knowledge-Level Modeling" (PDF). International Journal of Human-Computer Studies. 45 (3): 305–335. doi:10.1006/ijhc.1996.0054

- Minsky, Marvin (2006). The Emotion Machine: Commonsense Thinking, Artificial Intelligence, and the Future of the Human Mind. New York: Simon and Schuster. ISBN 0-7432-7663-9

- MacGregor, Robert (June 1991). "Using a description classifier to enhance knowledge representation". IEEE Expert. 6 (3): 41–46. doi:10.1109/64.87683. Retrieved 10 November 2013

- Rejón Altable, C (October 2012). "Logic structure of clinical judgment and its relation to medical and psychiatric semiology". Psychopathology. 45 (6): 344–51. doi:10.1159/000337968. PMID 22854297. Retrieved 17 January 2014

- Cialdea Mayer, Marta and Pirri, Fiora (1995) "Propositional Abduction in Modal Logic", Logic Jnl IGPL 1995 3: 907–919; doi:10.1093/jigpal/3.6.907 Oxford Journals

4

Machine Learning

A subset of artificial intelligence is machine learning. It is concerned with the use of statistical techniques for simulating the ability to learn in computers. The topics elaborated in this chapter will help in gaining a better perspective about the key elements of machine learning, such as hyperparameter, ensemble averaging, supervised learning and reinforcement learning.

Machine learning is an application of artificial intelligence (AI) that provides systems the ability to automatically learn and improve from experience without being explicitly programmed. Machine learning focuses on the development of computer programs that can access data and use it learn for themselves.

The process of learning begins with observations or data, such as examples, direct experience, or instruction, in order to look for patterns in data and make better decisions in the future based on the examples that we provide. The primary aim is to allow the computers learn automatically without human intervention or assistance and adjust actions accordingly.

Machine learning enables analysis of massive quantities of data. While it generally delivers faster, more accurate results in order to identify profitable opportunities or dangerous risks, it may also require additional time and resources to train it properly. Combining machine learning with AI and cognitive technologies can make it even more effective in processing large volumes of information.

Tom M. Mitchell provided a widely quoted, more formal definition of the algorithms studied in the machine learning field: "A computer program is said to learn from experience E with respect to some class of tasks T and performance measure P if its performance at tasks in T, as measured by P, improves with experience E." This definition of the tasks in which machine learning is concerned offers a fundamentally operational definition rather than defining the field in cognitive terms. This follows Alan Turing's proposal in his paper "Computing Machinery and Intelligence", in which the question "Can machines think?" is replaced with the question "Can machines do what we (as thinking entities) can do?". In Turing's proposal the various characteristics that could be possessed by a *thinking machine* and the various implications in constructing one are exposed.

Machine Learning Tasks

Machine learning tasks are typically classified into two broad categories, depending on whether there is a learning "signal" or "feedback" available to a learning system:

- Supervised learning: The computer is presented with example inputs and their desired outputs, given by a "teacher", and the goal is to learn a general rule that maps inputs to outputs. As special cases, the input signal can be only partially available, or restricted to special feedback:

  o Semi-supervised learning: the computer is given only an incomplete training signal: a training set with some (often many) of the target outputs missing.

  o Active learning: the computer can only obtain training labels for a limited set of instances (based on a budget), and also has to optimize its choice of objects to acquire labels for. When used interactively, these can be presented to the user for labeling.

  o Reinforcement learning: training data (in form of rewards and punishments) is given only as feedback to the program's actions in a dynamic environment, such as driving a vehicle or playing a game against an opponent.

- Unsupervised learning: No labels are given to the learning algorithm, leaving it on its own to find structure in its input. Unsupervised learning can be a goal in itself (discovering hidden patterns in data) or a means towards an end (feature learning).

Machine Learning Applications

Another categorization of machine learning tasks arises when one considers the desired *output* of a machine-learned system:

- In classification, inputs are divided into two or more classes, and the learner must produce a model that assigns unseen inputs to one or more (multi-label classification) of these classes. This is typically tackled in a supervised manner. Spam filtering is an example of classification, where the inputs are email (or other) messages and the classes are "spam" and "not spam".

- In regression, also a supervised problem, the outputs are continuous rather than discrete.

- In clustering, a set of inputs is to be divided into groups. Unlike in classification, the groups are not known beforehand, making this typically an unsupervised task.

- Density estimation finds the distribution of inputs in some space.

- Dimensionality reduction simplifies inputs by mapping them into a lower-dimensional space. Topic modeling is a related problem, where a program is given a list of human language documents and is tasked with finding out which documents cover similar topics.

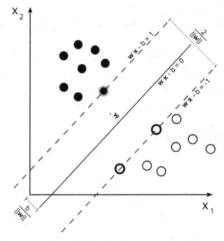

A support vector machine is a classifier that divides its input space into two regions, separated by a linear boundary. Here, it has learned to distinguish black and white circles.

Among other categories of machine learning problems, learning to learn learns its own inductive bias based on previous experience. Developmental learning, elaborated for robot learning, generates its own sequences (also called curriculum) of learning situations to cumulatively acquire repertoires of novel skills through autonomous self-exploration and social interaction with human teachers and using guidance mechanisms such as active learning, maturation, motor synergies, and imitation.

Machine Learning Algorithms

Decision Tree Learning

Decision tree learning uses a decision tree as a predictive model, which maps observations about an item to conclusions about the item's target value.

Association Rule Learning

Association rule learning is a method for discovering interesting relations between variables in large databases.

Artificial Neural Networks

An artificial neural network (ANN) learning algorithm, usually called "neural network" (NN), is a learning algorithm that is vaguely inspired by biological neural networks. Computations are structured in terms of an interconnected group of artificial neurons, processing information using a connectionist approach to computation. Modern neural networks are non-linear statistical data modeling tools. They are usually used to model complex relationships between inputs and outputs, to find patterns in data, or to capture the statistical structure in an unknown joint probability distribution between observed variables.

Deep Learning

Falling hardware prices and the development of GPUs for personal use in the last few years have contributed to the development of the concept of deep learning which consists of multiple hidden layers in an artificial neural network. This approach tries to model the way the human brain processes light and sound into vision and hearing. Some successful applications of deep learning are computer vision and speech recognition.

Inductive Logic Programming

Inductive logic programming (ILP) is an approach to rule learning using logic programming as a uniform representation for input examples, background knowledge, and hypotheses. Given an encoding of the known background knowledge and a set of examples represented as a logical database of facts, an ILP system will derive a hypothesized logic program that entails all positive and no negative examples. Inductive programming is a related field that considers any kind of programming languages for representing hypotheses (and not only logic programming), such as functional programs.

Support Vector Machines

Support vector machines (SVMs) are a set of related supervised learning methods used for classification and regression. Given a set of training examples, each marked as belonging to one of two categories, an SVM training algorithm builds a model that predicts whether a new example falls into one category or the other.

Clustering

Cluster analysis is the assignment of a set of observations into subsets (called *clusters*) so that observations within the same cluster are similar according to some predesignated criterion or criteria, while observations drawn from different clusters are dissimilar. Different clustering techniques make different assumptions on the structure of the data, often defined by some *similarity metric* and evaluated for example by *internal compactness* (similarity between members of the same cluster) and *separation* between different clusters. Other methods are based on *estimated density* and *graph connectivity*. Clustering is a method of unsupervised learning, and a common technique for statistical data analysis.

Bayesian Networks

A Bayesian network, belief network or directed acyclic graphical model is a probabilistic graphical model that represents a set of random variables and their conditional independencies via a directed acyclic graph (DAG). For example, a Bayesian network could represent the probabilistic relationships between diseases and symptoms. Given symptoms, the network can be used to compute the probabilities of the presence of various diseases. Efficient algorithms exist that perform inference and learning.

Reinforcement Learning

Reinforcement learning is concerned with how an *agent* ought to take *actions* in an *environment* so as to maximize some notion of long-term *reward*. Reinforcement learning algorithms attempt to find a *policy* that maps *states* of the world to the actions the agent ought to take in those states. Reinforcement learning differs from the supervised learning problem in that correct input/output pairs are never presented, nor suboptimal actions explicitly corrected.

Representation Learning

Several learning algorithms, mostly unsupervised learning algorithms, aim at discovering better representations of the inputs provided during training. Classical examples include principal components analysis and cluster analysis. Representation learning algorithms often attempt to preserve the information in their input but transform it in a way that makes it useful, often as a pre-processing step before performing classification or predictions, allowing reconstruction of the inputs coming from the unknown data generating distribution, while not being necessarily faithful for configurations that are implausible under that distribution.

Manifold learning algorithms attempt to do so under the constraint that the learned representation is low-dimensional. Sparse codingalgorithms attempt to do so under the constraint that the learned representation is sparse (has many zeros). Multilinear subspace learningalgorithms aim to learn low-dimensional representations directly from tensor representations for multidimensional data, without reshaping them into (high-dimensional) vectors. Deep learning algorithms discover multiple levels of representation, or a hierarchy of features, with higher-level, more abstract features defined in terms of (or generating) lower-level features. It has been argued that an intelligent machine is one that learns a representation that disentangles the underlying factors of variation that explain the observed data.

Similarity and Metric Learning

In this problem, the learning machine is given pairs of examples that are considered similar and pairs of less similar objects. It then needs to learn a similarity function (or a distance metric function) that can predict if new objects are similar. It is sometimes used in Recommendation systems.

Sparse Dictionary Learning

In this method, a datum is represented as a linear combination of basis functions, and the coefficients are assumed to be sparse. Let x be a d-dimensional datum, D be a d by n matrix, where each column of D represents a basis function. r is the coefficient to represent x using D. Mathematically, sparse dictionary learning means solving where r is sparse. Generally speaking, n is assumed to be larger than d to allow the freedom for a sparse representation.

Learning a dictionary along with sparse representations is strongly NP-hard and also difficult to solve approximately. A popular heuristic method for sparse dictionary learning is K-SVD.

Sparse dictionary learning has been applied in several contexts. In classification, the problem is to determine which classes a previously unseen datum belongs to. Suppose a dictionary for each class has already been built. Then a new datum is associated with the class such that it's best sparsely represented by the corresponding dictionary. Sparse dictionary learning has also been applied in image de-noising. The key idea is that a clean image patch can be sparsely represented by an image dictionary, but the noise cannot.

Genetic Algorithms

A genetic algorithm (GA) is a search heuristic that mimics the process of natural selection, and uses methods such as mutation and crossover to generate new genotype in the hope of finding good solutions to a given problem. In machine learning, genetic algorithms found some uses in the 1980s and 1990s. Conversely, machine learning techniques have been used to improve the performance of genetic and evolutionary algorithms.

Rule-based Machine Learning

Rule-based machine learning is a general term for any machine learning method that identifies, learns, or evolves "rules" to store, manipulate or apply, knowledge. The defining characteristic of a rule-based machine learner is the identification and utilization of a set of relational rules that collectively represent the knowledge captured by the system. This is in contrast to other machine learners that commonly identify a singular model that can be universally applied to any instance in order to make a prediction. Rule-based machine learning approaches include learning classifier systems, association rule learning, and artificial immune systems.

Learning Classifier Systems

Learning classifier systems (LCS) are a family of rule-based machine learning algorithms that combine a discovery component (e.g. typically a genetic algorithm) with a learning component (performing either supervised learning, reinforcement learning, or unsupervised learning). They seek to identify a set of context-dependent rules that collectively store and apply knowledge in a piecewise manner in order to make predictions.

Feature Selection Approach

Feature selection is the process of selecting an optimal subset of relevant features for use in model construction. It is assumed the data contains some features that are either redundant or irrelevant, and can thus be removed to reduce calculation cost without incurring much loss of information. Common optimality criteria include accuracy, similarity and information measures.

Applications

Applications for machine learning include:

- Agriculture
- Automated theorem proving
- Adaptive websites
- Affective computing
- Bioinformatics
- Brain–machine interfaces
- Cheminformatics
- Classifying DNA sequences
- Computational anatomy
- Computer Networks
- Telecommunication
- Computer vision, including object recognition
- Detecting credit-card fraud
- General game playing
- Information retrieval

- Internet fraud detection
- Linguistics
- Marketing
- Machine learning control
- Machine perception
- Medical diagnosis
- Economics
- Insurance
- Natural language processing
- Natural language understanding
- Optimization and metaheuristic
- Online advertising
- Recommender systems
- Robot locomotion
- Search engines
- Sentiment analysis (or opinion mining)
- Multimodal sentiment analysis
- Sequence mining
- Software engineering
- Speech and handwriting recognition
- Space mapping
- Financial market analysis
- Structural health monitoring
- Syntactic pattern recognition
- Time series forecasting
- User behavior analytics
- Translation

In 2006, the online movie company Netflix held the first "Netflix Prize" competition to find a program to better predict user preferences and improve the accuracy on its existing Cinematch movie recommendation algorithm by at least 10%. A joint team made up of researchers from AT&T Labs-Research in collaboration with the teams Big Chaos and Pragmatic Theory built an ensemble model to win the Grand Prize in 2009 for $1 million. Shortly after the prize was awarded, Netflix realized that viewers' ratings were not the best indicators of their viewing patterns ("everything is a recommendation") and they changed their recommendation engine accordingly.

In 2010 The Wall Street Journal wrote about the firm Rebellion Research and their use of Machine Learning to predict the financial crisis.

In 2012, co-founder of Sun Microsystems Vinod Khosla predicted that 80% of medical doctors jobs would be lost in the next two decades to automated machine learning medical diagnostic software.

In 2014, it has been reported that a machine learning algorithm has been applied in Art History to study fine art paintings, and that it may have revealed previously unrecognized influences between artists.

Model Assessments

Although machine learning has been very transformative in some fields, effective machine learning is difficult because finding patterns is hard and often not enough training data are available; as a result, machine-learning programs often fail to deliver.

Classification machine learning models can be validated by accuracy estimation techniques like the Holdout method, which splits the data into a training and test sets (conventionally 2/3 training set and 1/3 test set designation) and evaluates the performance of the training model on the test set. In comparison, the k-fold-cross-validation method randomly splits the data into k subsets where the k - 1 instances of the data subsets are used to train the model while the kth subset instance is used to test the predictive ability of the training model. In addition to the holdout and cross-validation methods, bootstrap, which samples n instances with replacement from the dataset, can be used to assess model accuracy.

In addition to overall accuracy, investigators frequently report sensitivity and specificity meaning True Positive Rate (TPR) and True Negative Rate (TNR) respectively. Similarly, investigators sometimes report the False Positive Rate (FPR) as well as the False Negative Rate (FNR). However, these rates are ratios that fail to reveal their numerators and denominators. The Total Operating Characteristic(TOC) is an effective method to express a model's diagnostic ability. TOC shows the numerators and denominators of the previously mentioned rates, thus TOC provides more information than the commonly used Receiver Operating Characteristic (ROC) and ROC's associated Area Under the Curve (AUC).

Examples of Machine Learning

Machine learning is being used in a wide range of applications today. One of the most well-known examples is Facebook's News Feed. The News Feed uses machine learning to personalize each member's feed. If a member frequently stops scrolling to read or like a particular friend's posts, the News Feed will start to show more of that friend's activity earlier in the feed. Behind the scenes, the software is simply using statistical analysis and predictive analytics to identify patterns in the user's data and use those patterns to populate the News Feed. Should the member no longer stop to read, like or comment on the friend's posts, that new data will be included in the data set and the News Feed will adjust accordingly.

Machine learning is also entering an array of enterprise applications. Customer relationship management (CRM) systems use learning models to analyze email and prompt sales team members to respond to the most important messages first. More advanced systems can even recommend potentially effective responses. Business intelligence (BI) and analytics vendors use machine learning in their software to help users automatically identify potentially important data points. Human resource (HR) systems use learning models to identify characteristics of effective employees and rely on this knowledge to find the best applicants for open positions.

Machine learning also plays an important role in self-driving cars. Deep learning neural networks are used to identify objects and determine optimal actions for safely steering a vehicle down the road.

Virtual assistant technology is also powered through machine learning. Smart assistants combine several deep learning models to interpret natural speech, bring in relevant context -- like a user's personal schedule or previously defined preferences -- and take an action, like booking a flight or pulling up driving directions.

Automated Machine Learning

AutoML is not automated data science. While there is undoubtedly overlap, machine learning is but one of many tools in the data science toolkit, and its use does not actually factor in to all data science tasks. For example, if prediction will be part of a given data science task, machine learning will be a useful component; however, machine learning may not play in to a descriptive analytics task at all.

Even for predictive tasks, data science encompasses much more than the actual predictive modeling. Data scientist Sandro Saitta, when discussing the potential confusion between AutoML and automated data science, had this to say:

> "The misconception comes from the confusion between the whole Data Science process and the sub-tasks of data preparation (feature extraction, etc.) and modeling (algorithm selection, hyper-parameters tuning, etc.) which I call Machine Learning."

Further, data scientist and leading automated machine learning proponent Randy Olson states that effective machine learning design requires us to:

1. Always tune the hyperparameters for our models

2. Always try out many different models

3. Always explore numerous feature representations for our data

Taking all of the above into account, if we consider AutoML to be the tasks of algorithm selection, hyperparameter tuning, iterative modeling, and model assessment, we can start to define what AutoML actually is. There will not be total agreement on this definition (for comparison, ask 10 people to define "data science," and then compare the 11 answers you get), but it arguably starts us off on the right foot.

Automated machine learning represents a fundamental shift in the way organizations of all sizes approach machine learning and data science. Applying traditional machine learning methods to real-world business problems is time-consuming, resource-intensive, and challenging. It requires experts in the several disciplines, including data scientists – some of the most sought-after professionals in the job market right now.

Automated machine learning changes that, making it easier to build and use machine learning models in the real world by running systematic processes on raw data and selecting models that pull the most relevant information from the data – what is often referred to as "the signal in the noise." Automated machine learning incorporates machine learning best practices from top-ranked data scientists to make data science more accessible across the organization.

Here is the standard machine learning process at a high level:

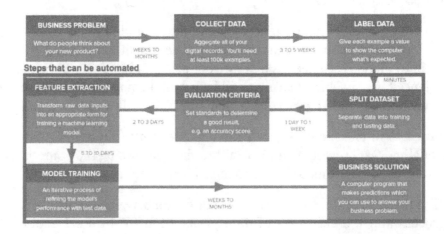

When developing a model with the traditional process, as you can see from figure above, the only automatic task is model training. Automated machine learning software automatically executes all the steps outlined in red – manual, tedious modeling tasks that used to require skilled data scientists. The traditional process often takes weeks or months, but with automated machine learning, it takes days at most for business professionals and data scientists to develop and compare dozens of models, find insights and predictions, and solve more business problems much faster.

shows the automated machine learning process after uploading a dataset and choose the target variable for the business problem:

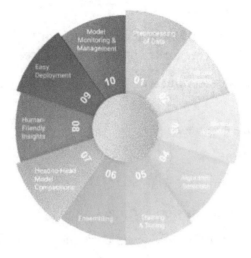

Automating these steps allows for greater agility in problem-solving and the democratization of data science to include those without extensive programming knowledge.

Importance of Machine Learning

Manually constructing a machine learning model is a multistep process that requires domain knowledge, mathematical expertise, and computer science skills – which is a lot to ask of one company, let alone one data scientist (provided you can hire and retain one). Not only that, there are countless opportunities for human error and bias, which gets in the way of model accuracy and devalues the insights you might get from the model. Automated machine learning enables organizations to use the baked-in knowledge of data scientists without having to develop the capabilities themselves, simultaneously improving return on investment in data science initiatives and reducing the amount of time it takes to capture value.

Automated machine learning makes it possible for businesses in every industry – healthcare, fintech, banking, the public sector, marketing, and more – to leverage machine learning and AI technology that was previously limited to organizations with vast resources at their disposal. By automating most of the manual modeling tasks that used to be necessary in order to develop and deploy machine learning models, automated machine learning enables business users to implement machine learning solutions with ease and frees up data scientists to focus on more complex problems.

Targets of Automation

Automated machine learning can target various stages of the machine learning process:

- Automated data preparation and ingestion (from raw data and miscellaneous formats)

  o Automated column type detection; e.g., boolean, discrete numerical, continuous numerical, or text

  o Automated column intent detection; e.g., target/label, stratification field, numerical feature, categorical text feature, or free text feature

  o Automated task detection; e.g., binary classification, regression, clustering, or ranking

- Automated feature engineering

  o Feature selection

  o Feature extraction

  o Meta learning and transfer learning

  o Detection and handling of skewed data and/or missing values

- Automated model selection

- Hyperparameter optimization of the learning algorithm and featurization

- Automated pipeline selection under time, memory, and complexity constraints

- Automated selection of evaluation metics / validation procedures

- Automated problem checking

  o Leakage detection

  o Misconfiguration detection

- Automated analysis of results obtained

- User interfaces and visualizations for automated machine learning

Examples

Software tackling various stages of AutoML:

Hyperparameter optimization and model selection

- H2O AutoML provides automated data preparation, hyperparameter tuning via random search, and stacked ensembles in a distributed machine learning platform.

- mlr is a R package that contains several hyperparameter optimization techniques for machine learning problems.

Full Pipeline Optimization

- Auto-WEKA is a Bayesian hyperparameter optimization layer on top of WEKA.

- auto-sklearn is a Bayesian hyperparameter optimization layer on top of scikit-learn.

- TPOT is a Python library that automatically creates and optimizes full machine learning pipelines using genetic programming.

Deep Neural Network Architecture Search

- devol is a Python package that performs Deep Neural Network architecture search using genetic programming.

- Google AutoML for deep learning model architecture selection.

Automated Machine Learning will lessen the scientists' and programmers' dependency on intuition by trying out an algorithm, scoring, testing and refining other models. In fact, it will automate the machine learning process of the data science workflow in the organisation.

Randy Olson, Senior Data Scientist at University of Pennsylvania Institute for Biomedical Informatics, and lead developer of TPOT has gone on record to say:

"In the near future, I see automated machine learning (AutoML) taking over the machine learning model-building process: once a data set is in a (relatively) clean format, the AutoML system will be able to design and optimise a machine learning pipeline faster than 99% of the humans out there. Perhaps AutoML systems will be able to expand out to cover a larger portion of the data cleaning process, but many tasks — such as being able to pose a problem as a machine learning problem in the first place — will remain solely a human endeavour in the near future."

Feature

In machine learning, feature vectors are used to represent numeric or symbolic characteristics, called features, of an object in a mathematical, easily analyzable way. They are important for many different areas of machine learning and pattern processing. Machine learning algorithms typically require a numerical representation of objects in order for the algorithms to do processing and statistical analysis. Feature vectors are the equivalent of vectors of explanatory variables that are used in statistical procedures such as linear regression.

An example of a feature vector you might be familiar with is RGB (red-green-blue) color descriptions. A color can be described by how much red, blue, and green there is in it. A feature vector for this would be color = [R, G, B].

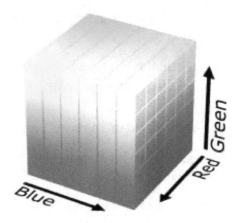

A vector is a series of numbers, like a matrix with one column but multiple rows, that can often be represented spatially. A feature is a numerical or symbolic property of an aspect of an object. A feature vector is a vector containing multiple elements about an object. Putting feature vectors for objects together can make up a feature space.

The features may represent, as a whole, one mere pixel or an entire image. The granularity depends on what someone is trying to learn or represent about the object. You could describe a 3-dimensional shape with a feature vector indicating its height, width, depth, etc.

$$X = \begin{bmatrix} X_1 \\ X_2 \\ \\ X_d \end{bmatrix}$$

Feature vector   **Feature space (3D)**   **Scatter plot (2D)**

The basics of feature vectors

Uses of Feature Vectors

Feature vectors are used widely in machine learning because of the effectiveness and practicality of representing objects in a numerical way to help with many kinds of analyses. They are good for analysis because there are many techniques for comparing feature vectors. One simple way to compare the feature vectors of two objects is to take the Euclidean distance.

In image processing, features can be gradient magnitude, color, grayscale intensity, edges, areas, and more. Feature vectors are particularly popular for analyses in image processing because of the convenient way attributes about an image, like the examples listed, can be compared numerically once put into feature vectors.

In speech recognition, features can be sound lengths, noise level, noise ratios, and more.

In spam-fighting initiatives, features are abundant. They can be IP location, text structure, frequency of certain words, or certain email headers.

Feature vectors are used in classification problems, artificial neural networks, and k-nearest neighbors algorithms in machine learning.

Examples

In character recognition, features may include histograms counting the number of black pixels along horizontal and vertical directions, number of internal holes, stroke detection and many others.

In speech recognition, features for recognizing phonemes can include noise ratios, length of sounds, relative power, filter matches and many others.

In spam detection algorithms, features may include the presence or absence of certain email headers, the email structure, the language, the frequency of specific terms, the grammatical correctness of the text.

In computer vision, there are a large number of possible features, such as edges and objects.

Extensions

In pattern recognition and machine learning, a feature vector is an n-dimensional vector of numerical features that represent some object. Many algorithms in machine learning require a numerical representation of objects, since such representations facilitate processing and statistical analysis. When representing images, the feature values might correspond to the pixels of an image, while when representing texts the features might be the frequencies of occurrence of textual terms. Feature vectors are equivalent to the vectors of explanatory variables used in statistical procedures such as linear regression. Feature vectors are often combined with weights using a dot product in order to construct a linear predictor function that is used to determine a score for making a prediction.

The vector space associated with these vectors is often called the feature space. In order to reduce the dimensionality of the feature space, a number of dimensionality reduction techniques can be employed.

Higher-level features can be obtained from already available features and added to the feature vector; for example, for the study of diseases the feature 'Age' is useful and is defined as *Age = 'Year of death' minus 'Year of birth'*. This process is referred to as feature construction. Feature construction is the application of a set of constructive operators to a set of existing features resulting in construction of new features. Examples of such constructive operators include checking for the equality conditions {=, ≠}, the arithmetic operators {+,−,×, /}, the array operators {max-(S), min(S), average(S)} as well as other more sophisticated operators, for example count(S,C) that counts the number of features in the feature vector S satisfying some condition C or, for example, distances to other recognition classes generalized by some accepting device. Feature construction has long been considered a powerful tool for increasing both accuracy and understanding of structure, particularly in high-dimensional problems. Applications include studies of disease and emotion recognition from speech.

Selection and Extraction

The initial set of raw features can be redundant and too large to be managed. Therefore, a preliminary step in many applications of machine learning and pattern recognition consists of selecting a subset of features, or constructing a new and reduced set of features to facilitate learning, and to improve generalization and interpretability.

Extracting or selecting features is a combination of art and science; developing systems to do so is known as feature engineering. It requires the experimentation of multiple possibilities and the combination of automated techniques with the intuition and knowledge of the domain expert. Automating this process is feature learning, where a machine not only uses features for learning, but learns the features itself.

Importance of Feature Selection

Machine learning works on a simple rule – if you put garbage in, you will only get garbage to come out.

This becomes even more important when the number of features are very large. You need not use every feature at your disposal for creating an algorithm. You can assist your algorithm by feeding in only those features that are really important.

Not only in the competitions but this can be very useful in industrial applications as well. You not only reduce the training time and the evaluation time, you also have less things to worry about.

Top reasons to use feature selection are:

- It enables the machine learning algorithm to train faster.

- It reduces the complexity of a model and makes it easier to interpret.

- It improves the accuracy of a model if the right subset is chosen.

- It reduces overfitting.

Filter Methods

Filter methods are generally used as a preprocessing step. The selection of features is independent of any machine learning algorithms. Instead, features are selected on the basis of their scores in various statistical tests for their correlation with the outcome variable. The correlation is a subjective term here. For basic guidance, you can refer to the following table for defining correlation co-efficients.

Feature\Response	Continuous	Categorical
Continuous	Pearson's Correlation	LDA
Categorical	Anova	Chi-Square

- Pearson's Correlation: It is used as a measure for quantifying linear dependence between two continuous variables X and Y. Its value varies from -1 to +1. Pearson's correlation is given as:

$$\rho_{X,Y} = \frac{\text{cov}(X,Y)}{\sigma_X \sigma_Y}$$

- LDA: Linear discriminant analysis is used to find a linear combination of features that characterizes or separates two or more classes (or levels) of a categorical variable.

- ANOVA: ANOVA stands for Analysis of variance. It is similar to LDA except for the fact that it is operated using one or more categorical independent features and one continuous dependent feature. It provides a statistical test of whether the means of several groups are equal or not.

- Chi-Square: It is a is a statistical test applied to the groups of categorical features to evaluate the likelihood of correlation or association between them using their frequency distribution.

One thing that should be kept in mind is that filter methods do not remove multicollinearity. So, you must deal with multicollinearity of features as well before training models for your data.

Wrapper Methods

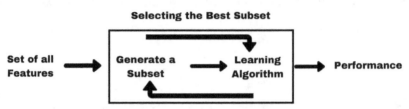

In wrapper methods, we try to use a subset of features and train a model using them. Based on the inferences that we draw from the previous model, we decide to add or remove features from your subset. The problem is essentially reduced to a search problem. These methods are usually computationally very expensive.

Some common examples of wrapper methods are forward feature selection, backward feature elimination, recursive feature elimination, etc.

- Forward Selection: Forward selection is an iterative method in which we start with having no feature in the model. In each iteration, we keep adding the feature which best improves our model till an addition of a new variable does not improve the performance of the model.

- Backward Elimination: In backward elimination, we start with all the features and removes the least significant feature at each iteration which improves the performance of the model. We repeat this until no improvement is observed on removal of features.

- Recursive Feature elimination: It is a greedy optimization algorithm which aims to find the best performing feature subset. It repeatedly creates models and keeps aside the best or the worst performing feature at each iteration. It constructs the next model with the left features until all the features are exhausted. It then ranks the features based on the order of their elimination.

One of the best ways for implementing feature selection with wrapper methods is to use Boruta package that finds the importance of a feature by creating shadow features.

It works in the following steps:

1. Firstly, it adds randomness to the given data set by creating shuffled copies of all features (which are called shadow features).

- Then, it trains a random forest classifier on the extended data set and applies a feature importance measure (the default is Mean Decrease Accuracy) to evaluate the importance of each feature where higher means more important.

- At every iteration, it checks whether a real feature has a higher importance than the best of its shadow features (i.e. whether the feature has a higher Z-score than the maximum Z-score of its shadow features) and constantly removes features which are deemed highly unimportant.

- Finally, the algorithm stops either when all features get confirmed or rejected or it reaches a specified limit of random forest runs.

For more information on the implementation of Boruta package, you can refer to this article:

Embedded Methods

Selecting the best subset

Set of all Features → Generate the Subset → Learning Algorithm + Performance

Embedded methods combine the qualities' of filter and wrapper methods. It's implemented by algorithms that have their own built-in feature selection methods.

Some of the most popular examples of these methods are LASSO and RIDGE regression which have inbuilt penalization functions to reduce overfitting.

- Lasso regression performs L1 regularization which adds penalty equivalent to absolute value of the magnitude of coefficients.

- Ridge regression performs L2 regularization which adds penalty equivalent to square of the magnitude of coefficients.

Other examples of embedded methods are Regularized trees, Memetic algorithm, Random multinomial logit.

Difference between Filter and Wrapper methods

The main differences between the filter and wrapper methods for feature selection are:

- Filter methods measure the relevance of features by their correlation with dependent variable while wrapper methods measure the usefulness of a subset of feature by actually training a model on it.

- Filter methods are much faster compared to wrapper methods as they do not involve training the models. On the other hand, wrapper methods are computationally very expensive as well.

- Filter methods use statistical methods for evaluation of a subset of features while wrapper methods use cross validation.

- Filter methods might fail to find the best subset of features in many occasions but wrapper methods can always provide the best subset of features.

- Using the subset of features from the wrapper methods make the model more prone to overfitting as compared to using subset of features from the filter methods.

Hyperparameter

Model optimization is one of the toughest challenges in the implementation of machine learning solutions. Entire branches of machine learning and deep learning theory have been dedicated to the optimization of models. Typically, we think about model optimization as a process of regularly modifying the code of the model in order to minimize the testing error. However, the are of machine learning optimization often entails fine tuning elements that live outside the model but that can heavily influence its behavior. Machine learning often refers to those hidden elements as hyperparameters as they are one of the most critical components of any machine learning application.

Hyperparameters are settings that can be tuned to control the behavior of a machine learning algorithm. Conceptually, hyperparameters can be considered orthogonal to the learning model itself in the sense that, although they live outside the model, there is a direct relationship between them.

The criteria of what defines a hyperparameter is incredibly abstract and flexible. Sure, there are well established hyperparameters such as the number of hidden units or the learning rate of a model but there are also an arbitrarily number of settings that can play the role of hyperparameters for specific models. In general, hyperparameters are very specific to the type of machine learning mode you are trying to optimize. Sometimes, a setting is modeled as a hyperparameter because is not appropriate to learn it from the training set. A classic example are settings that control the capacity of a model(the spectrum of functions that the model can represent). If a machine learning algorithm learns those settings directly from the training set, then it is likely to try to maximize them which will cause the model to overfit(poor generalization).

If hyperparameters are not learned from the training set, then how does a model learn them? Remember that classic role in machine learning models to split the input dataset in an 80/20 percent ratio between the training set and the validation set respectively? Well, part of the role of that 20% validation set is to guide the selection of hyperparameters. Technically, the validation set is used to "train" the hyperparameters prior to optimization.

Types

Most hyperparameters are one of two types (Fred et. al):

- Numerical (H_{num}): can be a real number or an integer value; these are usually bounded by a reasonable minimum value and maximum value.

- Categorical (H_{cat}): one value is chosen from a set of possible values.

Considerations

The time required to train and test a model can depend upon the choice of its hyperparameters. A hyperparameter is usually of continuous or integer type, leading to mixed-type optimization problems. The existence of some hyperparameters is conditional upon the value of others, e.g. the size of each hidden layer in a neural network can be conditional upon the number of layers.

Tunability

Most performance variation can be attributed to just a few hyperparameters. The tunability of an algorithm, hyperparameter, or interacting hyperparameters is a measure of how much performance can be gained by tuning it. For an LSTM, while the learning rate followed by the network size are its most crucial hyperparameters, whereas batching and momentum have no significant effect on its performance.

Although some research has advocated the use of mini-batch sizes in the thousands, other work has found the best performance with mini-batch sizes between 2 and 32.

Robustness

An inherent stochasticity in learning directly implies that the empirical hyperparameter performance is not necessarily its true performance. Methods that are not robust to simple changes in hyperparameters, random seeds, or even different implementations of the same algorithm cannot be integrated into mission critical control systems without significant simplification and robustification.

Reinforcement learning algorithms, in particular, require measuring their performance over a large number of random seeds, and also measuring their sensitivity to choices of hyperparameters. Their evaluation with a small number of random seeds does not capture performance adequately due to high variance. Some reinforcement learning methods, e.g. DDPG (Deep Deterministic Policy Gradient), are more sensitive to hyperparameter choices than others.

Optimization

Hyperparameter optimization finds a tuple of hyperparameters that yields an optimal model which minimizes a predefined loss function on given test data. The objective function takes a tuple of hyperparameters and returns the associated loss.

Reproducibility

Apart from tuning hyperparameters, machine learning involves storing and organizing the parameters and results, and making sure they are reproducible. In the absence of a robust infrastructure for this purpose, research code often evolves quickly and compromises essential aspects like bookkeeping and reproducibility. Online collaboration platforms for machine learning go further by allowing scientists to automatically share, organize and discuss experiments, data, and algorithms.

A number of relevant services and open source software exist:

Services

Name	Interfaces
Comet ml	Pylthon
OpenML	REST, Python, Java, R

Software

Name	Interfaces	Store
OpenMl Docker	REST, Python, Java, R	MySQL
sacred	Python	file, MongoDB, TinyDB, SQL

Examples

The number and diversity of hyperparameters in machine learning algorithms is very specific to each model. However, there some classic hyperparameters that we should always keep our eyes on and that should help you think about this aspect of machine learning solutions:

— Learning Rate: The mother of all hyperparameters, the learning rate quantifies the learning progress of a model in a way that can be used to optimize its capacity.

— Number of Hidden Units: A classic hyperparameter in deep learning algorithms, the number of hidden units is key to regulate the representational capacity of a model.

— Convolution Kernel Width: In convolutional Neural Networks(CNNs), the Kernel Width influences the number of parameters in a model which, in turns, influences its capacity.

Ensemble Averaging

In general, ensembling is a technique of combining two or more algorithms of similar or dissimilar types called base learners. This is done to make a more robust system which incorporates the predictions from all the base learners. It can be understood as conference room meeting between multiple traders to make a decision on whether the price of a stock will go up or not.

Since all of them have a different understanding of the stock market and thus a different mapping function from the problem statement to the desired outcome. Therefore, they are supposed to make varied predictions on the stock price based on their own understandings of the market.

Now we can take all of these predictions into account while making the final decision. This will make our final decision more robust, accurate and less likely to be biased. The final decision would have been opposite if one of these traders would have made this decision alone.

You can consider another example of a candidate going through multiple rounds of job interviews. The final decision of candidate's ability is generally taken based on the feedback of all the interviewers. Although a single interviewer might not be able to test the candidate for each required skill and trait. But the combined feedback of multiple interviewers usually helps in better assessment of the candidate.

Ensemble averaging is one of the simplest types of committee machines. Along with boosting, it is one of the two major types of static committee machines. In contrast to standard network design in which many networks are generated but only one is kept, ensemble averaging keeps the less satisfactory networks around, but with less weight. The theory of ensemble averaging relies on two properties of artificial neural networks:

1.   In any network, the bias can be reduced at the cost of increased variance

2.   In a group of networks, the variance can be reduced at no cost to bias

Ensemble averaging creates a group of networks, each with low bias and high variance, then combines them to a new network with (hopefully) low bias and low variance. It is thus a resolution of the bias-variance dilemma. The idea of combining experts has been traced back to Pierre-Simon Laplace.

Method

Create a set of experts with low bias and high variance, and then average them. Generally, what this means is to create a set of experts with varying parameters; frequently, these are the initial synaptic weights, although other factors (such as the learning rate, momentum etc.) may be varied as well. Some authors recommend against varying weight decay and early stopping. The steps are therefore:

1. Generate N experts, each with their own initial values. (Initial values are usually chosen randomly from a distribution.)

2. Train each expert separately.

3. Combine the experts and average their values.

Alternatively, domain knowledge may be used to generate several *classes* of experts. An expert from each class is trained, and then combined.

A more complex version of ensemble average views the final result not as a mere average of all the experts, but rather as a weighted sum. If each expert is y_i, then the overall result $\tilde{y}$ can be defined as:

$$\tilde{y}(X;\alpha) = \sum_{j=1}^{p} \alpha_j y_j(X)$$

where α is a set of weights. The optimization problem of finding alpha is readily solved through neural networks, hence a "meta-network" where each "neuron" is in fact an entire neural network can be trained, and the synaptic weights of the final network is the weight applied to each expert. This is known as a *linear combination of experts*.

It can be seen that most forms of neural networks are some subset of a linear combination: the standard neural net (where only one expert is used) is simply a linear combination with all $\alpha_j = 0$ and one $\alpha_k = 1$. A raw average is where all α_j are equal to some constant value, namely one over the total number of experts.

A more recent ensemble averaging method is negative correlation learning, proposed by Y. Liu and X. Yao. Now this method has been widely used in evolutionary computing.

Benefits

- The resulting committee is almost always less complex than a single network which would achieve the same level of performance

- The resulting committee can be trained more easily on smaller input sets

- The resulting committee often has improved performance over any single network

- The risk of overfitting is lessened, as there are fewer parameters (weights) which need to be set

Types of Ensembling

Some of the basic concepts which you should be aware of before we go into further detail are:

- Averaging: It's defined as taking the average of predictions from models in case of regression problem or while predicting probabilities for the classification problem.

Model1	Model2	Model3	AveragePrediction
45	40	65	50

- Majority vote: It's defined as taking the prediction with maximum vote / recommendation from multiple models predictions while predicting the outcomes of a classification problem.

Model1	Model2	Model3	VotingPrediction
1	0	1	1

- Weighted average: In this, different weights are applied to predictions from multiple models then taking the average which means giving high or low importance to specific model output.

	Model1	Model2	Model3	WeightAveragePrediction
Weight	0.4	0.3	0.3	
Prediction	45	40	60	48

Practically speaking, there can be a countless number of ways in which you can ensemble different models. But these are some techniques that are mostly used:

1. Bagging: Bagging is also referred to as bootstrap aggregation. To understand bagging, we first need to understand bootstrapping. Bootstrapping is a sampling technique in which we choose 'n' observations or rows out of the original dataset of 'n' rows as well. But the key is that each row is selected with replacement from the original dataset so that each row is equally likely to be selected in each iteration. Let's say we have 3 rows numbered 1, 2 and 3.

Data	Bootstraped Sample
Row 1	
Row 2	
Row 3	

For bootstrapped sample, we choose one out of these three randomly. Say we chose Row

Data		Bootstraped Sample
Row 1		Row 2
Row 2		
Row 3		

You see that even though Row 2 is chosen from the data to the bootstrap sample, it's still present in the data. Now, each of the three:

Data		Bootstraped Sample
Row 1		Row 2
Row 2		Row 1
Row 3		

Rows have the same probability of being selected again. Let's say we choose Row 1 this time.

Again, each row in the data has the same probability to be chosen for Bootstrapped sample. Let's say we randomly choose Row 1 again.

Data		Bootstraped Sample
Row 1		Row 2
Row 2		Row 1
Row 3		Row 1

Thus, we can have multiple bootstrapped samples from the same data. Once we have these multiple bootstrapped samples, we can grow trees for each of these bootstrapped samples and use the majority vote or averaging concepts to get the final prediction. This is how bagging works.

One important thing to note here is that it's done mainly to reduce the variance. Now, random forest actually uses this concept but it goes a step ahead to further reduce the variance by randomly choosing a subset of features as well for each bootstrapped sample to make the splits while training.

2. Boosting: Boosting is a sequential technique in which, the first algorithm is trained on the entire dataset and the subsequent algorithms are built by fitting the residuals of the first algorithm, thus giving higher weight to those observations that were poorly predicted by the previous model.

It relies on creating a series of weak learners each of which might not be good for the entire dataset but is good for some part of the dataset. Thus, each model actually boosts the performance of the ensemble.

It's really important to note that boosting is focused on reducing the bias. This makes the boosting algorithms prone to overfitting. Thus, parameter tuning becomes a crucial part of boosting algorithms to make them avoid overfitting.

Some examples of boosting are XGBoost, GBM, ADABOOST, etc.

3. Stacking: In stacking multiple layers of machine learning models are placed one over another where each of the models passes their predictions to the model in the layer above it and the top layer model takes decisions based on the outputs of the models in layers below it.

Let's understand it with an example:

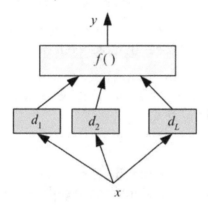

Here, we have two layers of machine learning models:

- Bottom layer models (d_1, d_2, d_3) which receive the original input features(x) from the dataset.

- Top layer model, f() which takes the output of the bottom layer models (d_1, d_2, d_3) as its input and predicts the final output.

- One key thing to note here is that out of fold predictions are used while predicting for the training data.

Here, we have used only two layers but it can be any number of layers and any number of models in each layer. Two of the key principles for selecting the models:

- The individual models fulfill particular accuracy criteria.

- The model predictions of various individual models are not highly correlated with the predictions of other models.

One thing that you might have realized is that we have used the top layer model which takes as input the predictions of the bottom layer models. This top layer model can also be replaced by many other simpler formulas like:

- Averaging

- Majority vote

- Weighted average

Advantages and Disadvantages of ensembling

Advantages

- Ensembling is a proven method for improving the accuracy of the model and works in most of the cases.

- It is the key ingredient for winning almost all of the machine learning hackathons.

- Ensembling makes the model more robust and stable thus ensuring decent performance on the test cases in most scenarios.

- You can use ensembling to capture linear and simple as well non-linear complex relationships in the data. This can be done by using two different models and forming an ensemble of two.

Disadvantages

- Ensembling reduces the model interpretability and makes it very difficult to draw any crucial business insights at the end.

- It is time-consuming and thus might not be the best idea for real-time applications.

- The selection of models for creating an ensemble is an art which is really hard to master.

Supervised Learning

Supervised learning, in the context of artificial intelligence (AI) and machine learning, is a type of system in which both input and desired output data are provided. Input and output data are labelled for classification to provide a learning basis for future data processing.

Supervised learning is where you have input variables (x) and an output variable (Y) and you use an algorithm to learn the mapping function from the input to the output.

$$Y = f(X)$$

The goal is to approximate the mapping function so well that when you have new input data (x) that you can predict the output variables (Y) for that data.

It is called supervised learning because the process of an algorithm learning from the training dataset can be thought of as a teacher supervising the learning process. We know the correct answers, the algorithm iteratively makes predictions on the training data and is corrected by the teacher. Learning stops when the algorithm achieves an acceptable level of performance.

Steps

In order to solve a given problem of supervised learning, one has to perform the following steps:

1. Determine the type of training examples. Before doing anything else, the user should decide what kind of data is to be used as a training set. In case of handwriting analysis, for example, this might be a single handwritten character, an entire handwritten word, or an entire line of handwriting.

2. Gather a training set. The training set needs to be representative of the real-world use of the function. Thus, a set of input objects is gathered and corresponding outputs are also gathered, either from human experts or from measurements.

3. Determine the input feature representation of the learned function. The accuracy of the learned function depends strongly on how the input object is represented. Typically, the input object is transformed into a feature vector, which contains a number of features that are descriptive of the object. The number of features should not be too large, because of the curse of dimensionality; but should contain enough information to accurately predict the output.

4. Determine the structure of the learned function and corresponding learning algorithm. For example, the engineer may choose to use support vector machines or decision trees.

5. Complete the design. Run the learning algorithm on the gathered training set. Some supervised learning algorithms require the user to determine certain control parameters. These parameters may be adjusted by optimizing performance on a subset (called a *validation* set) of the training set, or via cross-validation.

6. Evaluate the accuracy of the learned function. After parameter adjustment and learning, the performance of the resulting function should be measured on a test set that is separate from the training set.

Algorithm Choice

A wide range of supervised learning algorithms are available, each with its strengths and weaknesses. There is no single learning algorithm that works best on all supervised learning problems.

There are four major issues to consider in supervised learning:

Bias-variance Tradeoff

A first issue is the tradeoff between *bias* and *variance*. Imagine that we have available several different, but equally good, training data sets. A learning algorithm is biased for a particular input x if, when trained on each of these data sets, it is systematically incorrect when predicting the correct output for x. A learning algorithm has high variance for a particular input x if it predicts different output values when trained on different training sets. The prediction error of a learned classifier is related to the sum of the bias and the variance of the learning algorithm. Generally, there is a tradeoff between bias and variance. A learning algorithm with low bias must be "flexible" so that it can fit the data well. But if the learning algorithm is too flexible, it will fit each training data set differently, and hence have high variance. A key aspect of many supervised learning methods is that they are able to adjust this tradeoff between bias and variance (either automatically or by providing a bias/variance parameter that the user can adjust).

Function Complexity and Amount of Training Data

The second issue is the amount of training data available relative to the complexity of the "true" function (classifier or regression function). If the true function is simple, then an "inflexible" learning algorithm with high bias and low variance will be able to learn it from a small amount of data. But if the true function is highly complex (e.g., because it involves complex interactions among many different input features and behaves differently in different parts of the input space), then the function will only be learnable from a very large amount of training data and using a "flexible" learning algorithm with low bias and high variance.

Dimensionality of the Input Space

A third issue is the dimensionality of the input space. If the input feature vectors have very high dimension, the learning problem can be difficult even if the true function only depends on a small number of those features. This is because the many "extra" dimensions can confuse the learning algorithm and cause it to have high variance. Hence, high input dimensionality typically requires tuning the classifier to have low variance and high bias. In practice, if the engineer can manually remove irrelevant features from the input data, this is likely to improve the accuracy of the learned function. In addition, there are many algorithms for feature selection that seek to identify the relevant features and discard the irrelevant ones. This is an instance of the more general strategy of dimensionality reduction, which seeks to map the input data into a lower-dimensional space prior to running the supervised learning algorithm.

Noise in the Output Values

A fourth issue is the degree of noise in the desired output values (the supervisory target variables). If the desired output values are often incorrect (because of human error or sensor errors), then the learning algorithm should not attempt to find a function that exactly matches the training examples. Attempting to fit the data too carefully leads to overfitting. You can overfit even when there are no measurement errors (stochastic noise) if the function you are trying to learn is too complex for your learning model. In such a situation, the part of the target function that cannot be modeled "corrupts" your training data - this phenomenon has been called deterministic noise. When either type of noise is present, it is better to go with a higher bias, lower variance estimator.

In practice, there are several approaches to alleviate noise in the output values such as early stopping to prevent overfitting as well as detecting and removing the noisy training examples prior to training the supervised learning algorithm. There are several algorithms that identify noisy training examples and removing the suspected noisy training examples prior to training has decreased generalization error with statistical significance.

Other Factors to Consider

Other factors to consider when choosing and applying a learning algorithm include the following:

- Heterogeneity of the data. If the feature vectors include features of many different kinds (discrete, discrete ordered, counts, continuous values), some algorithms are easier to apply than others. Many algorithms, including Support Vector Machines, linear regression, logistic regression, neural networks, and nearest neighbor methods, require that the input features be numerical and scaled to similar ranges (e.g., to the [-1,1] interval). Methods that employ a distance function, such as nearest neighbor methods and support vector machines with Gaussian kernels, are particularly sensitive to this. An advantage of decision trees is that they easily handle heterogeneous data.

- Redundancy in the data. If the input features contain redundant information (e.g., highly correlated features), some learning algorithms (e.g., linear regression, logistic regression, and distance based methods) will perform poorly because of numerical instabilities. These problems can often be solved by imposing some form of regularization.

- Presence of interactions and non-linearities. If each of the features makes an independent contribution to the output, then algorithms based on linear functions (e.g., linear regression, logistic regression, Support Vector Machines, naive Bayes) and distance functions (e.g., nearest neighbor methods, support vector machines with Gaussian kernels) generally perform well. However, if there are complex interactions among features, then algorithms such as decision trees and neural networks work better, because they are specifically designed to discover these interactions. Linear methods can also be applied, but the engineer must manually specify the interactions when using them.

When considering a new application, the engineer can compare multiple learning algorithms and experimentally determine which one works best on the problem at hand. Tuning the performance of a learning algorithm can be very time-consuming. Given fixed resources, it is often better to spend more time collecting additional training data and more informative features than it is to spend extra time tuning the learning algorithms.

Algorithms

The most widely used learning algorithms are:

- Support Vector Machines
- linear regression
- logistic regression
- naive Bayes
- linear discriminant analysis
- decision trees
- k-nearest neighbor algorithm
- Neural Networks (Multilayer perceptron)

Working of Supervised Learning Algorithms

Given a set of N training examples of the form $\{(x_1, y_1), ..., (x_N, y_N)\}$ such that x_i is the feature vector of the i-th example and y_i is its label (i.e., class), a learning algorithm seeks a function $g : X \to Y$, where X is the input space and Y is the output space. The function g is an element of some space of possible functions G, usually called the *hypothesis space*. It is sometimes convenient to represent g using a scoring function $f : X \times Y \to \mathbb{R}$ such that g is defined as returning the y value that gives the highest score: $g(x) = \arg\max_y f(x, y)$. Let F denote the space of scoring functions.

Although G and F can be any space of functions, many learning algorithms are probabilistic models where g takes the form of a conditional probability model $g(x) = P(y \mid x)$, or f takes the form of a joint probability model $f(x, y) = P(x, y)$. For example, naive

Bayes and linear discriminant analysis are joint probability models, whereas logistic regression is a conditional probability model.

There are two basic approaches to choosing f or g: empirical risk minimization and structural risk minimization. Empirical risk minimization seeks the function that best fits the training data. Structural risk minimization includes a *penalty function* that controls the bias/variance tradeoff.

In both cases, it is assumed that the training set consists of a sample of independent and identically distributed pairs, (x_i, y_i). In order to measure how well a function fits the training data, a loss function $L: Y \times Y \to \mathbb{R}^{\geq 0}$ is defined. For training example (x_i, y_i), the loss of predicting the value $\hat{y}$ is $L(y_i, \hat{y})$.

The *risk* $R(g)$ of function g is defined as the expected loss of g. This can be estimated from the training data as

$$R_{emp}(g) = \frac{1}{N} \sum_i L(y_i, g(x_i)).$$

Empirical Risk Minimization

In empirical risk minimization, the supervised learning algorithm seeks the function g that minimizes $R(g)$. Hence, a supervised learning algorithm can be constructed by applying an optimization algorithm to find g.

When g is a conditional probability distribution $P(y \mid x)$ and the loss function is the negative log likelihood: $L(y, \hat{y}) = -\log P(y \mid x)$, then empirical risk minimization is equivalent to maximum likelihood estimation.

When G contains many candidate functions or the training set is not sufficiently large, empirical risk minimization leads to high variance and poor generalization. The learning algorithm is able to memorize the training examples without generalizing well. This is called overfitting.

Structural Risk Minimization

Structural risk minimization seeks to prevent overfitting by incorporating a regularization penalty into the optimization. The regularization penalty can be viewed as implementing a form of Occam's razor that prefers simpler functions over more complex ones.

A wide variety of penalties have been employed that correspond to different definitions of complexity. For example, consider the case where the function g is a linear function of the form

$$g(x) = \sum_{j=1}^{d} \beta_j x_j.$$

A popular regularization penalty is $\sum_j \beta_j^2$, which is the squared Euclidean norm of the weights, also known as the L_2 norm. Other norms include the L_1 norm, $\sum_j |\beta_j|$, and the L_0 norm, which is the number of non-zero β_j s. The penalty will be denoted by $C(g)$.

The supervised learning optimization problem is to find the function g that minimizes

$$J(g) = R_{emp}(g) + \lambda C(g).$$

The parameter λ controls the bias-variance tradeoff. When $\lambda = 0$, this gives empirical risk minimization with low bias and high variance. When λ is large, the learning algorithm will have high bias and low variance. The value of λ can be chosen empirically via cross validation.

The complexity penalty has a Bayesian interpretation as the negative log prior probability of g, $-\log P(g)$, in which case $J(g)$ is the posterior probabability of g.

Generative Training

The training methods described above are *discriminative training* methods, because they seek to find a function g that discriminates well between the different output values. For the special case where $f(x, y) = P(x, y)$ is a joint probability distribution and the loss function is the negative log likelihood $-\sum \log P(x_i, y_i)$, a risk minimization algorithm is said to perform *generative training*, because f can be regarded as a generative model that explains how the data were generated. Generative training algorithms are often simpler and more computationally efficient than discriminative training algorithms. In some cases, the solution can be computed in closed form as in naive Bayes and linear discriminant analysis.

Generalizations

There are several ways in which the standard supervised learning problem can be generalized:

- Semi-supervised learning: In this setting, the desired output values are provided only for a subset of the training data. The remaining data is unlabeled.

- Active learning: Instead of assuming that all of the training examples are given at the start, active learning algorithms interactively collect new examples, typically by making queries to a human user. Often, the queries are based on unlabeled data, which is a scenario that combines semi-supervised learning with active learning.

- Structured prediction: When the desired output value is a complex object, such as a parse tree or a labeled graph, then standard methods must be extended.

- Learning to rank: When the input is a set of objects and the desired output is a ranking of those objects, then again the standard methods must be extended.

Approaches and Algorithms

- Analytical learning
- Artificial neural network
- Backpropagation
- Boosting (meta-algorithm)
- Bayesian statistics
- Case-based reasoning
- Decision tree learning
- Inductive logic programming
- Gaussian process regression
- Genetic Programming
- Group method of data handling
- Kernel estimators
- Learning Automata
- Learning Classifier Systems
- Minimum message length (decision trees, decision graphs, etc.)
- Multilinear subspace learning
- Naive bayes classifier
- Maximum entropy classifier
- Conditional random field
- Nearest Neighbor Algorithm
- Probably approximately correct learning (PAC) learning
- Ripple down rules, a knowledge acquisition methodology
- Symbolic machine learning algorithms
- Subsymbolic machine learning algorithms
- Support vector machines
- Minimum Complexity Machines (MCM)
- Random Forests

- Ensembles of Classifiers
- Ordinal classification
- Data Pre-processing
- Handling imbalanced datasets
- Statistical relational learning
- Proaftn, a multicriteria classification algorithm

Applications

- Bioinformatics
- Cheminformatics
  - o   Quantitative structure–activity relationship
- Database marketing
- Handwriting recognition
- Information retrieval
  - o   Learning to rank
- Information extraction
- Object recognition in computer vision
- Optical character recognition
- Spam detection
- Pattern recognition
- Speech recognition
- Supervised learning is a special case of Downward causation in biological systems

Semi-supervised Learning

Semi-supervised learning(SSL) is one of the artificial intelligence(AI) methods that have become popular in the last few months. Companies such as Google have been advancing the tools and frameworks relevant for building semi-supervised learning applications. Google Expander is a great example of a tool that reflects the advancements in semi-supervised learning applications.

Conceptually, semi-supervised learning can be positioned halfway between unsupervised and supervised learning models. A semi-supervised learning problem starts with a series of labeled data points as well as some data point for which labels are not known.

The goal of a semi-supervised model is to classify some of the unlabeled data using the labeled information set.

Some AI practitioners see semi-supervised learning as a form of supervised learning with additional information. At the end, the goal of semi-supervised learning models is to sesame as supervised ones: to predict a target value for a specific input data set. Alternatively, other segments of the AI community see semi-supervised learning as a form of unsupervised learning with constraints.

Assumptions used

In order to make any use of unlabeled data, we must assume some structure to the underlying distribution of data. Semi-supervised learning algorithms make use of at least one of the following assumptions.

Continuity Assumption

Points which are close to each other are more likely to share a label. This is also generally assumed in supervised learning and yields a preference for geometrically simple decision boundaries. In the case of semi-supervised learning, the smoothness assumption additionally yields a preference for decision boundaries in low-density regions, so that there are fewer points close to each other but in different classes.

Cluster Assumption

The data tend to form discrete clusters, and points in the same cluster are more likely to share a label (although data sharing a label may be spread across multiple clusters). This is a special case of the smoothness assumption and gives rise to feature learning with clustering algorithms.

Manifold Assumption

The data lie approximately on a manifold of much lower dimension than the input space. In this case we can attempt to learn the manifold using both the labeled and unlabeled data to avoid the curse of dimensionality. Then learning can proceed using distances and densities defined on the manifold.

The manifold assumption is practical when high-dimensional data are being generated by some process that may be hard to model directly, but which only has a few degrees of freedom. For instance, human voice is controlled by a few vocal folds, and images of various facial expressions are controlled by a few muscles. We would like in these cases to use distances and smoothness in the natural space of the generating problem, rather than in the space of all possible acoustic waves or images respectively.

Methods

Generative Models

Generative approaches to statistical learning first seek to estimate $p(x \mid y)$, the distribution of data points belonging to each class. The probability $p(y \mid x) p(y \mid x)$ that a given point has label y is then proportional $p(x \mid y) p(y)$ to by Bayes' rule. Semi-supervised learning with generative models can be viewed either as an extension of supervised learning (classification plus information about $p(x)$) or as an extension of unsupervised learning (clustering plus some labels).

Generative models assume that the distributions take some particular form $p(x \mid y, \theta)$ parameterized by the vector θ. If these assumptions are incorrect, the unlabeled data may actually decrease the accuracy of the solution relative to what would have been obtained from labeled data alone. However, if the assumptions are correct, then the unlabeled data necessarily improves performance.

The unlabeled data are distributed according to a mixture of individual-class distributions. In order to learn the mixture distribution from the unlabeled data, it must be identifiable, that is, different parameters must yield different summed distributions. Gaussian mixture distributions are identifiable and commonly used for generative models.

The parameterized joint distribution can be written as $p(x, y \mid \theta) = p(y \mid \theta) p(x \mid y, \theta) p(x, y \mid \theta)$ by using the Chain rule. Each parameter vector θ is associated with a decision function $f_\theta(x) = \text{argmax } p(y \mid x, \theta)$. The parameter is then chosen based on fit to both the labeled and unlabeled data, weighted by λ:

$$\underset{\Theta}{\text{argmax}} \left(\log p(\{x_i, y_i\}_{i=1}^l \mid \theta) + \lambda \log p(\{x_i\}_{i=l+1}^{l+u} \mid \theta) \right)$$

Low-density Separation

Another major class of methods attempts to place boundaries in regions where there are few data points (labeled or unlabeled). One of the most commonly used algorithms is the transductive support vector machine, or TSVM (which, despite its name, may be used for inductive learning as well). Whereas support vector machines for supervised learning seek a decision boundary with maximal margin over the labeled data, the goal of TSVM is a labeling of the unlabeled data such that the decision boundary has maximal margin over all of the data. In addition to the standard hinge loss $(1 - yf(x))_+$ for labeled data, a loss function $(1 - |f(x)|)_+$ is introduced over the unlabeled data by letting $y = \text{sign } f(x)$. TSVM then selects $f^*(x) = h^*(x) + b$ from a reproducing kernel Hilbert space $\mathcal{H}$ by minimizing the regularized empirical risk:

$$f^* = \underset{f}{\text{argmin}} \left(\sum_{i=1}^l (1 - y_i f(x_i))_+ + \lambda_1 \|h\|_{\mathcal{H}}^2 + \lambda_2 \sum_{i=l+1}^{l+u} (1 - |f(x_i)|)_+ \right)$$

An exact solution is intractable due to the non-convex term $(1-|f(x)|)_+$, so research has focused on finding useful approximations.

Other approaches that implement low-density separation include Gaussian process models, information regularization, and entropy minimization (of which TSVM is a special case).

Graph-based Methods

Graph-based methods for semi-supervised learning use a graph representation of the data, with a node for each labeled and unlabeled example. The graph may be constructed using domain knowledge or similarity of examples; two common methods are to connect each data point to its k nearest neighbors or to examples within some distance ϵ. The weight W_{ij} of an edge between x_i and x_j is then set to.

$$e^{\dfrac{-\|x_i - x_j\|^2}{\epsilon}}.$$

Within the framework of manifold regularization, the graph serves as a proxy for the manifold. A term is added to the standard Tikhonov regularization problem to enforce smoothness of the solution relative to the manifold (in the intrinsic space of the problem) as well as relative to the ambient input space. The minimization problem becomes

$$\underset{f \in \mathcal{H}}{\operatorname{argmin}}\left(\frac{1}{l}\sum_{i=1}^{l} V(f(x_i), y_i) + \lambda_A \| f \|_{\mathcal{H}}^2 + \lambda_I \int_M \| \nabla_M f(x) \|^2 dp(x) \right)$$

where $\mathcal{H}$ is a reproducing kernel Hilbert space and $\mathcal{M}$ is the manifold on which the data lie. The regularization parameters λ_A and λ_I control smoothness in the ambient and intrinsic spaces respectively. The graph is used to approximate the intrinsic regularization term. Defining the graph Laplacian $L = D - W$ where $D_{ii} = \sum_{j=1}^{l+u} W_{ij}$ and f the vector $[f(x_1)...f(x_{l+u})]$ we have

$$\mathbf{f}^T L \mathbf{f} = \sum_{i,j=1}^{l+u} W_{ij}(f_i - f_j)^2 \approx \int_M \| \nabla_M f(x) \|^2 dp(x)$$

The Laplacian can also be used to extend the supervised learning algorithms: regularized least squares and support vector machines (SVM) to semi-supervised versions Laplacian regularized least squares and Laplacian SVM.

Heuristic Approaches

Some methods for semi-supervised learning are not intrinsically geared to learning from both unlabeled and labeled data, but instead make use of unlabeled data within a supervised learning framework. For instance, the labeled and unlabeled examples may inform a choice of representation, distance metric, or kernel for the data in an unsupervised first step. Then supervised learning proceeds from only the labeled examples.

Self-training is a wrapper method for semi-supervised learning. First a supervised learning algorithm is trained based on the labeled data only. This classifier is then applied to the unlabeled data to generate more labeled examples as input for the supervised learning algorithm. Generally only the labels the classifier is most confident of are added at each step.

Co-training is an extension of self-training in which multiple classifiers are trained on different (ideally disjoint) sets of features and generate labeled examples for one another.

In Human Cognition

Human responses to formal semi-supervised learning problems have yielded varying conclusions about the degree of influence of the unlabeled data. More natural learning problems may also be viewed as instances of semi-supervised learning. Much of human concept learning involves a small amount of direct instruction (e.g. parental labeling of objects during childhood) combined with large amounts of unlabeled experience (e.g. observation of objects without naming or counting them, or at least without feedback).

Human infants are sensitive to the structure of unlabeled natural categories such as images of dogs and cats or male and female faces. More recent work has shown that infants and children take into account not only the unlabeled examples available, but the sampling process from which labeled examples arise.

Semi-Supervised Learning in the Real World

Semi-supervised learning models are becoming widely applicable in scenarios across a large variety of industries. Let's explore a few of the most well-known examples:

- Speech Analysis: Speech analysis is a classic example of the value of semi-supervised learning models. Labeling audio files typically is a very intensive tasks that requires a lot of human resources. Applying SSL techniques can really help to improve traditional speech analytic models.

- Protein Sequence Classification: Inferring the function of proteins typically requires active human intervention.

- Web Content Classification: Organizing the knowledge available iun billions of web pages will advance different segments of AI. Unfortunately, that task typically requires human intervention to classify the content.

There are plenty of other scenarios for SSL models. However, not all AI scenarios can directly be tackled using SSL. There are a few essential characteristics that should be present on a problem to be effectively solvable using SSL.

1. Sizable Unlabeled Dataset: In SSL scenarios, the seize of the unlabeled dataset should be substantially bigger than the labeled data. Otherwise, the problem can be simply addressed using supervised algorithms.

2. Input-Output Proximity Symmetry: SSL operates by inferring classification for unlabeled data based on proximity with labeled data points. Inverting that reasoning, SSL scenarios entail that if two data points are part of the same cluster (determined by a K-means algo or similar) their outputs are likely to be in close proximity as well. Complementarily, if two data points are separated by a low density area, their output should not be close.

3. Relatively Simple Labeling & Low-Dimension Nature of the Problem: In SSL scenarios, it is important that the inference of the labeled data doesn't become a problem more complicated than the original problem. This is known in AI circles as the "Vapnik Principle" which essentially states that in order to solve a problem we should not pick an intermediate problem of a higher order of complexity. Also, problems that use datasets with many dimensions or attributes are likely to become really challenging for SSL algorithms as the labeling task will become very complex.

Active Learning

The main hypothesis in active learning is that if a learning algorithm can choose the data it wants to learn from, it can perform better than traditional methods with substantially less data for training.

But what are these traditional methods exactly?

These are tasks which involve gathering a large amount of data randomly sampled from the underlying distribution and using this large dataset to train a model that can perform some sort of prediction. You will call this typical method *passive learning*.

One of the more time-consuming tasks in passive learning is collecting labelled data. In many settings, there can be limiting factors that hamper gathering large amounts of labelled data.

Let's take the example of studying pancreatic cancer. You might want to predict whether a patient will get pancreatic cancer, however, you might only have the opportunity to give a small number of patients further examinations to collect features, etc. In this case, rather than selecting patients at random, we can select patients based on certain criteria. An example criteria might be if the patient drinks alcohol and is over 40 years. This criteria does not have to be static but can change depending on results from previous patients. For example, if you realised that your model is good at predicting pancreatic cancer for those over 50 years, but struggle to make accurate prediction for those between 40-50 years, this might be your new criteria.

The process of selecting these patients (or more generally instances) based upon the data we have collected so far is called *active learning*.

Let T be the total set of all data under consideration. For example, in a protein engineering problem, T would include all proteins that are known to have a certain interesting activity and all additional proteins that one might want to test for that activity.

During each iteration, i, T is broken up into three subsets

1. $T_{K,i}$: Data points where the label is known.

2. $T_{U,i}$: Data points where the label is unknown.

3. $T_{C,i}$: A subset of $T_{U,i}$ that is chosen to be labeled.

Most of the current research in active learning involves the best method to choose the data points for $T_{C,i}$.

Query Strategies

Algorithms for determining which data points should be labeled can be organized into a number of different categories:

- Uncertainty sampling: label those points for which the current model is least certain as to what the correct output should be.

- Query by committee: a variety of models are trained on the current labeled data, and vote on the output for unlabeled data; label those points for which the "committee" disagrees the most.

- Expected model change: label those points that would most change the current model.

- Expected error reduction: label those points that would most reduce the model's generalization error.

- Variance reduction: label those points that would minimize output variance, which is one of the components of error.

- Balance exploration and exploitation: the choice of examples to label is seen as a dilemma between the exploration and the exploitation over the data space representation. This strategy manages this compromise by modelling the active learning problem as a contextual bandit problem. For example, Bouneffouf et al. propose a sequential algorithm named Active Thompson Sampling (ATS), which, in each round, assigns a sampling distribution on the pool, samples one point from this distribution, and queries the oracle for this sample point label.

- Exponentiated Gradient Exploration for Active Learning: In this paper, the author proposes a sequential algorithm named exponentiated gradient (EG)-active that can improve any active learning algorithm by an optimal random exploration.

- Querying from diverse subspaces or partitions: When the underlying model is a forest of trees, the leaf nodes might represent (overlapping) partitions of the original feature space. This offers the possibility of selecting instances from non-overlapping or minimally overlapping partitions for labeling.

A wide variety of algorithms have been studied that fall into these categories.

Minimum Marginal Hyperplane

Some active learning algorithms are built upon Support vector machines (SVMs) and exploit the structure of the SVM to determine which data points to label. Such methods usually calculate the margin, W, of each unlabeled datum in $T_{U,i}$ and treat W as an n-dimensional distance from that datum to the separating hyperplane.

Minimum Marginal Hyperplane methods assume that the data with the smallest W are those that the SVM is most uncertain about and therefore should be placed in $T_{C,i}$ to be labeled. Other similar methods, such as Maximum Marginal Hyperplane, choose data with the largest W. Tradeoff methods choose a mix of the smallest and largest Ws.

Applications and Modern Research into Active Learning

One of the most popular areas in active learning is natural language processing (NLP). This is because many applications in NLP require lots of labelled data (for example, Part-of-Speech Tagging, Named Entity Recognition) and there is a very high cost to labelling this data.

In fact, there are only a handful datasets in NLP that are freely available and fully tagged for these applications. Hence, using active learning can significantly reduce the amount of labelled data that is needed and the experts required to accurately label them. This same reasoning can be applied to many speech recognition tasks and even tasks such as information retrieval.

Active learning is still being heavily researched. Many people have begun research into using different deep learning algorithms like CNNs and LSTMS as the learner and how to improve their efficiency when using active learning frameworks. There is also research being done on implementing Generative Adversarial Networks (GANs) into the active learning framework. With the increasing interest into deep reinforcement learning, researchers are trying to reframe active learning as a reinforcement learning problem. Also, there are papers which try to learn active learning strategies via a meta-learning setting.

Reinforcement Learning

Reinforcement learning, in the context of artificial intelligence, is a type of dynamic programming that trains algorithms using a system of reward and punishment.

A reinforcement learning algorithm, or agent, learns by interacting with its environment. The agent receives rewards by performing correctly and penalties for performing incorrectly. The agent learns without intervention from a human by maximizing its reward and minimizing its penalty.

Reinforcement learning is an approach to machine learning that is inspired by behaviorist psychology. It is similar to how a child learns to perform a new task. Reinforcement learning contrasts with other machine learning approaches in that the algorithm is not explicitly told how to perform a task, but works through the problem on its own.

As an agent, which could be a self-driving car or a program playing chess, interacts with its environment, receives a reward state depending on how it performs, such as driving to destination safely or winning a game. Conversely, the agent receives a penalty for performing incorrectly, such as going off the road or being checkmated.

The agent over time makes decisions to maximize its reward and minimize its penalty using dynamic programming. The advantage of this approach to artificial intelligence is that it allows an AI program to learn without a programmer spelling out how an agent should perform the task.

In machine learning, the environment is typically formulated as a Markov Decision Process (MDP), as many reinforcement learning algorithms for this context utilize dynamic programming techniques. The main difference between the classical dynamic programming methods and reinforcement learning algorithms is that the latter do not assume knowledge of an exact mathematical model of the MDP and they target large MDPs where exact methods become infeasible.

Reinforcement learning differs from standard supervised learning in that correct input/output pairs need not be presented, and sub-optimal actions need not be explicitly corrected. Instead the focus is on performance, which involves finding a balance between exploration (of uncharted territory) and exploitation (of current knowledge). The exploration vs. exploitation trade-off has been most thoroughly studied through the multi-armed bandit problem and in finite MDPs.

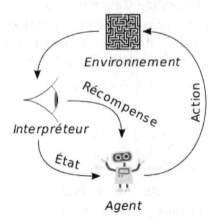

Agent

The typical framing of a Reinforcement Learning (RL) scenario: an agent takes actions in an environment, which is interpreted into a reward and a representation of the state, which are fed back into the agent.

Basic reinforcement is modeled as a Markov decision process:

- a set of environment and agent states, S;

- a set of actions, A, of the agent;

- $P_a(s, s') = Pr(s_{t+1} = s' \mid s_t = s, a_t = a)$ is the probability of transition from state s to state s' under action a.

- $R_a(s, s')$ is the immediate reward after transition from s to s' with action a.

- rules that describe what the agent observes

Rules are often stochastic. The observation typically involves the scalar, immediate reward associated with the last transition. In many works, the agent is assumed to observe the current environmental state (*full observability*). If not, the agent has *partial observability*. Sometimes the set of actions available to the agent is restricted (a zero balance cannot be reduced).

A reinforcement learning agent interacts with its environment in discrete time steps. At each time t, the agent receives an observation o_t which typically includes the reward r_t. It then chooses an action a_t from the set of available actions, which is subsequently sent to the environment. The environment moves to a new state s_{t+1} and the reward r_{t+1} associated with the *transition* (s_t, a_t, s_{t+1}) is determined. The goal of a reinforcement learning agent is to collect as much reward as possible. The agent can (possibly randomly) choose any action as a function of the history.

When the agent's performance is compared to that of an agent that acts optimally, the difference in performance gives rise to the notion of *regret*. In order to act near optimally, the agent must reason about the long term consequences of its actions (i.e., maximize future income), although the immediate reward associated with this might be negative.

Thus, reinforcement learning is particularly well-suited to problems that include a long-term versus short-term reward trade-off. It has been applied successfully to various problems, including robot control, elevator scheduling, telecommunications, backgammon, checkers and go (AlphaGo).

Two elements make reinforcement learning powerful: the use of samples to optimize performance and the use of function approximation to deal with large environments. Thanks to these two key components, reinforcement learning can be used in large environments in the following situations:

- A model of the environment is known, but an analytic solution is not available;

- Only a simulation model of the environment is given (the subject of simulation-based optimization);

- The only way to collect information about the environment is to interact with it.

The first two of these problems could be considered planning problems (since some form of model is available), while the last one could be considered to be a genuine learning problem. However, reinforcement learning converts both planning problems to machine learning problems.

Exploration

Reinforcement learning requires clever exploration mechanisms. Randomly selecting actions, without reference to an estimated probability distribution, shows poor performance. The case of (small) finite Markov decision processes is relatively well understood. However, due to the lack of algorithms that provably scale well with the number of states (or scale to problems with infinite state spaces), simple exploration methods are the most practical.

One such method is ϵ–greedy, when the agent chooses the action that it believes has the best long-term effect with probability $1-\epsilon$, and it chooses an action uniformly at random, otherwise. Here, $0 < \epsilon < 1$ is a tuning parameter, which is sometimes changed, either according to a fixed schedule (making the agent explore progressively less), or adaptively based on heuristics.

Algorithms for Control Learning

Even if the issue of exploration is disregarded and even if the state was observable (assumed hereafter), the problem remains to use past experience to find out which actions are good.

Criterion of Optimality

Policy

The agent's action selection is modeled as a map called *policy*:

$$\pi : S \times A \rightarrow [0,1]$$

$$\pi(a \mid s) = P(a_t = a \mid s_t = s)$$

The policy map gives the probability of taking action a when in state s. There are also non-probabilistic policies.

State-value Function

Value function $V_\pi(s)$ is defined as the *expected return* starting with state s, i.e. $s_0 = s$, and successively following policy π. Hence, roughly speaking, the value function estimates "how good" it is to be in a given state.

$$V_\pi(s) = E[R] = E[\sum_{t=0}^\infty \gamma^t r_t \mid s_0 = s],$$

where the random variable R denotes the return, and is defined as the sum of future discounted rewards

$$R = \sum_{t=0}^\infty \gamma^t r_t,$$

where r_t is the reward at step t, $\gamma \in [0,1]$ is the discount-rate.

The algorithm must find a policy with maximum expected return. From the theory of MDPs it is known that, without loss of generality, the search can be restricted to the set of so-called *stationary* policies. A policy is *stationary* if the action-distribution returned by it depends only on the last state visited (from the observation agent's history). The search can be further restricted to *deterministic* stationary policies. A *deterministic stationary* policy deterministically selects actions based on the current state. Since any such policy can be identified with a mapping from the set of states to the set of actions, these policies can be identified with such mappings with no loss of generality.

Brute Force

The brute force approach entails two steps:

- For each possible policy, sample returns while following it
- Choose the policy with the largest expected return

One problem with this is that the number of policies can be large, or even infinite. Another is that variance of the returns may be large, which requires many samples to accurately estimate the return of each policy.

These problems can be ameliorated if we assume some structure and allow samples generated from one policy to influence the estimates made for others. The two main approaches for achieving this are value function estimation and direct policy search.

Value Function

Value function approaches attempt to find a policy that maximizes the return by maintaining a set of estimates of expected returns for some policy (usually either the "current" [on-policy] or the optimal [off-policy] one).

These methods rely on the theory of MDPs, where optimality is defined in a sense that is stronger than the above one: A policy is called optimal if it achieves the best expected return from *any* initial state (i.e., initial distributions play no role in this definition). Again, an optimal policy can always be found amongst stationary policies.

To define optimality in a formal manner, define the value of a policy π by

$$V^\pi(s) = E[R \,|\, s, \pi],$$

where R stands for the random return associated with following π from the initial state. Defining s as the maximum possible value of $V^*(s)$, where π is allowed to change,

$$V^*(s) = \max_\pi V^\pi(s).$$

A policy that achieves these optimal values in each state is called *optimal*. Clearly, a policy that is optimal in this strong sense is also optimal in the sense that it maximizes the expected return ρ^π, since $\rho^\pi = E[V^\pi(S)]$, where S is a state randomly sampled from the distribution μ.

Although state-values suffice to define optimality, it is useful to define action-values. Given a state s, an action a and a policy π, the action-value of the pair (s, a) under π is defined by

$$Q^\pi(s, a) = E[R \,|\, s, a, \pi],$$

where R now stands for the random return associated with first taking action a in state s and following π, thereafter.

The theory of MDPs states that if π^* is an optimal policy, we act optimally (take the optimal action) by choosing the action from $Q^{\pi^*}(s, \cdot)$ with the highest value at each state, s. The *action-value function* of such an optimal policy (Q^{π^*}) is called the *optimal action-value function* and is commonly denoted by Q^*. In summary, the knowledge of the optimal action-value function alone suffices to know how to act optimally.

Assuming full knowledge of the MDP, the two basic approaches to compute the optimal action-value function are value iteration and policy iteration. Both algorithms compute a sequence of functions Q_k ($k = 0, 1, 2, \ldots$) that converge to Q^*. Computing these functions involves computing expectations over the whole state-space, which is impractical for all but the smallest (finite) MDPs. In reinforcement learning methods, expectations are approximated by averaging over samples and using function approximation techniques to cope with the need to represent value functions over large state-action spaces.

Monte Carlo Methods

Monte Carlo methods can be used in an algorithm that mimics policy iteration. Policy iteration consists of two steps: *policy evaluation* and *policy improvement*.

Monte Carlo is used in the policy evaluation step. In this step, given a stationary, deterministic policy π, the goal is to compute the function values $Q^\pi(s,a)$ (or a good approximation to them) for all state-action pairs (s,a). Assuming (for simplicity) that the MDP is finite, that sufficient memory is available to accommodate the action-values and that the problem is episodic and after each episode a new one starts from some random initial state. Then, the estimate of the value of a given state-action pair (s,a) can be computed by averaging the sampled returns that originated from (s,a) over time. Given sufficient time, this procedure can thus construct a precise estimate Q of the action-value function Q^π. This finishes the description of the policy evaluation step.

In the policy improvement step, the next policy is obtained by computing a *greedy* policy with respect to Q: Given a state s, this new policy returns an action that maximizes $Q(s,\cdot)$. In practice lazy evaluation can defer the computation of the maximizing actions to when they are needed.

Problems with this procedure include:

- The procedure may spend too much time evaluating a suboptimal policy.

- It uses samples inefficiently in that a long trajectory improves the estimate only of the *single* state-action pair that started the trajectory.

- When the returns along the trajectories have *high variance*, convergence is slow.

- It works in episodic problems only;

- It works in small, finite MDPs only.

Temporal Difference Methods

The first problem is corrected by allowing the procedure to change the policy (at some or all states) before the values settle. This too may be problematic as it might prevent convergence. Most current algorithms do this, giving rise to the class of *generalized policy iteration* algorithms. Many *actor critic* methods belong to this category.

The second issue can be corrected by allowing trajectories to contribute to any state-action pair in them. This may also help to some extent with the third problem, although a better solution when returns have high variance is Sutton's temporal difference (TD) methods that are based on the recursive Bellman equation. Note that the computation in TD methods can be incremental (when after each transition the memory is changed and the transition is thrown away), or batch (when the transitions are batched and the estimates are computed once based on the batch). Batch methods, such as the least-squares temporal difference method, may use the information in the samples better, while incremental methods are the only choice when batch methods are infeasible due to their high computational or memory complexity. Some methods try to combine the two approaches. Methods based on temporal differences also overcome the fourth issue.

In order to address the fifth issue, *function approximation methods* are used. *Linear function approximation* starts with a mapping ϕ that assigns a finite-dimensional vector to each state-action pair. Then, the action values of a state-action pair (s,a) are obtained by linearly combining the components of $\phi(s,a)$ with some *weights* θ:

$$Q(s,a) = \sum_{i=1}^{d} \theta_i \phi_i(s,a).$$

The algorithms then adjust the weights, instead of adjusting the values associated with the individual state-action pairs. Methods based on ideas from nonparametric statistics (which can be seen to construct their own features) have been explored.

Value iteration can also be used as a starting point, giving rise to the Q-Learning algorithm and its many variants.

The problem with using action-values is that they may need highly precise estimates of the competing action values that can be hard to obtain when the returns are noisy. Though this problem is mitigated to some extent by temporal difference methods. Using the so-called compatible function approximation method compromises generality and efficiency. Another problem specific to TD comes from their reliance on the recursive Bellman equation. Most TD methods have a so-called λ parameter $(0 \le \lambda \le 1)$ that can continuously interpolate between Monte Carlo methods that do not rely on the Bellman equations and the basic TD methods that rely entirely on the Bellman equations. This can be effective in palliating this issue.

Direct Policy Search

An alternative method is to search directly in (some subset of) the policy space, in which case the problem becomes a case of stochastic optimization. The two approaches available are gradient-based and gradient-free methods.

Gradient-based methods (*policy gradient methods*) start with a mapping from a finite-dimensional (parameter) space to the space of policies: given the parameter vector θ, let π_θ denote the policy associated to θ. Defining the performance function by

$$\rho(\theta) = \rho^{\pi_\theta}.,$$

under mild conditions this function will be differentiable as a function of the parameter vector θ. If the gradient of ρ was known, one could use gradient ascent. Since an analytic expression for the gradient is not available, only a noisy estimate is available. Such an estimate can be constructed in many ways, giving rise to algorithms such as

Williams' REINFORCE method (which is known as the likelihood ratio method in the simulation-based optimization literature). Policy search methods have been used in the robotics context. Many policy search methods may get stuck in local optima (as they are based on local search).

A large class of methods avoids relying on gradient information.These include simulated annealing, cross-entropy search or methods of evolutionary computation. Many gradient-free methods can achieve (in theory and in the limit) a global optimum. In multiple domains they have demonstrated performance.

Policy search methods may converge slowly given noisy data. For example, this happens in episodic problems when the trajectories are long and the variance of the returns is large. Value-function based methods that rely on temporal differences might help in this case. In recent years, *actor–critic methods* have been proposed and performed well on various problems.

Theory

Both the asymptotic and finite-sample behavior of most algorithms is well understood. Algorithms with provably good online performance (addressing the exploration issue) are known.

Efficient exploration of large MDPs is largely unexplored (except for the case of bandit problems). Although finite-time performance bounds appeared for many algorithms, these bounds are expected to be rather loose and thus more work is needed to better understand the relative advantages and limitations.

For incremental algorithms, asymptotic convergence issues have been settled. Temporal-difference-based algorithms converge under a wider set of conditions than was previously possible (for example, when used with arbitrary, smooth function approximation).

Research

Research topics include

- adaptive methods that work with fewer (or no) parameters under a large number of condition

- addressing the exploration problem in large MDPs

- large-scale empirical evaluations

- learning and acting under partial information (e.g., using Predictive State Representation)

- modular and hierarchical reinforcement learning

- improving existing value-function and policy search methods

- algorithms that work well with large (or continuous) action spaces
- transfer learning
- lifelong learning
- efficient sample-based planning (e.g., based on Monte Carlo tree search).

Multiagent or distributed reinforcement learning is a topic of interest. Applications are expanding.

Reinforcement learning algorithms such as TD learning are under investigation as a model for dopamine-based learning in the brain. In this model, the dopaminergic projections from the substantia nigra to the basal ganglia function as the prediction error. Reinforcement learning has been used as a part of the model for human skill learning, especially in relation to the interaction between implicit and explicit learning in skill acquisition.

End-to-end Reinforcement Learning

The work on learning ATARI TV games by Google DeepMind increased attention to end-to-end reinforcement learning or deep reinforcement learning. This approach extends reinforcement learning to the entire process from observation to action (sensors to motors or end to end) by forming it using a deep network and without explicitly designing state space or action space.

Inverse Reinforcement Learning

In inverse reinforcement learning (IRL), no reward function is given. Instead, the reward function is inferred given an observed behavior from an expert. The idea is to mimic observed behavior, which is often optimal or close to optimal.

Apprenticeship Learning

In apprenticeship learning, an expert demonstrates the target behavior. The system tries to recover the policy via observation.

Recent Advancements in Reinforcement Learning

With the recent success in Deep Learning, now the focus is slowly shifting to applying deep learning to solve reinforcement learning problems. The news recently has been flooded with the defeat of Lee Sedol by a deep reinforcement learning algorithm developed by Google DeepMind. Similar breakthroughs are being seen in video games, where the algorithms developed are achieving human-level accuracy and beyond. Research is still at par, with both industrial and academic masterminds working together to accomplish the goal of building better self-learning robots.

Some major domains where RL has been applied are as follows:

- Game Theory and Multi-Agent Interaction

- Robotics

- Computer Networking

- Vehicular Navigation

- Medicine and

- Industrial Logistic.

References

- Mohri, Mehryar; Rostamizadeh, Afshin; Talwalkar, Ameet (2012). Foundations of Machine Learning. USA, Massachusetts: MIT Press. ISBN 9780262018258

- Goldberg, David E.; Holland, John H. (1988). "Genetic algorithms and machine learning". Machine Learning. 3 (2): 95–99. doi:10.1007/bf00113892

- Cornell University Library. "Breiman: Statistical Modeling: The Two Cultures (with comments and a rejoinder by the author)". Retrieved 8 August 2015

- Char, D. S.; Shah, N. H.; Magnus, D. (2018). "Implementing Machine Learning in Health Care – Addressing Ethical Challenges". New England Journal of Medicine. 378 (11): 981–983. doi:10.1056/nejmp1714229. PMID 29539284

- Mehryar Mohri, Afshin Rostamizadeh, Ameet Talwalkar (2012) Foundations of Machine Learning, The MIT Press ISBN 9780262018258

- M. Belkin; P. Niyogi (2004). "Semi-supervised Learning on Riemannian Manifolds". Machine Learning. 56 (Special Issue on Clustering): 209–239. doi:10.1023/b:mach.0000033120.25363.1e

- Settles, Burr (2010), "Active Learning Literature Survey" (PDF), Computer Sciences Technical Report 1648. University of Wisconsin–Madison, retrieved 2014-11-18

- Kaelbling, Leslie P.; Littman, Michael L.; Moore, Andrew W.(1996). "Reinforcement Learning: A Survey". Journal of Artificial Intelligence Research. 4: 237–285. Archived from the original on 2001-11-20

5

Applications of Artificial Intelligence

Artificial intelligence has diverse applications in the modern world, for instance in the fields of electronic trading, robot control, medical diagnosis and remote sensing. The significant applications of AI systems such as software agent, virtual assistant, video game bot, autonomous robot and domestic robot have been thoroughly discussed in this chapter.

Intelligent Agent

An intelligent agent is a type of software application that searches, retrieves and presents information from the Internet. This application automates the process of extracting data from the Internet, such as information selected based on a predefined criterion, keywords or any specified information/entity to be searched. Intelligent agents are often used as Web browsers, news retrieval services and online shopping. An intelligent agent may also be called an agent or bot.

An intelligent agent is primarily used to complement data retrieval tasks, which are traditionally performed manually by humans. Typically, an intelligent agent executes automatically on scheduled time or when manually initiated by the user. It then searches the entire Internet or on user-defined websites to work on the primary search query/request. When a relevancy or match is found, the intelligent agent copies, extracts or lists that data. The collected data is then presented in a raw or report-based format to the user. Some advanced-level intelligent agent utilities use artificial intelligence based data inference matching and retrieval techniques, which allows them to collect higher quality and more relevant data. Popular forms of intelligent agents include shopping agents/bots, news feed/alert agents and Web crawlers.

An example of an agent is Infogate, which alerts you about news on specified topics of interest. A number of similar agents compare shopping prices and bring the news back to the user. Other types of agents include specific site watchers that tell you when the site has been updated or look for other events and analyst agents that not only gather but organize and interpret information for you.

Structure of Agents

A simple agent program can be defined mathematically as an agent function which maps every possible percepts sequence to a possible action the agent can perform or to a coefficient, feedback element, function or constant that affects eventual actions:

$$f : P \to A$$

Agent function is an abstract concept as it could incorporate various principles of decision making like calculation of utility of individual options, deduction over logic rules, fuzzy logic, etc.

The program agent, instead, maps every possible percept to an action.

We use the term percept to refer to the agent's perceptional inputs at any given instant.

Architectures

Weiss (2013) said we should consider four classes of agents:

- Logic-based agents – in which the decision about what action to perform is made via logical deduction;

- Reactive agents – in which decision making is implemented in some form of direct mapping from situation to action;

- Belief-desire-intention agents – in which decision making depends upon the manipulation of data structures representing the beliefs, desires, and intentions of the agent; and finally,

- Layered architectures – in which decision making is realized via various software layers, each of which is more or less explicitly reasoning about the environment at different levels of abstraction.

Classes

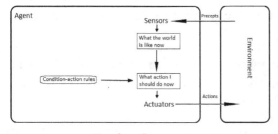

Simple reflex agent

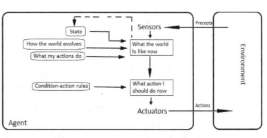

Model-based reflex agent

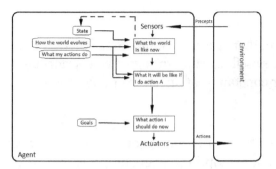

Model-based, goal-based agent

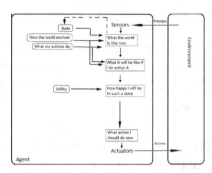

Model-based, utility-based agent

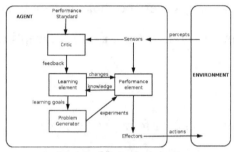

A general learning agent

Russell & Norvig (2003) group agents into five classes based on their degree of perceived intelligence and capability:

1. simple reflex agents

2. model-based reflex agents

3. goal-based agents

4. utility-based agents

5. learning agents

Simple Reflex Agents

Simple reflex agents act only on the basis of the current percept, ignoring the rest of the percept history. The agent function is based on the *condition-action rule*: if condition then action.

This agent function only succeeds when the environment is fully observable. Some reflex agents can also contain information on their current state which allows them to disregard conditions whose actuators are already triggered.

Infinite loops are often unavoidable for simple reflex agents operating in partially observable environments. Note: If the agent can randomize its actions, it may be possible to escape from infinite loops.

Model-based Reflex Agents

A model-based agent can handle partially observable environments. Its current state is stored inside the agent maintaining some kind of structure which describes the part of the world which cannot be seen. This knowledge about "how the world works" is called a model of the world, hence the name "model-based agent".

A model-based reflex agent should maintain some sort of internal model that depends on the percept history and thereby reflects at least some of the unobserved aspects of the current state. Percept history and impact of action on the environment can be determined by using internal model. It then chooses an action in the same way as reflex agent.

Goal-based Agents

Goal-based agents further expand on the capabilities of the model-based agents, by using "goal" information. Goal information describes situations that are desirable. This allows the agent a way to choose among multiple possibilities, selecting the one which reaches a goal state. Search and planning are the subfields of artificial intelligence devoted to finding action sequences that achieve the agent's goals.

Utility-based Agents

Goal-based agents only distinguish between goal states and non-goal states. It is possible to define a measure of how desirable a particular state is. This measure can be obtained through the use of a *utility function* which maps a state to a measure of the utility of the state. A more general performance measure should allow a comparison of different world states according to exactly how happy they would make the agent. The term utility can be used to describe how "happy" the agent is.

A rational utility-based agent chooses the action that maximizes the expected utility of the action outcomes - that is, what the agent expects to derive, on average, given the probabilities and utilities of each outcome. A utility-based agent has to model and keep track of its environment, tasks that have involved a great deal of research on perception, representation, reasoning, and learning.

Learning Agents

Learning has the advantage that it allows the agents to initially operate in unknown environments and to become more competent than its initial knowledge alone might allow. The most important distinction is between the "learning element", which is responsible for making improvements, and the "performance element", which is responsible for selecting external actions.

The learning element uses feedback from the "critic" on how the agent is doing and determines how the performance element should be modified to do better in the future.

The performance element is what we have previously considered to be the entire agent: it takes in percepts and decides on actions.

The last component of the learning agent is the "problem generator". It is responsible for suggesting actions that will lead to new and informative experiences.

Hierarchies of Agents

To actively perform their functions, Intelligent Agents today are normally gathered in a hierarchical structure containing many "sub-agents". Intelligent sub-agents process and perform lower level functions. Taken together, the intelligent agent and sub-agents create a complete system that can accomplish difficult tasks or goals with behaviors and responses that display a form of intelligence.

Applications

An example of an automated online assistant providing automated customer service on a webpage.

Intelligent agents are applied as automated online assistants, where they function to perceive the needs of customers in order to perform individualized customer service. Such an agent may basically consist of a dialog system, an avatar, as well an expert system to provide specific expertise to the user. They can also be used to optimize coordination of human groups online.

Software Agent

A Software Agent (or Autonomous Agent or Intelligent Agent) is a computer program which works toward goals (as opposed to discrete tasks) in a dynamic environment (where change is the norm) on behalf of another entity (human or computational), possibly over an extended period of time, without continuous direct supervision or control, and exhibits a significant degree of flexibility and even creativity in how it seeks to transform goals into action tasks.

A Software Agent System (or Multi-Agent System (MAS)) is a computational environment (such as the Web or a grid computing environment overlay network) in which individual software agents interact with each other, sometime in a cooperative manner, sometimes in a competitive manner, and sometimes autonomously pursuing their individual goals, accessing resources and services of the environment, and occasionally producing results for the entities that initiated those software agents.

A simpler, more structured definition is to say that a software agent is a computer program that exhibits the characteristics of agency or software agency.

The other entity could be a human, a traditional, "legacy" computer program, a robot, or another software agent. A software agent is similar to a robot, but operates in cyberspace, on a computer network.

Concepts

The basic attributes of an autonomous software agent are that agents

- are not strictly invoked for a task, but activate themselves,

- may reside in wait status on a host, perceiving context,

- may get to run status on a host upon starting conditions,

- do not require interaction of user,

- may invoke other tasks including communication.

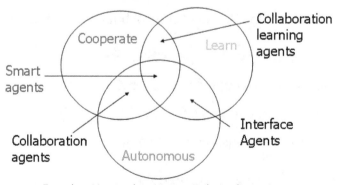

Based on Nwanna's primary attribute dimension

Nwana's Category of Software Agent

The term "agent" describes a software abstraction, an idea, or a concept, similar to OOP terms such as methods, functions, and objects. The concept of an agent provides a convenient and powerful way to describe a complex software entity that is capable of acting with a certain degree of autonomy in order to accomplish tasks on behalf of its host. But unlike objects, which are defined in terms of *methods* and *attributes*, an agent is defined in terms of its behavior.

Various authors have proposed different definitions of agents, these commonly include concepts such as:

- *persistence* (code is not executed on demand but runs continuously and decides for itself when it should perform some activity).

- *autonomy* (agents have capabilities of task selection, prioritization, goal-directed behavior, decision-making without human intervention).

- *social ability* (agents are able to engage other components through some sort of communication and coordination, they may collaborate on a task).

- *reactivity* (agents perceive the context in which they operate and react to it appropriately).

Distinguishing Agents from Programs

All agents are programs, but not all programs are agents. Contrasting the term with related concepts may help clarify its meaning. Franklin & Graesser (1997) discuss four key notions that distinguish agents from arbitrary programs: reaction to the environment, autonomy, goal-orientation and persistence.

Intuitive Distinguishing Agents from Objects

- Agents are more autonomous than objects.

- Agents have flexible behaviour: reactive, proactive, social.

- Agents have at least one thread of control but may have more.

Distinguishing Agents from Expert Systems

- Expert systems are not coupled to their environment.

- Expert systems are not designed for reactive, proactive behavior.

- Expert systems do not consider social ability.

Distinguishing Intelligent Software Agents from Intelligent Agents in AI

- Intelligent agents (also known as rational agents) are not just computer programs: they may also be machines, human beings, communities of human beings (such as firms) or anything that is capable of goal-directed behavior.

Impact of Software Agents

Software agents may offer various benefits to their end users by automating complex or repetitive tasks. However, there are organizational and cultural impacts of this technology that need to be considered prior to implementing software agents.

Organizational Impact

Work Contentment and Job Satisfaction Impact

People like to perform easy tasks providing the sensation of success unless the repetition of the simple tasking is affecting the overall output. In general implementing software agents to perform administrative requirements provides a substantial increase in work contentment, as administering their own work does never please the worker. The effort freed up serves for a higher degree of engagement in the substantial tasks of individual work. Hence, software agents may provide the basics to implement self-controlled work, relieved from hierarchical controls and interference. Such conditions may be secured by application of software agents for required formal support.

Cultural Impact

The cultural effects of the implementation of software agents include trust affliction, skills erosion, privacy attrition and social detachment. Some users may not feel entirely comfortable fully delegating important tasks to software applications. Those who start relying solely on intelligent agents may lose important skills, for example, relating to information literacy. In order to act on a user's behalf, a software agent needs to have a complete understanding of a user's profile, including his/her personal preferences. This, in turn, may lead to unpredictable privacy issues. When users start relying on their software agents more, especially for communication activities, they may lose contact with other human users and look at the word with the eyes of their agents. These consequences are what agent researchers and users must consider when dealing with intelligent agent technologies.

Examples of Intelligent Software Agents

Haag suggests that there are only four essential types of intelligent software agents:

1. Buyer agents or shopping bots

2. User or personal agents

3. Monitoring-and-surveillance agents

4. Data-mining agents

Buyer Agents

Buyer agents travel around a network (e.g. the internet) retrieving information about goods and services. These agents, also known as 'shopping bots', work very efficiently for commodity products such as CDs, books, electronic components, and other one-size-fits-all products. Buyer agents are typically optimized to allow for digital payment services used in e-commerce and traditional businesses.

User Agents

User agents, or personal agents, are intelligent agents that take action on your behalf. In this category belong those intelligent agents that already perform, or will shortly perform, the following tasks:

- Check your e-mail, sort it according to the user's order of preference, and alert you when important emails arrive.

- Play computer games as your opponent or patrol game areas for you.

- Assemble customized news reports for you. There are several versions of these, including CNN.

- Find information for you on the subject of your choice.

- Fill out forms on the Web automatically for you, storing your information for future reference.

- Scan Web pages looking for and highlighting text that constitutes the "important" part of the information there.

- Discuss topics with you ranging from your deepest fears to sports.

- Facilitate with online job search duties by scanning known job boards and sending the resume to opportunities who meet the desired criteria.

- Profile synchronization across heterogeneous social networks.

Monitoring-and-surveillance Agents

Monitoring and Surveillance Agents are used to observe and report on equipment, usually computer systems. The agents may keep track of company inventory levels, observe competitors' prices and relay them back to the company, watch stock manipulation by insider trading and rumors, etc.

For example, NASA's Jet Propulsion Laboratory has an agent that monitors inventory, planning, schedules equipment orders to keep costs down, and manages food storage facilities. These agents usually monitor complex computer networks that can keep track of the configuration of each computer connected to the network.

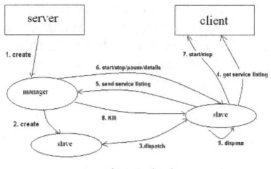

service monitoring

A special case of Monitoring-and-Surveillance agents are organizations of agents used to emulate the Human Decision-Making process during tactical operations. The agents monitor the status of assets (ammunition, weapons available, platforms for transport, etc.) and receive Goals (Missions) from higher level agents. The Agents then pursue the Goals with the Assets at hand, minimizing expenditure of the Assets while maximizing Goal Attainment.

Data-mining Agents

This agent uses information technology to find trends and patterns in an abundance of information from many different sources. The user can sort through this information in order to find whatever information they are seeking.

A data mining agent operates in a data warehouse discovering information. A 'data warehouse' brings together information from lots of different sources. "Data mining" is the process of looking through the data warehouse to find information that you can use to take action, such as ways to increase sales or keep customers who are considering defecting.

'Classification' is one of the most common types of data mining, which finds patterns in information and categorizes them into different classes. Data mining agents can also detect major shifts in trends or a key indicator and can detect the presence of new information and alert you to it. For example, the agent may detect a decline in the construction industry for an economy; based on this relayed information construction companies will be able to make intelligent decisions regarding the hiring/firing of employees or the purchase/lease of equipment in order to best suit their firm.

Networking and Communicating Agents

Some other examples of current intelligent agents include some spam filters, game bots, and server monitoring tools. Search engine indexing bots also qualify as intelligent agents.

- User agent - for browsing the World Wide Web

- Mail transfer agent - For serving E-mail, such as *Microsoft Outlook*. Why? It communicates with the POP3 mail server, without users having to understand POP3 command protocols. It even has rule sets that filter mail for the user, thus sparing them the trouble of having to do it themselves.

- SNMP agent.

- In Unix-style networking servers, *httpd* is an HTTP daemon that implements the Hypertext Transfer Protocol at the root of the World Wide Web.

- Management agents used to manage telecom devices.

- Crowd simulation for safety planning or 3D computer graphics.

- Wireless *beaconing agent* is a simple process hosted single tasking entity for implementing wireless lock or electronic leash in conjunction with more complex software agents hosted e.g. on wireless receivers.

- Use of autonomous agents (deliberately equipped with noise) to optimize coordination in groups online.

Design Issues

Issues to consider in the development of agent-based systems include:

- how tasks are scheduled and how synchronization of tasks is achieved.

- how tasks are prioritized by agents.

- how agents can collaborate, or recruit resources.

- how agents can be re-instantiated in different environments, and how their internal state can be stored.

- how the environment will be probed and how a change of environment leads to behavioral changes of the agents.

- how messaging and communication can be achieved.

- what hierarchies of agents are useful (e.g. task execution agents, scheduling agents, resource providers).

For software agents to work together efficiently they must share semantics of their data elements. This can be done by having computer systems publish their metadata.

The definition of *agent processing* can be approached from two interrelated directions:

- internal state processing and ontologies for representing knowledge.

- interaction protocols – standards for specifying communication of tasks.

Agent systems are used to model real-world systems with concurrency or parallel processing.

- Agent Machinery – Engines of various kinds, which support the varying degrees of intelligence.

- Agent Content – Data employed by the machinery in Reasoning and Learning.

- Agent Access – Methods to enable the machinery to perceive content and perform actions as outcomes of Reasoning.

- Agent Security – Concerns related to distributed computing, augmented by a few special concerns related to agents.

The agent uses its access methods to go out into local and remote databases to forage for content. These access methods may include setting up news stream delivery to the agent, or retrieval from bulletin boards, or using a spider to walk the Web. The content that is retrieved in this way is probably already partially filtered – by the selection of the newsfeed or the databases that are searched. The agent next may use its detailed searching or language-processing machinery to extract keywords or signatures from the body of the content that has been received or retrieved. This abstracted content (or event) is then passed to the agent's Reasoning or inferencing machinery in order to decide what to do with the new content. This process combines the event content with the rule-based or knowledge content provided by the user. If this process finds a good hit or match in the new content, the agent may use another piece of its machinery to do a more detailed search on the content. Finally, the agent may decide to take an action based on the new content; for example, to notify the user that an important event has occurred. This action is verified by a security function and then given the authority of the user. The agent makes use of a user-access method to deliver that message to the user. If the user confirms that the event is important by acting quickly on the notification, the agent may also employ its learning machinery to increase its weighting for this kind of event.

Bots can act on behalf of their creators to do good as well as bad. There are a few ways which bots can be created to demonstrate that they are designed with the best intention and are not built to do harm. This is first done by having a bot identify itself in the user-agent HTTP header when communicating with a site. The source IP address must also be validated to establish itself as legitimate. Next, the bot must also always respect a site's robots.txt file since it has become the standard across most of the web. And like respecting the robots.txt file, bots should shy away from being too aggressive and respect any crawl delay instructions

Next Step

Software agents are the next evolutionary step beyond objects and programs. Objects tend to be passive with only one object active at a time, and objects tend to be 'hidden' inside programs. Programs tend to be relatively static and designing a distributed computation with an indeterminate number of collaborating programs is not an easy task. Software agents offer opportunities for parallelism and inter-program collaboration, and on a large scale, and to do it easily and in a robust, reliable, flexible, and secure manner.

Virtual Assistant

A virtual assistant, also called AI assistant or digital assistant, is an application program that understands natural language voice commands and completes tasks for the user.

Such tasks, historically performed by a personal assistant or secretary, include taking dictation, reading text or email messages aloud, looking up phone numbers, scheduling, placing phone calls and reminding the end user about appointments. Popular virtual assistants currently include Amazon Alexa, Apple's Siri, Google Now and Microsoft's Cortana -- the digital assistant built into Windows Phone 8.1 and Windows 10.

Method of Interaction

Virtual assistants make work via:

- Text (online chat), especially in an instant messaging app or other app.

- Voice, for example with Amazon Alexa on the Amazon Echo device, or Siri on an iPhone.

- By taking and/or uploading images, as in the case of Samsung Bixby on the Samsung Galaxy S8.

Some virtual assistants are accessible via multiple methods, such as Google Assistant via chat on the Google Allo app and via voice on Google Home smart speakers.

Virtual assistants use natural language processing (NLP) to match user text or voice input to executable commands. Many continually learn using artificial intelligence techniques including machine learning.

To activate a virtual assistant using the voice, a wake word might be used. This is a word or groups of words such as "Alexa", "Hey Siri" or "OK Google".

Devices and Objects Where Found

Virtual assistants may be integrated into many types of platforms or, like Amazon Alexa, across several of them:

- Into devices like smart speakers such as Amazon Echo, Google Home and Apple HomePod.

- In instant messaging apps on both smartphones and via the Web, e.g. Facebook's M (virtual assistant) on both Facebook and Facebook Messenger apps or via the Web.

- Built into a mobile operating system (OS), as are Apple's Siri on iOS devices and BlackBerry Assistant on BlackBerry 10 devices, or into a desktop OS such as Cortana on Microsoft Windows OS.

- Built into a smartphone independent of the OS, as is Bixby on the Samsung Galaxy S8 and Note 8.

- On other mobile apps such as Google Allo.

- Within instant messaging platforms, assistants from specific organizations, such as Aeromexico's Aerobot on Facebook Messenger or Wechat Secretary on WeChat.

- Within mobile apps from specific companies and other organizations, such as Dom from Domino's Pizza.

- On smartwatches.

- In appliances, cars, and Android Wear clothing.

- Previous generations of virtual assistants often worked on websites, such as Alaska Airlines' Ask Jenn, or on interactive voice response (IVR) systems such as American Airlines' IVR by Nuance.

- Orange Djingo

Services

Virtual assistants can provide a wide variety of services, and particularly those from Amazon Alexa and Google Assistant grow by the day. These include:

- Provide information such as weather, facts from e.g. Wikipedia or IMDB, set an alarm, make to-do lists and shopping lists

- Play music from streaming services such as Spotify and Pandora; play radio stations; read audiobooks

- Play videos, TV shows or movies on televisions, streaming from e.g. Netflix

- Conversational commerce

- Complement and/or replace customer service by humans. One report estimated that an automated online assistant produced a 30% decrease in the work-load for a human-provided call centre.

Conversational Commerce

Conversational commerce is e-commerce via various means of messaging, including via voice assistants but also live chat on e-commerce Web sites, live chat on messaging apps such as WeChat, Facebook Messenger and WhatsApp and chatbots on messaging apps or Web sites.

Third-party Services

Amazon enables Alexa "Skills" and Google "Actions", essentially apps that run on the assistant platforms.

Developer Platforms

The platforms that power the most widely used virtual assistants are also used to power other solutions:

- Amazon Lex was opened to developers in April 2017. It involves natural language understanding technology combined with automatic speech recognition and had been introduced in November 2016.

- Google provides the Actions on Google and Dialogflow platforms for developers to create "Actions" for Google Assistant

- Apple provides SiriKit for developers to create extensions for Siri

- IBM's Watson, while sometimes spoken of as a virtual assistant is in fact an entire artificial intelligence platform and community powering some virtual assistants, chatbots. and many other types of solutions.

Previous Generations

In previous generations of text chat-based virtual assistants, the assistant was often represented by an avatar of (a.k.a. 'interactive online character *or* automated character) — *this was known as an embodied agent.*

Virtual Assistant Privacy Concerns

Some consumers have expressed privacy concerns about virtual assistants, such as Amazon Alexa and Google Home, because these virtual assistants require large amounts of personal data and are always "listening" in order to respond to voice commands. Virtual assistants then retain voice interactions and personal information to improve the user experience.

Cortana, for example, works best by using data from a user's device, including emails and other communications, a user's contacts, location data, search history, and data from other Microsoft services and skills -- third-party applications -- that users choose to connect with. Users can choose not to sign in and share this data with Cortana, and adjust permissions to prevent certain data from being collected, though these actions limit the virtual assistant's usefulness.

Virtual assistant providers also maintain privacy policies, which define how each company uses and shares personal information. In most cases, companies do not share customer-identifiable information without a customer's consent.

The Future of Virtual Assistants

Virtual assistants are quickly evolving to provide more capabilities and value to users. As speech recognition and natural language processing advances, so too will a virtual assistant's ability to understand and perform requests. And as voice recognition technology improves, virtual assistant use will move deeper into business workflows.

Tomorrow's virtual assistants will be built with more advanced cognitive computing technologies, which will allow a virtual assistant to understand and carry out multistep requests and perform more complex tasks, such as making a plane reservation.

Video Game Bot

AI bots have been in video games since their debut. Typically the term "bot" refers to a computer-controlled player that takes the role of a human player in their absence. Bots have become most notable in first person shooters such as the Unreal franchise, which is renown for their adaptive and challenging AI. Other games, such as Timesplitters, have used bots on consoles prior to the advent of online console gaming in order to recreate battles of a bigger scale than four local players would allow. Another good example of an AI Bot is Sheva Alomar in Resident Evil 5. Through most of the game, the player is fighting cooperatively alongside Sheva, who, in the absence of a 2nd human player, is controlled by the computer.

Bots written for first-person shooters usually try to mimic how a human would play a game. Computer-controlled bots may play against other bots and/or human players in unison, either over the Internet, on a LAN or in a local session. Features and intelligence of bots may vary greatly, especially with community created content. Advanced bots feature machine learning for dynamic learning of patterns of the opponent as well as dynamic learning of previously unknown maps – whereas more trivial bots may rely completely on lists of waypoints created for each map by the developer, limiting the bot to play only maps with said waypoints.

Use in Games

Typically, bots are used to help familiarize players into the multiplayer experience without plunging them head on into player vs. player combat. Bots help players learn map layouts, weapon positions, cover points, and the general feel of the game itself. Some games, before online console gaming, used bots to create deeper, and more chaotic multiplayer environments that added an extra element to the simple 4 player splitscreen experience. For example, players could team up cooperatively against computer-controlled enemies, in the same multiplayer setting, as opposed to facing each other.

While first person shooter bots are well known, other games have used bots in many ways. For example the Super Smash Brothers series offers the player the ability to substitute a computer opponent in one of the four slots not filled by a player. This has become common practice in Nintendo games due to their lack of online play prior to the Nintendo Wii.

Using bots is generally against the rules of current massively multiplayer online role-playing games (MMORPGs), but a significant number of players still use MMORPG bots for games like RuneScape.

In MUDs, players may run bots to automate laborious tasks: this activity can sometimes make up the bulk of the gameplay. While a prohibited practice in most MUDs, there is an incentive for the player to save his/her time while the bot accumulates resources, such as experience, for the player character.

Bot Types

Bots may be either static or dynamic.

Static bots are designed to follow pre-made waypoints for each level or map. These bots need to have a unique waypoint file for each map, if they are to function. For example, *Quake III Arena* bots use an area awareness system file to move around the map, while *Counter-Strike* bots use a waypoint file.

Dynamic bots, dynamically learn the levels and maps as they play. RealBot, for *Counter-Strike*, is an example. Some bots are designed using both static and dynamic features.

Bot Decline

As online gaming has grown in popularity, the inclusion of AI bots in games has dropped. Developers have found it is not worth the effort when other human players are almost always available online.

Autonomous Robot

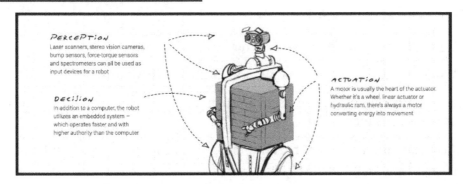

PERCEPTION
Laser scanners, stereo vision cameras, bump sensors, force-torque sensors and spectrometers can all be used as input devices for a robot

DECISION
In addition to a computer, the robot utilizes an embedded system – which operates faster and with higher authority than the computer

ACTUATION
A motor is usually the heart of the actuator. Whether it's a wheel, linear actuator or hydraulic ram, there's always a motor converting energy into movement

Autonomous robots, just like humans, also have the ability to make their own decisions and then perform an action accordingly. A truly autonomous robot is one that can perceive its environment, make decisions based on what it perceives and/or has been programmed to recognize and then actuate a movement or manipulation within that environment. With respect to mobility, for example, these decision-based actions include but are not limited to the following basics: starting, stopping, and maneuvering around obstacles that are in their way.

Simpler autonomous robots use infrared or ultrasound sensors to see obstacles, allowing them to navigate around the obstacles without human control. More advanced robots use stereo vision to see their environments; cameras give them depth perception, and software allows them to locate and classify objects in real time.

Autonomous robots are helpful in busy environments, like a hospital. Instead of employees leaving their posts, an autonomous robot can deliver lab results and patient samples expeditiously. Without traditional guidance, these robots can navigate the hospital hallways, and can even find alternate routes when another is blocked. They will stop at pick-up points, and collect samples to bring to the lab.

DARPA, the Defense Advanced Research Projects Agency, is a division of the US Defense Department with the mission to create technological surprise for our enemies. This organization represents the cutting edge of military and disaster relief technology, and after developing autonomous vehicles, they are focused on creating autonomous robots that are capable of performing complex tasks in dangerous environments.

Another place autonomous robots are useful is in our natural environment. In 2013, researchers at Virginia Tech developed an autonomous robotic jellyfish with the intent of one day conducting undersea military surveillance or monitoring the environment. The 5 foot 7 inch jellyfish has a long duration and range of operation.

While major robotics companies like FANUC, ABB, KUKA, Universal Robots, and Motoman all offer autonomous robots, the Robotarium X Zoo houses 45 autonomous robots powered by photo-voltaic energy. This "first zoo for artificial life" provides an ideal environment for robotic development.

A fully autonomous robot can:

- Gain information about the environment

- Work for an extended period without human intervention

- Move either all or part of itself throughout its operating environment without human assistance

- Avoid situations that are harmful to people, property, or itself unless those are part of its design specifications

An autonomous robot may also learn or gain new knowledge like adjusting for new methods of accomplishing its tasks or adapting to changing surroundings.

Examples

Self-maintenance

The first requirement for complete physical autonomy is the ability for a robot to take care of itself. Many of the battery-powered robots on the market today can find and connect to a charging station, and some toys like Sony's *Aibo* are capable of self-docking to charge their batteries.

Self-maintenance is based on "proprioception", or sensing one's own internal status. In the battery charging example, the robot can tell proprioceptively that its batteries are low and it then seeks the charger. Another common proprioceptive sensor is for heat monitoring. Increased proprioception will be required for robots to work autonomously near people and in harsh environments. Common proprioceptive sensors include thermal, optical, and haptic sensing, as well as the Hall effect (electric).

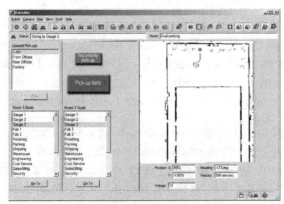

Robot GUI display showing battery voltage and other proprioceptive data in lower right-hand corner. The display is for user information only. Autonomous robots monitor and respond to proprioceptive sensors without human intervention to keep themselves safe and operating properly.

Sensing the Environment

Exteroception is sensing things about the environment. Autonomous robots must have a range of environmental sensors to perform their task and stay out of trouble.

- Common exteroceptive sensors include the electromagnetic spectrum, sound, touch, chemical (smell, odor), temperature, range to various objects, and altitude.

Some robotic lawn mowers will adapt their programming by detecting the speed in which grass grows as needed to maintain a perfectly cut lawn, and some vacuum cleaning robots have dirt detectors that sense how much dirt is being picked up and use this information to tell them to stay in one area longer.

Task Performance

The next step in autonomous behavior is to actually perform a physical task. A new area showing commercial promise is domestic robots, with a flood of small vacuuming robots beginning with iRobot and Electrolux in 2002. While the level of intelligence is not high in these systems, they navigate over wide areas and pilot in tight situations around homes using contact and non-contact sensors. Both of these robots use proprietary algorithms to increase coverage over simple random bounce.

The next level of autonomous task performance requires a robot to perform conditional tasks. For instance, security robots can be programmed to detect intruders and respond in a particular way depending upon where the intruder is.

Autonomous Navigation

Indoor Navigation

For a robot to associate behaviors with a place (localization) requires it to know where it is and to be able to navigate point-to-point. Such navigation began with wire-guidance in the 1970s and progressed in the early 2000s to beacon-based triangulation. Current commercial robots autonomously navigate based on sensing natural features. The first commercial robots to achieve this were Pyxus' HelpMate hospital robot and the CyberMotion guard robot, both designed by robotics pioneers in the 1980s. These robots originally used manually created CAD floor plans, sonar sensing and wall-following variations to navigate buildings. The next generation, such as MobileRobots' PatrolBot and autonomous wheelchair, both introduced in 2004, have the ability to create their own laser-based maps of a building and to navigate open areas as well as corridors. Their control system changes its path on the fly if something blocks the way.

At first, autonomous navigation was based on planar sensors, such as laser range-finders, that can only sense at one level. The most advanced systems now fuse information from various sensors for both localization (position) and navigation. Systems such as

Motivity can rely on different sensors in different areas, depending upon which provides the most reliable data at the time, and can re-map a building autonomously.

Rather than climb stairs, which requires highly specialized hardware, most indoor robots navigate handicapped-accessible areas, controlling elevators, and electronic doors. With such electronic access-control interfaces, robots can now freely navigate indoors. Autonomously climbing stairs and opening doors manually are topics of research at the current time.

As these indoor techniques continue to develop, vacuuming robots will gain the ability to clean a specific user-specified room or a whole floor. Security robots will be able to cooperatively surround intruders and cut off exits. These advances also bring concomitant protections: robots' internal maps typically permit "forbidden areas" to be defined to prevent robots from autonomously entering certain regions.

Outdoor Navigation

Outdoor autonomy is most easily achieved in the air, since obstacles are rare. Cruise missiles are rather dangerous highly autonomous robots. Pilotless drone aircraft are increasingly used for reconnaissance. Some of these unmanned aerial vehicles (UAVs) are capable of flying their entire mission without any human interaction at all except possibly for the landing where a person intervenes using radio remote control. Some drones are capable of safe, automatic landings, however.

Outdoor autonomy is the most difficult for ground vehicles, due to:

- Three-dimensional terrain
- Great disparities in surface density
- Weather exigencies
- Instability of the sensed environment

The Seekur and MDARS robots demonstrate their autonomous
navigation and security capabilities at an airbase.

The Seekur robot was the first commercially available robot to demonstrate MDARS-like capabilities for general use by airports, utility plants, corrections facilities and Homeland Security.

The Mars rovers MER-A and MER-B (now known as Spirit rover and Opportunity rover) can find the position of the sun and navigate their own routes to destinations on the fly by:

- Mapping the surface with 3D vision

- Computing safe and unsafe areas on the surface within that field of vision

- Computing optimal paths across the safe area towards the desired destination

- Driving along the calculated route;

- Repeating this cycle until either the destination is reached, or there is no known path to the destination

The planned ESA Rover, ExoMars Rover, is capable of vision based relative localisation and absolute localisation to autonomously navigate safe and efficient trajectories to targets by:

- Reconstructing 3D models of the terrain surrounding the Rover using a pair of stereo cameras

- Determining safe and unsafe areas of the terrain and the general "difficulty" for the Rover to navigate the terrain

- Computing efficient paths across the safe area towards the desired destination

- Driving the Rover along the planned path

- Building up a navigation map of all previous navigation data

During the final NASA Sample Return Robot Centennial Challenge in 2016, a rover, named Cataglyphis, successfully demonstrated fully autonomous navigation, decision-making, and sample detection, retrieval, and return capabilities. The rover relied on a fusion of measurements from inertial sensors, wheel encoders, Lidar, and camera for navigation and mapping, instead of using GPS or magnetometers. During the 2 hour challenge, Cataglyphis traversed over 2.6 km and returned five different samples to its starting position.

The DARPA Grand Challenge and DARPA Urban Challenge have encouraged development of even more autonomous capabilities for ground vehicles, while this has been the demonstrated goal for aerial robots since 1990 as part of the AUVSI International Aerial Robotics Competition.

Open Problems in Autonomous Robotics

There are several open problems in autonomous robotics which are special to the field rather than being a part of the general pursuit of AI. According to George A. Bekey's

Autonomous Robots: From Biological Inspiration to Implementation and Control, problems include things such as making sure the robot is able to function correctly and not run into obstacles autonomously.

Energy Autonomy and Foraging

Researchers concerned with creating true artificial life are concerned not only with intelligent control, but further with the capacity of the robot to find its own resources through foraging (looking for food, which includes both energy and spare parts).

This is related to autonomous foraging, a concern within the sciences of behavioral ecology, social anthropology, and human behavioral ecology; as well as robotics, artificial intelligence, and artificial life.

Delivery Robot

A delivery robot is an autonomous robot used for delivering goods. As of February 2017 there were several notable companies developing delivery robots (some with pilot deliveries in progress):

- Starship Technologies
- Dispatch
- Marble

Legislature

In March 2016 a bill was introduced in Washington, D.C., allowing pilot ground robotic deliveries. The program was to take place from September 15 through the end of December 2017. The robots were limited to a weight of 50 pounds unloaded and maximum speed of 10 miles per hour. In case the robot stopped moving because of malfunction the company was required to remove it from the streets within 24 hours. There were allowed only 5 robots to be tested per company at a time. A 2017 version of the Personal Delivery Device Act bill was under review as of March 2017.

In February 2017 a bill was passed in the US state of Virginia (the House bill, HB2016, and the Senate bill, SB1207) that will allow autonomous delivery robots to travel on sidewalks and use crosswalks statewide beginning on July 1, 2017. The robots will be limited to a maximum speed of 10 mph and maximum weight of 50 pounds. In the states of Idaho and Florida there are also talks about passing similar legislation.

It has been discussed that robots with similar characteristics to invalid carriages (e.g. 10 mph maximum, limited battery life) might be a workaround for certain classes of applications. If the robot was sufficiently intelligent and able to recharge itself using existing electric vehicle (EV) charging infrastructure it would only need minimal supervision and a single arm with low dexterity might be enough to enable this function if its visual systems had enough resolution.

In November 2017, the San Francisco Board of Supervisors announced that companies would need to get a city permit in order to test these robots. In addition, sidewalk delivery robots have been banned from making non-research deliveries.

Future

As emerging technologies become more prominent, the relationship between humans and robots is evolving. Autonomous robots have the ability to replace humans, such as a cognitive virtual assistant acting as an automated customer representative. Autonomous robots even have the ability to understand the emotion in a human's voice. These trends towards robotic involvement in industry processes will allow companies to improve productivity and customer experience, and gain a competitive advantage.

Domestic Robot

Domestic robots, also known as home or service robots, are essentially programmable computers integrated with electrically powered machines that perform household chores. They typically have some capacity for movement, either for moving themselves or manipulating objects, or both. Home robots differ from appliances (dishwashers, for example) or even internet-connected appliances in that they do all the work, as opposed to simply making a task easier. These labor-saving devices not only free people to do other things, but may also assist disabled or elderly people.

Depending on its uses and design, a robot may contain sensors (cameras, microphones, accelerometers, etc.); tool parts that do the work (effectors); circuit boards and electronic components; software; wireless components and Wi-Fi microcontrollers; displays; speakers; LED lights; motors; gear boxes; belts for drives, wheels, and tracks; dust bins; pumps; batteries and power supplies; nuts, bolts, and screws; casings and covers; on/off switches; and so on.

Indoor Robots

This type of domestic robot does chores around and inside homes. Different kinds include:

Robotic vacuum cleaners and floor-washing robots that clean floors with sweeping and wet mopping functions. Some use Swiffer or other disposable cleaning cloths to dry-sweep, or reusable microfiber cloths to wet-mop.

Within the ironing robots, Dressman is a mannequin to dry and iron shirts using hot air. Other ones also includes manneqin for down parts (pants, trousers and skirts). More advanced ones fold and organizes the clothes, as Laundroid (using image analysis and artificial intelligence), Effie (irons 12 items of clothing at once) and FoldiMate.

Cat litter robots are automatic self-cleaning litter boxes that filter clumps out into a built-in waste receptacle that can be lined with an ordinary plastic bag.

Between kitchen robots can find Rotimatic (that makes rotis, tortillas, puris out of flour in just few minutes) and Moley Robotics MK1.

Security robots such as Knightscope have a night-vision-capable wide-angle camera that detects movements and intruders. It can patrol places and shoot video of suspicious activities, too, and send alerts via email or text message; the stored history of past alerts and videos are accessible via the Web. The robot can also be configured to go into action at any time of the day.

Atlas is a robot built to perform in house task such as sweeping, opening doors, climbing stairs, etc. Robots such as Atlas can be utilized to making the average person's day just that much more interesting and easy.

Outdoor Robots

A robotic lawn mower is a lawn mower that is able to mow a lawn by itself after being programmed. Once programmed, this invention repeats the operation by itself according to its programming. Robotic lawn mowers comes with a power unit which may be an electric motor or internal combustion engine. This provides power to the robot and allows it to move itself and its cutting blades. There is also a control unit which helps the mower move itself. This unit also contains a memory unit which records and memorizes its operation programming. Its memorized route includes the length of travel in a given direction and turn angles. This allows the same lawn to be mowed repeatedly without having to reprogram. The steering unit acquires an operation signal and propels the lead wheel, which leads the mower, go guide along the programmed route.

Some models can mow complicated and uneven lawns that are up to three-quarters of an acre in size. Others can mow a lawn as large as 40,000 square feet (3,700 m²), can handle a hill inclined up to 27 degrees.

There are also automated pool cleaners that clean and maintain swimming pools autonomously by scrubbing in-ground pools from the floor to the waterline in 3 hours, cleaning and circulating more than 70 US gallons (260 l) of water per minute, and removing debris as small as 2 μm in size.

Gutter-cleaning robots such as Looj use brushes and rubber blades to remove debris from rain gutters; users operate the device using a remote.

Window cleaning robots are most commonly used to clean outdoor windows, more specifically house windows. However, it may be used on other types of windows, such as ones on tall buildings and structures. This robot contains a movement system which allows the robot to navigate itself across the window surface in a defined direction. It also has a powered agitator located by the cleaning pad. When activated, the agitator gets rid of debris and dirt from the window surface. The cleaning pad directly interacts with the window surface and is directly responsible for removing the dirt by filling itself with specialized window cleaning fluid.

A window-washing robot commonly uses two magnetic modules to navigate windows as it sprays cleaning solution onto microfiber pads to wash them. It covers about 1,601 square feet (148.7 m^2) per charge.

Toys

Robotic toys, such as the well known Furby, have been popular since 1998. There are also small humanoid remote controlled robots. Electronic pets, such as robotic dogs, can be companions for children. They have also have been used by many universities in competitions such as the RoboCup.

There are many different kind of toy robots that have been invented since the late 1900s. There were many robotic toys invented that was used for entertainment. One example that is popular known as Furby, a toy that children nourished every day. The toy robot, made it seem like it was alive like a pet that you have to watch on and give it attention. There are many different kind of toy robots that are animal related, like, robotic dogs. Another type of robotic toy is the phone-powered robots. Using this toy, you are able to connect with your phone and control the toy while using an application. Now, robotic toys are becoming more mobile device platformed. This in turn is creating a larger demand for these types of products. The increase in demand has a direct effect on the escalation of the technology used in the toys.

There are also phone-powered robots for fun and games, such as Romo which is a small robot that employs smartphones as its brain. By using another mobile device and a cross-platform app, the user can drive it, make it produce animated facial expressions, direct it to dance, or turn it into a spybot.

Social Robots

Social robots take on the function of social communication. Domestic humanoid robots are used by elderly and immobilized residents to keep them company. Wakamaru is a domestic humanoid robot developed in Japan. Its function is to act as a care taker. Wakamaru has a number of operations and "can be programmed to remind patients to take their medicine and even call a doctor when it appears that someone is in distress." Paro, a robotic baby seal, is intended to provide comfort to nursing home patients.

Home-telepresence robots can move around in a remote location and let one communicate with people there via its camera, speaker, and microphone. Through other remote-controlled telepresence robots, the user can visit a distant location and explore it as if they were physically present. These robots can, among other applications, permit health-care workers to monitor patients or allow children who are homebound because of injuries, illnesses, or other physical challenges to attend school remotely. Kuri, JIBO and ConnectR are family robots that includes telepresence.

Entertainment

Network robots link ubiquitous networks with robots, contributing to the creation of new lifestyles and solutions to address a variety of social problems including the aging of population and nursing care.

Advantages of Domestic Robot

The robotics at home have the prime benefit of making the life effortless for the families that they reside with, Especially for the mothers, if even the couple of chores such as vacuuming and washing the dishes could be eliminated, it would leave more time to focus on being rearing their children.

The Roomba is the robot that specializes in vacuum cleaning. The features include a superb built in, automatic adjustment between the floor types and also strong cleaning functions to pick up the pet hair.

The robotics in the home has the ability to help the handicapped maneuver and serve as companions for the elderly. The robot becomes more advanced and robotic cameras become cheaper, the rest of society will have access to them and be able to make use of them in their households.

The disabled people have been using the dogs and the monkeys for years to help them with the household tasks they are unable to take care of. The EI-E robot can use the laser recognition, so, you can point to the task and you can voice the commands to control the robot.

The employing robots in the home can provide the personal security. The cameras are self automated and they can take the pictures and videos of the environment such as WowWee Robotics that aid the families who have been robbed in catching the thief or deflect any intruders.

Disadvantages of Domestic Robot

The robots help us, they make the life easier, and they are harmless, but in retrospect, giving the robots too much access to our daily lives could lead to the disaster worldwide.

The people depend on technology and the robotics at home, and they could not bear to live without them.

The robotics can not respond in times of danger as the humans can, the production and purchasing of robots is very expensive and this could harm the global economy, but the robotics in the home can cause conflict because everyone will not be able to own one, even if they need it and they just do trivial tasks.

The robotics in the home have high cost for both the production and the purchasing, robots cost millions of dollars to build and many companies invest much money in programming and the involved research.

The robots have the specific job to do that is ordered by their operator, and if the robot has malfunctions, the chaos will happen, we become overly dependent upon the robot technology.

The robots can aid the disabled and elderly. If the people find themselves in dangerous situations, the robots can not help them, we can not invest our entire trust in the robots to care and give the companionship to our family members. If the emergency occur, the robot will not be able to dial type emergency number and it will not give the vital information to the emergency services.

References

- Russell, Stuart J.; Norvig, Peter (2003), Artificial Intelligence: A Modern Approach (2nd ed.), Upper Saddle River, New Jersey: Prentice Hall, ISBN 0-13-790395-2

- Nwana, H. S. (1996). "Software Agents: An Overview". Knowledge Engineering Review. Cambridge University Press. 21(3): 205–244. doi:10.1017/s026988890000789x

- Morrison, Maureen (2014-10-05). "Domino's Pitches Voice-Ordering App in Fast-Food First | CMO Strategy". AdAge. Retrieved 2017-12-10

- Memeti, Suejb; Pllana, Sabri (January 2018). "PAPA: A parallel programming assistant powered by IBM Watson cognitive computing technology". Journal of Computational Science.

- Schermer,, B. W. (2007). "Software agents, surveillance, and the right to privacy: A legislative framework for agent-enabled surveillance" (paperback). 21 (3). Leiden University Press: 140, 205–244. hdl:1887/11951. ISBN 978-0-596-00712-6

- Dan O'Shea (2017-01-04). "LG introduces smart refrigerator with Amazon Alexa-enabled grocery ordering". Retail Dive. Retrieved 2017-12-10

Permissions

All chapters in this book are published with permission under the Creative Commons Attribution Share Alike License or equivalent. Every chapter published in this book has been scrutinized by our experts. Their significance has been extensively debated. The topics covered herein carry significant information for a comprehensive understanding. They may even be implemented as practical applications or may be referred to as a beginning point for further studies.

We would like to thank the editorial team for lending their expertise to make the book truly unique. They have played a crucial role in the development of this book. Without their invaluable contributions this book wouldn't have been possible. They have made vital efforts to compile up to date information on the varied aspects of this subject to make this book a valuable addition to the collection of many professionals and students.

This book was conceptualized with the vision of imparting up-to-date and integrated information in this field. To ensure the same, a matchless editorial board was set up. Every individual on the board went through rigorous rounds of assessment to prove their worth. After which they invested a large part of their time researching and compiling the most relevant data for our readers.

The editorial board has been involved in producing this book since its inception. They have spent rigorous hours researching and exploring the diverse topics which have resulted in the successful publishing of this book. They have passed on their knowledge of decades through this book. To expedite this challenging task, the publisher supported the team at every step. A small team of assistant editors was also appointed to further simplify the editing procedure and attain best results for the readers.

Apart from the editorial board, the designing team has also invested a significant amount of their time in understanding the subject and creating the most relevant covers. They scrutinized every image to scout for the most suitable representation of the subject and create an appropriate cover for the book.

The publishing team has been an ardent support to the editorial, designing and production team. Their endless efforts to recruit the best for this project, has resulted in the accomplishment of this book. They are a veteran in the field of academics and their pool of knowledge is as vast as their experience in printing. Their expertise and guidance has proved useful at every step. Their uncompromising quality standards have made this book an exceptional effort. Their encouragement from time to time has been an inspiration for everyone.

The publisher and the editorial board hope that this book will prove to be a valuable piece of knowledge for students, practitioners and scholars across the globe.

Index

CPSIA information can be obtained
at www.ICGtesting.com
Printed in the USA
BVHW011517280519
549456BV00003B/34/P

9 781632 409027